THE WEB PAGE
RECIPE BOOK

BARRIE SOSINSKY

ELISABETH PARKER

For book and bookstore information

http://www.prenhall.com

Prentice Hall PTR
Upper Saddle River, NJ 07458

Library of Congress Cataloging-in-Publication Data

Sosinsky, Barrie A.
    The Web page recipe book / Barrie Sosinsky and Elisabeth Parker.
       p.   cm.
   Includes index.
   ISBN 0-13-460296-X
   1. Hypertext systems.   2. HTML (Document markup language)
3. World Wide Web (Information retrieval system) I. Parker,
Elisabeth. II. Title.
QA76.76.H94S67   1996
005.75--dc20   96-13211
                                 CIP

Acquisitions editor: Mark Taub
Editorial/production supervision: Betty Letizia
Interior design: Gail Cocker-Bogusz
Manufacturing manager: Alexis R. Heydt
Cover design: Talar Agasyan
Cover illustration: Don Martinetti
Page layout/formatting: Bear Type & Graphics

© 1996 Prentice Hall P T R
Prentice-Hall, Inc.
A Simon & Schuster Company
Upper Saddle River, NJ 07458

The publisher offers discounts on this book when ordered in bulk quantities. For more information, contact:

Corporate Sales Department / Prentice Hall P T R
1 Lake Street
Upper Saddle River, New Jersey 07458
Phone: 800-382-3419
FAX: 201-236-7141
E-mail: corpsales@prenhall.com

Printed in the United States of America

10 9 8 7 6 5 4 3 2

ISBN 0-13-460296-X

Prentice-Hall International (UK) Limited, *London*
Prentice-Hall of Australia Pty. Limited, *Sydney*
Prentice-Hall of Canada, Inc., *Toronto*
Prentice-Hall Hispanoamericana S.A., *Mexico*
Prentice-Hall of India Private Limited, *New Delhi*
Prentice-Hall of Japan, Inc., *Tokyo*
Simon & Schuster Asia Pte. Ltd., *Singapore*
Editora Prentice-Hall do Brasil, Ltda., *Rio de Janeiro*

CONTENTS

Chapter 5   Some Sample Meals   189

Chapter 6   Setting the Table: Getting Your Web Pages Posted   269

Chapter 7   Coffee and Dessert: Learning More About the Web   295

Acknowledgements

The authors wish to thank the many people who contributed to this book's conception and production, including our editors at PTR: Steve Guty, who signed the book and sponsored the project at its inception; and Mark Taub, who was the project manager. We hope this book repays their efforts. Also involved in the production of the book at PTR was Dori Steinhauff.

As always, thanks goes to our literary agent, Matt Wagner, at Waterside Productions in Cardiff-by-the-Sea, California for negotiating a good contract.

We owe a great debt of gratitude to our technical editor, Thomas Powell, who did a very thorough and thoughtful job in reviewing our manuscript. His comments and suggestions nearly always led to corrections and improvements in the text. We rarely get such a a quality review of our work by a technical editor. There were so many great catches that he earns our "Golden Glove" award for technical editing. He saved us from many embarrassing mistakes.

Elisabeth Parker wishes to thank Barrie Sosinsky for his help in co-authoring the book and creating the concept, his work on correcting the manuscript at author review, and his managing the project. She is particularly grateful for his help in launching a technical writing career and for his gentle and considerate suggestions and guidance.

Barrie Sosinsky wishes to thank his family for the time spent away from them during the course of working on this book.

About the Authors

Barrie Sosinsky is the author of 25 computer books on desktop computer technologies, publishing, graphics, and database software. Among his recent titles are: *Foundations of BackOffice* and *Microsoft Publisher for Dummies* by IDG Books Worldwide; *The Essential Works Book*, *The Essential Word Book*, *Web Browsing with America Online*, *Visio 4: Drawing Has Never Been Easier*, and *The Warp Book* all from Prima Publishing; and *The Acrobat Quick Tour* by Ventana Press. All these titles appeared in 1995 or 1996. He has also published over 70 articles on personal computer topics and was the Electronic Print columnist for *Techniques* magazine in 1995–96.

Barrie's company Killer Apps in Newton, Massachusetts specializes in database and workgroup solutions as commercial vertical market software and in custom solutions. Among the products they produce are *Granted!* a financial package for managing research grant accounting, and internetworking and Web based software solutions.

Elisabeth A. Parker is an author and consultant specializing in Web publishing and graphic design. Recent writings include Charles River Media's *The Netscape Navigator 2.0 Jumpstart Tutorial* (author) and Ventana Press *Acrobat QuickTour* (coauthor). Elisabeth has also written for *Technique* and *NetGuide* magazines. You can reach her at eparker@byteit.com, or check out her home page at http://www.cnsii.com/byteit/.

INTRODUCTION

This book is dedicated to the proposition that anyone can publish their own Web pages on the World Wide Web of the Internet. Although managing servers, connections, and the specialized software required to be a Webmaster or Webmistress may be more than most of us want to tackle, just about anybody can set up simple, attractive Web pages with text, graphics, and maybe even a few multimedia files. It's easy, and this book will show you how it's done.

Posting Web pages is electronic publishing at its finest. Whether you want to put up a family photo album, run an electronic newsletter on your favorite hobby, or publish information about your business, the World Wide Web offers unprecedented opportunities for distributing information across the street or around the world. And it costs a lot less than paper. Once you're up on the Web, you never know who may stumble across your home page.

Being an Internaut means being part of a vast, globally linked electronic community consisting of academics, corporations, and ordinary people like us. One minute you're in North Carolina, the next you're in Switzerland. Point, click, and shoot.

The place most people start their Web publishing experience is at their home page. A home page can be simple, and it can be complex. It can contain text, lists, pointers to other locations, images, and other hypertext constructs. When you're done reading this book, you'll be able to create your own very attractive home page from scratch, or by cutting and pasting from our work or the work of others. The underlying language for constructing Web pages is very straightforward and lets you examine the work of others and build on it.

You'll also be able to construct an entire site for people to wander around in, perusing the information you left for them. People who visit your home page can use it as a jumping-off place to the rest of your Web pages.

If you are new to the World Wide Web and the Internet, and don't know what a Web page looks like yet, take a look at Figure I.1. That figure shows a Web page viewed with the most popular Web browser at the moment, Netscape. The Unit Circle Cool Links Page appears in the main window of this program. This site is devoted to showing people interesting places to go.

There are many Web browsers out there, and even the major online services have gotten into the act. You'll find a World Wide Web browser in America Online, CompuServe, Prodigy, eWorld, the new Microsoft Network in Windows 95, and others. Netscape is the most popular for people connected to what are called "service providers." Most services offer you these browsers free of charge, and in some cases, like Netscape, they are commercial software or shareware that you try and buy. We will have much more to say about browsers later in this book, but they serve as the means for viewing the pages you are going to create.

All browsers work more or less the same way. You enter the location of the Web page you want to visit in the Location text box. To visit the Unit Circle Cool Links home page, type:

```
http://www.etext.org/Zines/UnitCircle/
cool_links.html
```

in the Location text box. This code is called a Uniform Resource Locator, more commonly referred to as a URL. You can think of a URL as an address for a particular Web page. Be careful entering a URL; they require that you enter them exactly. We'll break down the syntax of a URL later, in Chapter 1.

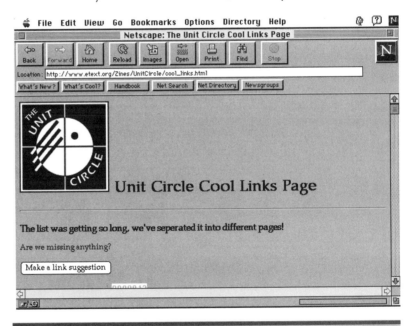

Figure I.1   The Unit Circle Cool Links Home Page.

○ WHAT'S A WEB PAGE?

A Web page is a file formatted in a special way using the Hypertext Markup Language, or HTML. If you have ever seen how computers handle PostScript, or word processors format documents in interchange formats like the Rich Text Format (RTF), then the constructs in creating a Web page will look pretty familiar to you. You can write and create a Web page in a word processor, although there are specialized tools that will make it easier for you to create them. What you view in a Web browser is the interpreted display of the text file you create.

A Web page can contain just about anything you want. Some people like to create huge lists and linked databases of places to go and things to check out. An example is the Ultimate Band List (http://american.recordings.com/wwwofmusic/ubl/ubl.shtml), shown in Figure I.2. This page offers what is often called a "jump map." As you move the cursor in your browser about the page, you find that each letter of the alphabet is a hot spot or link. Click once on them and you are transferred to another Web page. Underlying each link is the URL of the page listing bands whose names start with that letter.

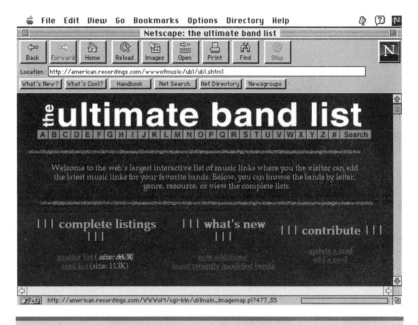

Figure I.2   The Ultimate Band List.

The ability to create hyperlinked sites and provide different pathways through the Web pages you choose to reference (whether they are yours and on your server, or someone else's around the world) makes browsing the World Wide Web a highly interactive experience. It also makes planning an attractive Web site more challenging than just writing a letter to the world.

Many organizations and individuals are also experimenting with creating electronic magazines, resulting in a wealth of both Web versions of established publications and underground independent "e-zines" devoted to a wide array of topics. Other sites, such as the Web 66 site (http://web66.coled.umn.edu/) are devoted to further developing the World Wide Web and offer on-line manuals, downloadable software, and links to other resources.

Surprisingly, some of the most fun and eclectic Web sites are the corporate ones. In addition to the expected product information, order forms, and such, you will also often find hot new links to different sites, downloadable goodies, and on-line contests and games. Netscape's home page (http://home.mcom.com/home/welcome.html), as shown in Figure I.3, is a definite must-see. The World Wide Web is organized anarchy, and surfin' the 'net is an addiction to many.

Figure I.3   Netscape's corporate home page.

Think of a home page as an interactive, electronic publication which people cruising the 'Net will visit during their travels. Notice, in Figure I.3 the hand cursor at the bottom of the screen over an underlined line of text. Web pages are called home pages when they refer to the central document for a site, enterprise, or person's files.

In Netscape, the cursor is normally an arrow, and only changes to a hand when it is over a pointer to another location. The location to which the text pointer points is a Web page whose address is shown in the bar at the very bottom of the screen.

Netscape has one other neat feature: when you click on a pointer, it changes color to indicate you've been there, done that, for a period of time that you can set as a preference.

Most browsers let you get in and view the underlying HTML code. In Netscape, for example, you can do this using the View Source command on the View menu. Just for grins, Figure I.4 shows you the underlying HTML code for the exact same portion of the Netscape home page you saw in Figure I.3.

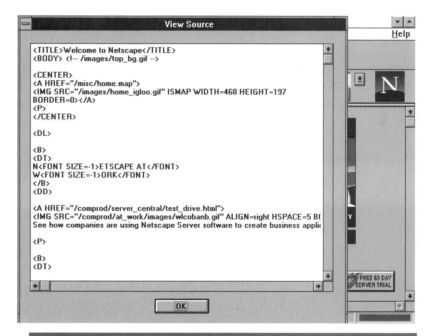

Figure I.4   The HTML description for Netscape's corporate home page.

HTML sounds scary, but it's actually pretty easy once you get the hang of how it works. You simply enter command tags in text-only documents to identify different parts of your Web page. These elements generally consist of headlines, body text, bulleted and numbered lists, images, and hypertext links. And, since all of these command tags are English-language constructs, Web pages are fairly easy to read in HTML once you've seen the styles to which the tags refer.

WORLD WIDE WEB FEVER

Hardly anyone had even heard of the World Wide Web three years ago, and now everyone's talking about it. And why not? The Web not only puts information from around the globe on practically every subject at your fingertips, it's also fun and easy to use. The Web is like a giant library that never closes.

Since its beginnings at the European Particle Physics Laboratory (CERN) in Geneva, Switzerland in 1991, the Web has undergone explosive growth. The growth is so large, in fact, that some industry analysts estimate that the number of users is doubling every month. That estimate is based on the number of searches on Web search engines which are judged to be a general indication of activity.

What started out as a project designed to make research findings and scientific texts available on a global network to the academic community has become a wild and wonderful free-for-all with people from all walks of life contributing their perspectives.

FOR WHOM WE WROTE THIS BOOK

If you've just gotten an Internet account with access to the World Wide Web, or you're about to, this book is for you. Maybe your company has wired your desktop and provided you with an Internet server in the office. Maybe you've seen some other people's home pages and think you would enjoy publishing one yourself, or want to create a set of Web pages for your research group, business, church, or temple. If you're interested in creating your own Web pages but aren't technologically inclined, this is the book for you.

We've written *The Web Page Recipe Book* in plain English, with easy-to-understand instructions—not in computerese or technobabble. So we don't spend a lot of time discussing intimidating things like setting up file servers, creating sockets or firewalls, or working on UNIX systems because we assume your interest is in just getting your Web pages created and posted. In the years to come millions of online computer users will have access to their own sites where they can store Web pages—it's almost a certainty.

And, if creating Web pages and life in Cyberspace really turns you on, we'll point you towards the resources you need for becoming a true Webmaster/Webmistress. Meanwhile, you don't need to be an Internet guru to weave attractive, interesting home pages.

You can still use this book even if you're not on-line yet. All you need is a copy of a Web browser so you can view the home pages you create. Open the Web pages you create in this book (or those you wish to view graphically) by choosing the <u>O</u>pen command on the browser's <u>F</u>ile menu, or its equivalent in the browser of your choice.

When you finish this book, you will know how to do the following:

- **Find your way around the Web:** *Use the Web's sophisticated search engines to find information and learn how to make your information available for others.*

  Learn how the Web is organized (insofar as one can call it "organized") and understand how Web browsers work. You will be able to find the information and resources you want.

- **Create HTML documents:** *Yes, believe it or not, you will understand hypertext markup language well enough to* enter tags for transforming ordinary text into exciting, interactive Web documents.

- **Work with images:** *You will be surprised at how easy it is to jazz up your home page with images. Not only will you find plenty of cool graphics on the CD-ROM, but if you are artistically inclined you can incorporate on-line images of your own.*

- **Generate interactive forms:** *The ability to interact with the creators of the home pages you visit and invite your home page visitors to interact with you is one of the most exciting things about publishing on the Web. You will learn how to solicit feedback and e-mail by creating electronic forms, like the one shown in Figure I.5.*

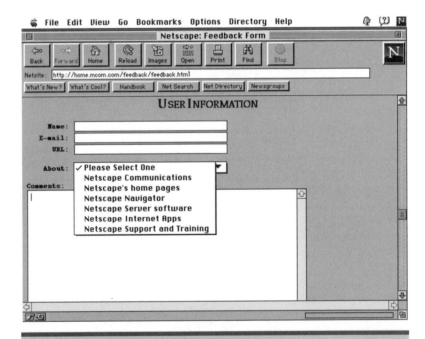

Figure I.5   You can get feedback from your visitors through electronic forms.

- **Make your Web page inviting:** *You can get your visitors to keep coming back by following a few guidelines for keeping your Web pages interesting, informative, well-organized, and attractive. You'll learn about these "Elements of Web Style" throughout this book.*

- **Let people know you're out there:** *What use is it to create a fabulous home page if no one knows it's out there? We will also explain how to announce your presence so people will stop by and visit.*

- **Learn more:** *As we have already mentioned, this book is mainly for beginners; however, if you want to learn more, we certainly don't want to stop you. We are happy to point you towards resources available on the Web that will help you become an expert.*

○ WHAT'S IN THIS BOOK

The Web Page Recipe Book tells you everything you need to know to whip up a home page. This book begins with a basic overview of the World Wide Web and how it works. Then you go on to learn how to format your documents with HTML, and how to add images, sounds, and movies to your home pages in a structured, step-by-step way that goes from simple projects to more complex ones.

- **Chapter 1, "What's Cooking on the Web?":** *We'll get you started by introducing you to the World Wide Web with a brief history, overview of browsers and search engines, and an explanation of how the Web works and why we love it so.*

- **Chapter 2, "Gathering Your Web Page Ingredients":** *In this chapter you'll learn about some of the nitty gritty you need to know to get started. This chapter will explain HTML, internal and external links, and handling different types of files in greater detail.*

- **Chapter 3, "Getting Your Kitchen in Order":** *This chapter addresses how to organize, present, and format your Web* *page so that your visitors will add your page to their browsers' bookmarks.*

■ ***Chapter 4, "Some Sample Dishes":*** *In this, the largest chapter in the book, you will find some basic templates and an overview of the types of documents you can create. Figure I.6 shows you an example to whet your whistle. Learn here how to work with headers, paragraphs, bulleted and numbered lists, text formatting, and adding and creating internal and external links. As an extra, we throw in some of the Netscape extensions into the mix.*

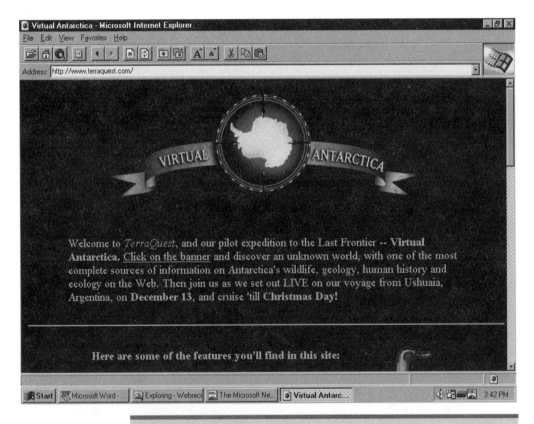

Figure I.6   Believe it or not, you will soon be able to create Web pages like the one shown here.

■ **Chapter 5, "Sample Meals":** *This chapter builds on what you'll learn in Chapter 4 and offers templates for more complex types of Web pages. Here, you'll learn how to add multimedia content, generate forms, set up an electronic resumé, and how to create an electronic magazine (e-zine) with a complex linking scheme.*

■ **Chapter 6, "Setting the Table: Getting Your Web Pages Posted":** *Once you have your Web page(s) set up, you should invite people to come and sample it. Here, we will explore various options for letting people know you're out there, including posting to Usenet groups, registering your location with the search engines' on-line forms, and linking up with other Web sites.*

■ **Chapter 7, "Coffee and Dessert: Learning More About the Web":** *This chapter will point you to resources for learning more about the Web and will overview HTML editor programs available.*

■ **Appendices:** *The appendices offer a glossary of terms, a listing of HTML tags, and a listing of what's on the CD-ROM.*

○ WHAT'S ON THE CD-ROM

We want to make creating your own Web pages as easy as possible. Therefore, the CD-ROM gives you the tools you need to generate your own Web pages. You will find HTML templates and graphics organized by subject and folder, so creating a home page will be as easy as cutting and pasting text in your word processor. All of the text and graphics files are designed with cross-platform compatibility in mind (as is the Internet itself).

Whether or not you use a Macintosh or a PC, you will be able to open all of the documents, use all of the graphics, and view all of the sample home pages in your browser application.

Some of the software and multimedia content can only be used on one platform or the other. These files will be divided into separate directories for Macintosh and Windows.

The CD-ROM provides you with the following:

- **HTML scripts/templates:** *We have set up templates for creating Web pages on a broad range of subjects including hobbies, businesses, and more, which are organized by topic. All you have to do is fill in the blanks with your own content, and leave the formatting tags intact. In addition, the "Parts" folder contains samples of each type of HTML code saved as individual documents, so you can cut and paste these elements to suit your Web page.*

- **Sample home pages for Chapters 4 and 5:** *All scripts and files discussed in Chapters 4 and 5 can be found in the Chapters 4 and 5 directories.*

- **Graphics:** *We have included an array of .JPG and .GIF graphics files for you to use when creating your home pages. You can jazz up your Web page by using the photographs, logos, horizontal rules, bullets, icons, and backgrounds on the CD-ROM, which will be organized in separate directories by category. In addition, you will find logos and artwork for specific templates included in the appropriate directory.*

- **Public domain software:** *We have also included some Web-related public domain freeware for Windows and Macintosh users so you can play around with it. You can copy it onto your hard drive from either the Windows or Macintosh directory.*

In the various folders for the public domain software, you will find a variety of Web pages that contain useful information about the software. In some cases the information tells you how to install the software; more generally, the information tells you what the vendor expects of you when you use their product. For example, most of the developers of these programs we are distributing restrict you from selling the software in a commercial product.

These pages are HTML files (or on the PC .HTM files), and can be read in your Web browser or in a word processor that is set up to read HTML files and their tags correctly. However, in cases where these pages point to graphics that were on the developer or vendor's server, those graphics were not copied along with the Web page. In those cases you will see a blank box or an icon in place of the missing graphic. You should still be able to read the page without difficulty.

○ BOOK CONVENTIONS

We like conventions. Elisabeth likes to attend conventions to go to fun places. Barrie likes to attend conventions to sleep unfettered by a three-year-old. But just to make sure we understand each other, we should explain the conventions used in this book:

■ ***Cross-platform compatibility:*** *Because we want both Windows and Macintosh users to be able to use this book, we have stuck with the eight-character file name/three-character suffix DOS file-naming conventions for all of the examples offered in the text and CD-ROM material. (We know some of you were waiting in line for Windows 95, but figure most of you with PCs are just getting around to the idea of it when this book goes to press.)*

■ ***Typefaces:*** *All ordinary text will appear in* this typeface. *If we offer a script or tell you to make a specific text entry, it will appear in* <u>this typeface</u>.

- **Note icons:** *When you see the Note icon, you will know that we want to call your attention to a specific detail or issue.*

- **Tip icons:** *These will alert you to fun tricks you can try or useful bits of advice.*

- **Caution icons:** *Pay attention to these so you don't run into any trouble; this is the Gotcha icon.*

○ WHY YOU WANT THIS BOOK

Once upon a time, only technogeeks could figure out how to put a home page up on the Web. Now, all of us can enjoy the thrill of Web publishing. If someone can devote a home page exclusively to the worst-looking stuff on the Web, then what's stopping you from creating a home page? Mirsky's Worst of the Web (http://turnpike.net/metro/mirsky/Worst.html) is shown in Figure I.7

Figure I.7　Mirsky's Worst of the Web.

The Web Page Recipe Book is an easy-to-read guide that makes it easy and fun for nontechnical people to create their own web pages. Simple HTML "recipes" along with appealing illustrations; a CD-ROM containing sample scripts and graphics files; and an appendix containing a glossary, complete HTML tag tables, and a list of the CD-ROM's contents will help you throw together some cool home pages in a snap. So what are you waiting for? Get your kitchen witch hung up over your computer, and let's get started.

PART 1

Cooking Tools

chapter 1

THIS CHAPTER WILL COVER THE FOLLOWING:

- WHAT THE WORLD WIDE WEB IS, ALONG WITH A BRIEF HISTORY OF IT

- BE THERE, DO THAT: WHAT YOU'LL FIND ON THE WEB

- WHAT YOU NEED TO GET ON THE WEB: BROWSERS, GRAZERS, FTP FILE TRANSFER UTILITIES, AND OTHER WEB CRITTERS

- FINDING YOUR WAY AROUND: SEARCH ENGINES

- A FEW COOL PLACES TO CHECK OUT

- WHY WE LIKE THE WEB SO MUCH, AND WHY WE THINK YOU'LL LIKE IT TOO

What's Cooking on the Web

In this chapter, we will introduce you to the World Wide Web. This chapter should give you the context necessary in which to understand why you would want to create Web pages, and provide some of the basic principles on how to do that.

○ WHAT IS IT, BATMAN?

Think of the World Wide Web as a giant library for just about any topic you can think of. Only instead of searching a card catalog and physically turning book pages, you can click your mouse pointer on hypertext links to jump from file to file without regard to where that file is physically stored. Navigating the Internet used to require knowledge of arcane UNIX commands and some technical knowledge, and it was only possible to view text. Now, just about anyone can access the Internet's treasures, thanks to the World Wide Web and browsers that make the information appear graphically.

3

UNIX is a complicated but powerful operating system. Most of the Internet—including the World Wide Web—uses servers running the UNIX operating system, not on DOS, Windows, or Macintosh operating system computers. Fortunately for non-programmers like ourselves, the Web disguises the ugliness of UNIX and allows servers to have desktop clients of all types.

The following ingredients make up the World Wide Web:

■ **Web sites:** *A Web site is a specific location with an Internet "address." That location is a domain, like ucsd.edu, killerapps.com, pbs.org, or whitehouse.gov. The suffixes refer to commercial (.com), education (.edu), organization (.org), and government (.gov).*

NOTE Domains are registered with a central registration service (Network Solutions, Inc.) in Virginia. This used to be a function of the organization InterNIC, but was spun off in Spring 1995. For information about registering domains, check the Web page at http://rs0.internic.net/rs-internic.html.

Web sites are groups of Web pages that can be accessed at a location, Figure 1.1 shows you the home page of our Internet provider, The Internet Access Company (TIAC) (http://www.ti-ac.net/index.cgi/). TIAC is a service provider with a large Web site, and its computers store the files that contain the Web pages of their customers. From here, you can access all of their customers' individual Web pages; some of those are shown in Figure 1.2 (http://www.tiac.net/index.cgi).

Figure 1.1   The TIAC Web site contains links to Web pages of its customers, and stores many of their Web pages on their servers.

■ ***Web pages:*** *When people refer to "Web pages" or "home pages," they're talking about an HTML document, or group of documents (some of which can be other types of files like image files), generated by a single person or organization, as shown in Figure 1.2.*

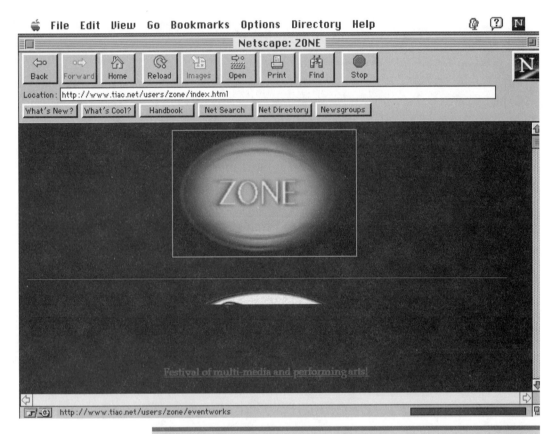

Figure 1.2   Individually generated Web page published on a larger Web site. (Courtesy of Eventworks. Designer: Robert Gabriel Abate)

■ **Web servers:** *A Web server is a computer (generally, but not necessarily, a UNIX workstation) that is attached full-time to the Internet using high-speed telephone connections.*

Most of us can't afford to dedicate a computer to set up our own Web servers, so we pay our Internet providers to provide Internet access for us as if they were an on-line service. Many service providers let us set up home pages on their Web site. Many companies are finding Web sites so useful for disseminating information that they outstrip the capabilities of a service provider and pull their Web sites in-house.

Many desktop computers and operating systems can be used as Web servers. It doesn't require a powerhouse PC or workstation to provide these capabilities. For example, a mid-range Macintosh using either a 68030 or a Power Macintosh with a 601 chip at 60 MHz will do nicely as a Web server.

Similarly, a 80486 DX2 66 computer will be serviceable. The most popular Web solutions on Windows use the Windows NT, and support a small or medium-sized workgroup of people connected to it at any one time. This single use for NT has led to great interest in that operating system.

Solutions on computers, such as those mentioned in the previous two paragraphs, will satisfy a workgroup, or 20 or so simultaneous connections. Factors such as hard drive and modem characteristics are seen to be more important at this low load level. As your need for more simultaneous connections grows, your need to move up to more powerful computers, more memory, and so on grows. Serious Web servers tend to run very fast Pentium systems or, more commonly, Sun servers.

■ *Universal Resource Location (URL): A URL is the cyberspace equivalent of a street address. Every Web page has an individual URL address so people can find it by entering the URL in the Open Location option in their browser application, as shown in Figure 1.3.*

A URL generally consists of the type of protocol for the file's viewing. If a URL begins with **http** (which stands for the hypertext transfer protocol), then you know it's a Web page. FTP (which stands for the File Transfer Protocol) site URLs begin with **ftp**, followed by the name of the host, the port, the name of a directory, and the name of a document.

Here's an important point for you to appreciate. If you examine the file structure of a Web server, what you see are a set of folders that contain the Web pages for the site. The syntax of the URLs calls the domain or address of the Internet address and maps it to its physical location (server). The remainder of the URL points to the path to the files for the Web page on the appropriate server.

Let's break down a sample URL or two for an example. Take the address shown in Figure 1.3:

```
http://www.sito.org/sito/artchives.html
```

CAUTION

Be very careful to enter the exact spelling and punctuation for a URL. Addresses on the Internet are case-insensitive (and generally entered in lower case), but documents are often case-sensitive. If you don't connect to a known site, check your address carefully. The effect is similar to sending a fax to the wrong phone number.

The above URL is the address of the Otis Online Art Gallery, featuring links to artists' collections and art museums. The "http:" tells you that it's a Web site; "sunsite.unc.edu" is the name of Sun Microsystem's file server located at the University of North Carolina, which is an educational institution. The portion "/otis" points to a folder or directory name on that file server where the Otis Online Art Gallery is set up. The main document or home page for the Otis Art Gallery is a file called "gallery.html."

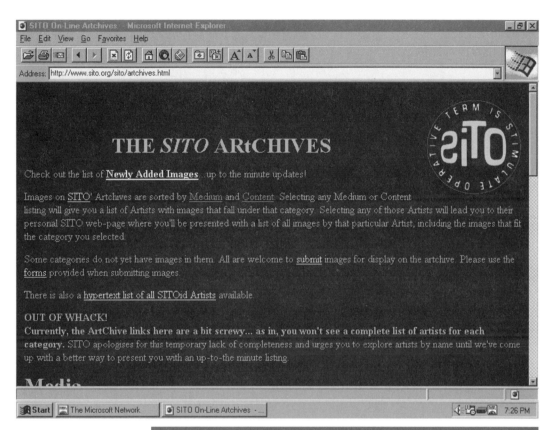

Figure 1.3   Entering a URL in the Find Location option of a browser application.

Many Web sites are more obvious than the address you saw above. They have an address like the following:

```
http://www.microsoft.com
```

The **www** in the address is a dead giveaway that the site requested is a World Wide Web site. The **.com** extension indicates that it is a commercial venture, as in fact we all know Microsoft Corporation to be.

- ***Hypertext Markup Language (HTML):*** *HTML is an easy-to-use standard markup language used for generating Web pages. It is an agreed-upon standard specified by an international committee and published for all to use. In a markup language, you insert tags that tell the reading application how to format the text it finds or work with the documents it references. (HTML is not a programming language!)*

NOTE

HTML is a subset of a broader markup language called SGML, or the Standard General Markup Language. This language was developed to make formatting documents distributed among government and military institutions in the United States easier to accomplish.

Command tags are entered in text-only documents to tell browsers how to display text and graphics. You can enter the tags yourself, or use special utilities to place tags (they often occur in pairs in HTML documents) as required. These utilities exist as stand-alone products, or as additions to word processors like Microsoft Word or Novell WordPerfect.

Text and graphic displays vary from browser to browser; that is, some browsers let you use tags others don't or display the effects of a tag in some special way. However, there are many standard tags that are basic in HTML, and don't change at all from browser to browser. We focus on those standard tags in this book before we move on to a few unique examples. In Chapters 4 and 5 of this book, we will use HTML to create our own home pages.

- ***Web Browsers:*** *Software applications designed for viewing the contents of the Web. Some software, like Lynx, display only text. The most popular ones, like Mosaic and Netscape, are more exciting because they also display* *color and graphics. It was the appearance of the first browser, NCSA Mosaic, that led to the popularization of the World Wide Web. More in a moment…*

■ **Search Engines:** *Think of search engines as enormous searchable databases for locating Web pages by topic, keywords, name, or location. Examples of search engines include WebCrawler and Lycos.*

Each of these search engines have different methods of gathering information so you can find what's out there. For example, several search engines use what is called a "software robot" to go out and visit Web sites, examine the keywords contained therein, and then index the content of that site.

■ **Directory Services:** *A directory service is a special kind of Web site that organizes other Web sites by category. The best example of a directory service is Yahoo (http://www.yahoo.com). When you visit Yahoo, you can navigate a tree of topics until you zero in on the listing of interest to you. Each listing contains jumps to one or more Web pages containing material of interest. Yahoo is also a searchable database of keywords and summary descriptions.*

■ **PPP/SLIP Connections:** *PPP stands for Point-to-Point Protocol. SLIP stands for Serial Line Internet Protocol. Both of these two protocols are TCP/IP protocols (see below) for transmitting IP datagrams over serial lines such as phone lines. With PPP, users connect to the Internet and still operate in their native environment (e.g., Macintosh or Windows) instead of UNIX.*

■ **TCP:** *Stands for Transmission Control Protocol, part of the TCP/IP protocol stack. This protocol or agreement lets different networks exchange information. The suite of protocols includes methods for remote login (telnet), file transfer (FTP), e-mail (SMTP), and so forth.*

TCP/IP works with any computer or operating system, and was developed by the Defense Advanced Research Projects Agency (DARPA) in the 1970s as a robust set of internetworking protocols that could withstand a nuclear attack. Windows users generally use Trumpet TCP, a $75 shareware program to create a TCP session to the Internet. For Macintosh users, Mac TCP comes with System 7.5. You can think of this software as a specialized form of telecommunications package. Once connected, you fire up your Internet browser, mail package, or file transfer utility to transfer information over the connection that the TCP communication package has created.

We will discuss all of the items just mentioned in greater detail later in this chapter.

○ A BRIEF HISTORY

The World Wide Web began in the late '80s with the World Wide Web Initiative, a group of developers seeking to put a friendlier face on the Internet. Their goal was to create an easy-to-use interface so that nontechnical users could easily share information, text, and graphics. Finally, the World Wide Web was launched in 1991 at the European Particle Physics Laboratory (CERN) in Geneva, Switzerland. The current widespread use of the Web testifies to their success! You can access a vast array of Web-related resources at the World Wide Web Consortium, which grew out of the CERN site, MIT, and other central sites. It is located at http://www.w3.org and shown in Figure 1.4. The CERN home page, which is generally credited as being the birthplace of the World Wide Web, is now found at http://www.cern.ch.

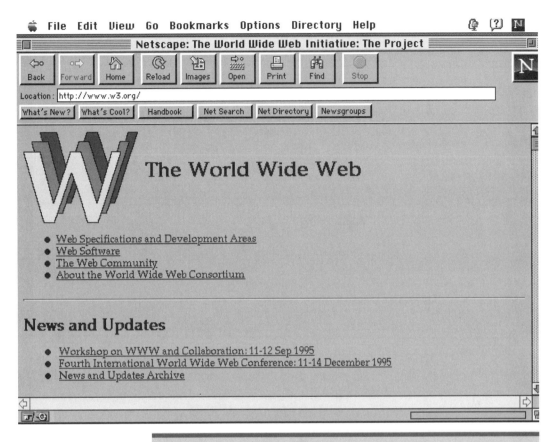

Figure 1.4 The World Wide Web Consortium Home page.

NOTE

The W3C site is one of the best sites to visit on the Web. However, it is heavily subscribed and can be hard to connect to. Try it in an off hour, late at night or early in the morning.

In 1991 the Web was primarily used by the scientific and academic community, and less than 100 Web sites existed. A year later, CERN started encouraging organizations outside of academia to check out the Web—and the Web expanded to over 500 locations. Ever since then, the number of Web sites has increased approximately tenfold every year. As of 1995 the World Wide Web had over 500,000 locations, and new ones keep popping up every hour.

At first, there were only text-mode browsers (the applications you need for viewing information on the Web) available, like Lynx. Then, the University of Illinois' National Center for Supercomputing Applications (NCSA) introduced Mosaic. The Mosaic browser generated excitement by allowing people to view Web pages with color graphics. You can download Mosaic at the NCSA ftp site (ftp://ftp.ncsa.uiuc.edu/Mosaic). Now there are a wide array of text and graphical browsers available. We will discuss these in detail later in this chapter.

○ WHY WE LIKE IT

Once you log on to the World Wide Web, it's hard to log out! The Web offers fascinating opportunities for seeing what other Webmasters are up to and for publishing your own information. One link leads to another, then to another, and before you know it, you get lost in this anarchic Internet playground. Although many groups and individuals have made admirable attempts to organize, catalog, and keep track of the Web's offerings, no one has quite succeeded. But you can be sure of one thing: if you're looking for something, it's out there somewhere on the Web. It's a rare search of the Web that doesn't yield some nugget of information on a topic of interest.

We like the Web for the following reasons:

- ■ **Ease of use:** *You no longer need to enter complicated strings of UNIX commands to navigate the Internet. Thanks to the World Wide Web, you can find your way around the Internet the same way as on your PC or Macintosh: by pointing and clicking your mouse.*

- ***Finding information:*** *You can use the Web's search engines to quickly locate information on just about any topic under the sun. Think of the Web as the biggest database in the world. If you're a serious researcher, a large number of academic sites offer a broad range of hard-to-find texts from around the globe, complete with indexes, footnotes, and citations. If you're looking for fun, the Web offers plenty of that, too.*

- ***The joyous anarchy of it all:*** *You never know what you'll find on the Web. Other communications vehicles like television, radio, and the print media are subject to high costs and government regulation. Meanwhile, publishing on the Web is relatively cheap, and it has proven almost impossible to regulate material on the Internet. Large corporate sites and small sites devoted to an eccentric array of topics jostle and compete for your attention on an equal footing. When looking up a topic, your search engine doesn't know the difference between Joe Schmoe's home page and Humongous Corporation's site. If Joe Schmoe's home page offers more relevant information pertaining to your topic, it will even appear further up on the list that is returned by your search!*

○ BE THERE, DO THAT

You don't need a car or a plane ticket to travel around on the Web. With a computer, a modem, and the right software, you can check out Web pages from around the globe while sitting in your home or office. Although cyberspace will (or should) never substitute for real-life experience, the ability to access such a broad range of information and individual perspectives holds an undeniable fascination. Some Web sites offer valuable resources and information, like the W3C site mentioned earlier in the chapter. Others are just plain silly. Whether you're a serious researcher looking for texts on a particular subject or a Bart Simpson fan, you'll find what you're looking for—and encounter many things that you never even knew existed along the way.

Here's what you'll find on the Web:

- **Information on just about anything:** *Are you taking a trip? (Try Travel Weekly at http://www.travel.net/) Seeking more information about the World Wide Web? (Try Web 66 at http://web66.coled.umn.edu/) Search your topic with the search engines and see what turns up. No matter how obscure your subject matter may be, there will probably be something out there. The Web's hypertext links are ideal for jumping from place to place until you find the information you want.*

- **Images:** *You will find a dizzying array of images on the World Wide Web, many of which can be downloaded to your hard drive for your personal use. Whether you want a photo of Newt Gingrich with an alien from the Newt Watch home page (http://www.cais.com/newtwatch/) or travel photographs from Kodak's corporate site (http://www.kodak.com/digitalImages/digitalImages.shtml), shown in Figure 1.5, you can find it on the Web.*

CAUTION

Of course, if you use images or data for any sort of widespread distribution, avoid possible legal difficulty by making sure they're not copyrighted. Get permission from whoever owns the rights to them. Since the information is so freely available, the Web lulls you into thinking that it's yours for the taking.

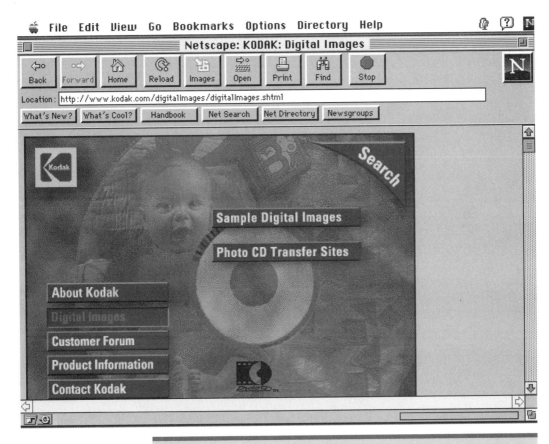

Figure 1.5   Many Web pages, including Kodak's corporate site, offer downloadable images. (Reprinted with permission from Eastman Kodak Company.)

■ ***Multimedia:*** *Sounds and movies are fun! Many Web pages offer downloadable sound and video files which you can download and listen to or view on your computer. To find sites with sounds, try Audio Clips (http://www.eecs.nwu.edu/~jmyers/other-sounds.html). For video clips, try the Yahoo Multimedia/Video Page (http://www.yahoo.com/Computers/Multimedia/Video).*

- **Portable document format (.PDF) files:** *Adobe Systems Incorporated has a program out called Acrobat, which has the potential of revolutionizing the publications industry. Acrobat lets you convert magazines, books, and other literature into .PDF files, which are based on the PostScript graphics language.*

Portable documents can be shared over networks, downloaded, or sent as e-mail attachments for viewing and printing on Windows, DOS, Macintosh, and UNIX workstations. Regardless of what program and operating system the piece was created with, you can see the publication in its full graphical glory—with all of the images, formatting, and design intact. All you need is the Acrobat Reader, a freely distributed helper application which you can download from the Adobe site (http://www.adobe.com/). We will further discuss helper applications in Chapter 2, "Gathering your Web Page Ingredients."

- **Computer games:** *The World Wide Web abounds with fun computer games that you can download to your computer and play. The Web is also a treasure trove to the game enthusiast because many sites are devoted to sneak previews, gaming strategies, and links to other game-related sites (try Ziff Davis' Computer Gaming World site at http://www.zdnet.com/~gaming/).*

- **Free goodies:** *Oh boy, free goodies! In addition to all the things mentioned above, you can get lots of software off of the Web. When you click on a pointer in a Web document that points to a downloadable file, your browser will prompt you to name and locate the file on your hard drive. Then your browser will transfer the file.*

Why would you want more software? Well, you need help-er applications in order to enjoy some of the Web's offerings mentioned above. There are also programs that make it easier for you to generate Web pages, format graphics as .GIF files, process files so you can serve them on your web site more ef-fectively and more. Plus, you may want to try some of the many Web browsers available. We will discuss downloadable Web-related software further in Chapter 2.

So what are you waiting for? Let's log on!

○ WHY YOU'LL LIKE IT

You'll like the Web because it's so easy to use and you can do so much with it. The accessibility and affordability of putting forth information on the Web offers a wealth of possibilities. The Web holds unprecedented opportunities for exchanging and distributing information within a vast global community.

Here are some of the things you'll be able to do on the World Wide Web.

■ ***Publish your own magazine:*** *Have you ever fantasized about publishing your own magazine about any subject you want? Well, now you can!*

Maintaining a basic Internet account with Web space costs well under $100 per month. Some Internet providers even give you space on their file server free of charge just for signing up with them. Whether you want to publish information about a fa-vorite hobby or simply rant and rave, putting up a home page costs a lot less than printing on paper.

One of us (Elisabeth) publishes her own on-line magazine, Byte It! (http//www.byteit.com), with a listing of the happenings in the Boston area. Her site is visited through a jump from the TIAC site.

- ■ ***Promote your small business:*** *Whether you have a small consulting firm or a growing company with a full product line, the Web is an ideal place to put forth your latest information so it reaches your customers.*

You can even provide on-line forms so customers can instantly order products, request more information, or give you feedback. And since it doesn't cost much, you can also provide fun tidbits, links to related sites, interesting graphics, and other offerings that will make people keep wanting to visit your site.

The other one of us (Barrie) has a small database and consulting company and advertises it via the Web at http://www.tiac.net/users/basman/.

- ■ ***Have fun:*** *Sure, the Web can be put to many practical uses. But part of the reason the Web has gotten so popular is because it's pure, unadulterated fun. You can put anything you want on your web page—photographs, artwork, silly sound clips, links to favorite web sites, and even home movies.*

Start a fan club for your favorite television show or band. Or devote your page to a pet subject of yours, whether it's gardening, rock and roll music, an obscure B-movie star, or something else—new content is always welcome. The Web page shown in Figure 1.6 is devoted to Mary Tyler Moore (http://rucs2.sunlab.cs.runet.edu/~msharov/mary/mary.html/).

Figure 1.6   The Mary Tyler Moore home page shows that Web sites can be devoted to just about any topic!

■ *Make new friends:* No matter what subject you choose to address on your Web page, you'll find people with common interests. By including response forms or at least an e-mail link, visitors can give you feedback, contribute material, and tell you about what they're doing on the Web. We'll show you how to include those types of links later in this book.

Now that you have some idea of what the Web has in store for you, we'll talk more about browsers.

○ CRUISE THE 'NET IN STYLE: WEB BROWSERS

In order to cruise the Web, you need a Web browser for viewing home pages. Web browsers interact with Web servers to locate and retrieve documents. They then process the information contained in the HTML documents, format it, and display the material. The browser also handles hypertext links, so that when you click on a linked item, it knows where you want to go. Many Web browsers are available, but the ones listed below are the most popular ones. Most browsers are either freeware (you can download the software free of charge) or shareware (you can try it out, but if you like them, please be nice and send a check to the developers).

Browsers make navigating the Web easy by offering options for opening locations, returning to your opening screen, reloading information, backtracking to where you just were, and adding "bookmarks" so you can visit places you like regularly without having to write down the URL somewhere. Some browsers, like Netscape, also offer additional options for displaying text and graphics.

As you begin cruising the Web, you will notice that it lacks formatting capabilities. If you are used to complex desktop publishing options and programs, formatted Web pages are going to look pretty crude to you. For example, text cannot be laid out in columns and grids as when publishing on paper and getting tables into a Web page is a chore. Most displays are pretty barebones, with headlines followed by text and a few images thrown in here and there. Although the Web's ability to display color graphics is impressive, we have a long way to go before saying goodbye to the print industry!

A list of browsers and pointers to them can be found on the CERN Web site at: http://www.w3.org/hypertext/WWW/ Clients.html.

Listed below are some of the many browsers available on the Web:

■ **Lynx:** *Lynx is a text-only application, meaning that it won't let you check out any graphics, sound, or video files.*

Versions of Lynx run on a variety of computers (DOS, Windows, OS/2, AIX), but not the Macintosh. With Lynx you can still download graphics, sound, and video, and enjoy them using an external helper application (we will discuss helper applications further in Chapter 2, "Gathering your Web Page Ingredients"). Lynx supports FTP transfers, Gopher, WAIS, and UseNet News services.

Many Web users (but not the majority at this point) still use text-style Web browsers. We use Lynx in this book to check out our Web pages and see what they look like to those kinds of viewers. A properly designed Web page accommodates all kinds of browsers, even ones that don't display images.

While cruising the Web, you may notice that graphics and multimedia take a frustratingly long time to view or download anyway. So if you want greater speed while cruising the Web, or if you have a DOS operating system or a slow modem, Lynx will deliver the information you want faster and more efficiently. Lynx was developed at the University of Kansas. You can get it from their FTP site at ftp://ftp2.cc.ukans.edu/pub/lynx. Since Lynx is a shareware application, the developers request a donation if you find it useful.

TIP

Many graphical browsers have an option that lets you turn off the display of graphic images to speed up the viewing of Web pages. Instead, a standard icon for an image is displayed. You can click on that icon to view the image. An example is shown in Figure 1.7.

- **Mosaic:** *Mosaic was developed at the University of Illinois' National Center for Supercomputing Applications (NCSA). (What you see in Figure 1.7 is an advanced version of the program.) Mosaic was the first browser that enabled users to view Web pages with embedded images. Many commercial versions of Mosaic have appeared. The NCSA offers versions of Mosaic for UNIX, Windows, and Macintosh. You can get Mosaic from the NCSA site at ftp://ftp.ncsa.uiuc.edu. Mosaic is a freeware application and can therefore be used and distributed free of charge.*

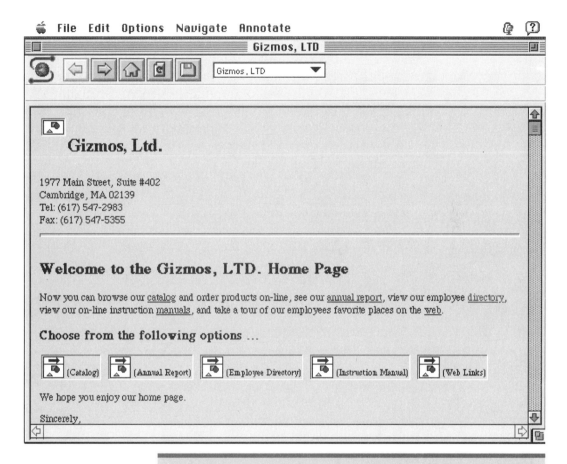

Figure 1.7   A Web page viewed with Mosaic. Note the icons; the graphics appear when you click on them.

■ ***Netscape:*** *The Netscape browser (shown in Figure 1.8) has many exciting features, such as the ability to display backgrounds, adjust font sizes, and align images, and extensive support for on-line forms.*

Netscape is brought to you by the Netscape Communications Corporation, which specializes in Internet-related software. This company was launched by some of the original developers of Mosaic, and has captured an estimated 70% of the

Internet World Wide Web (WWW) browser market. Although Netscape is a commercial product, you can often obtain a copy of the latest version of the product (even beta copies) through your Internet provider, or by downloading it from http://www.netscape.com. Many of the figures shown throughout this book use the Macintosh or Windows version of Netscape.

Figure 1.8 A Web page viewed in the Macintosh version of Netscape.

■ *MacWeb and WinWeb: TradeWave offers the WinWeb and MacWeb browsers. You can get these browsers from their ftp sites at ftp://ftp.einet.net/einet/pc/winweb (for Win-*

*dows users) or ftp://ftp.einet.net/einet/mac/macweb (for
Macintosh users). Although WinWeb and MacWeb lack
some of Mosaic's and Netscape's bells and whistles, they
support graphical displays and forms, and are speedier and
take up less disk space than their flashier counterparts.*

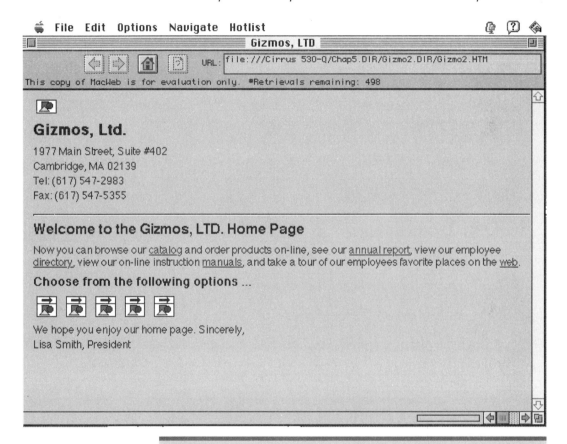

Figure 1.9   A Web page viewed with MacWeb.

Currently, two operating systems ship with Web browsers.
OS/2 Warp contains the WebExplorer in its BonusPak. WebExplorer is a very nice, fast, and slick 32-bit application running in
OS/2. In WebExplorer you can do the following: download files
with FTP, access and use Gopher sites, and use WAIS, Telnet,

UseNet News services, and e-mail. OS/2 Warp ships with individual applications in the Internet Connections folder that do these tasks with more features.

One of us (Barrie) is very impressed with the speed and stability of the WebExplorer, as he is with OS/2 Warp itself. With the WebExplorer you have a 32-bit piece of software that is fully drag-and-drop-enabled. If you see a file you want to download in WebExplorer, you simply drag and drop it to the OS/2 Desktop. Figure 1.10 shows you the WebExplorer.

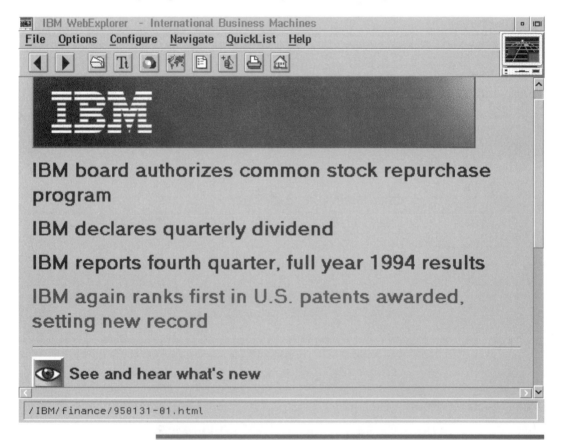

Figure 1.10 The OS/2 Warp WebExplorer. (Reprinted by permission from International Business Machines.)

The WebExplorer is also notable for a very nice Web Map of sites you have visited previously in a session.

The second common desktop operating system shipping with a Web browser is the one that comes with Windows 95. That browser is based on Spry Mosaic, and provides a direct connection to the Microsoft Network. It's not much of a jump to believe that in the next year or two all operating systems will ship with a Web browser. Apple has a number of Internet utilities under development. Their first product in this area is a suite called the Apple Internet kit, which includes Netscape Navigator as its browser.

And if these aforementioned browsers aren't enough, most of the major on-line services have or are integrating Web browsers into their services. America Online's browser, purchased from Internetworks, comes in version 3.0 in June for Macintosh and Windows. One of us (Barrie) who's worked extensively with AOL's Web browser is impressed with its speed, ease of use, and integration into the America Online suite of services. Figure 1.11 shows the AOL Internet connection screen that leads off to the Web browser, an FTP utility, Newsgroup reader, and Gopher browser. The home page for America Online shown in their Web browser appears in Figure 1.12.

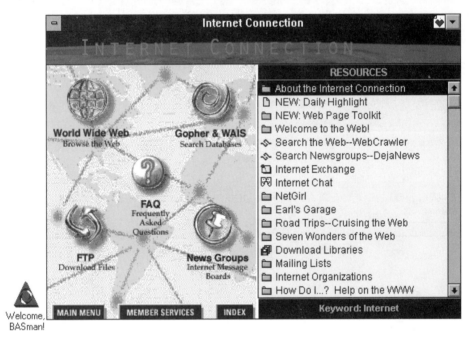

Figure 1.11 AOL's Internet Connection.

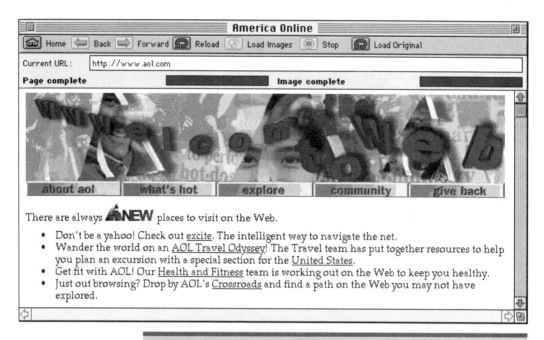

Figure 1.12 The AOL home page shown in the AOL browser.

CompuServe's Internet Web browser is slated for a late 1995 release, and should be out by the time you read this. Other services are also offering Web browsers, such as Prodigy and soon, Delphi. If you think it's raining Web browsers, you're right! We're finding Web browsers in our mail, browsers in our magazines, and browsers in our cereal boxes. And there's a lot of hopping around from service to service as subscribers check out the various offerings.

○ GETTING YOURS: UPLOADING AND DOWNLOADING FILES

Once you have your browser, downloading files is as easy as pointing and clicking on a link. But first, you have to get your Web software. If you are not given one by your service provider or your on-line service, consider using an FTP program to download one from an FTP site. FTP stands for File Transfer Protocol, and it is a fast, easy way to get your goodies from somebody's file server. FTP programs connect you to a remote computer, let you log in, search through directories and download the program you want.

When downloading files, you will generally be logging on to an "anonymous" FTP site. This means that the server offers a public FTP archive so that people who don't have accounts can log on by entering "anonymous" as their user name, and their e-mail address as their password. Private directories deny access to unauthorized users by requiring a specified name and password. For example, when uploading Web pages to the directory assigned to you by your Internet provider, you will generally enter your e-mail address at the user name prompt (e.g., basman@tiac.net), and your personal password at the password prompt.

The most commonly used FTP programs are Trumpet FTP for Windows users and Fetch for Macintosh users.

○ ANATOMY OF A WEB PAGE

The Hypertext Markup Language (HTML) is a formatting language used for creating the structure of a Web page and defining sets of elements within that document. Actually, HTML is less a language than a set of formatting codes that you apply to your page. If you are familiar with either PostScript or the Rich Text Format's method for formatting a graphics or text page, respectively, then HTML will look very unintimidating to you.

You'll be seeing a lot of HTML marked-up pages in the chapters to come.

A Web browser interprets a marked-up page using the tags or elements you have defined. What do we mean by the word "elements"? Think of them as the ingredients for your Web recipes, which will generally include titles, headings, paragraphs, lists, and graphics.

You can create your own home pages in any word processing program or even a simple text editor like Notepad on Windows 3.1, Wordpad in Windows 95, or SimpleText on the Macintosh; anything, in fact, that can save your documents in text-only (straight, Lower, or 7-bit ASCII) format.

In order to distinguish HTML documents from your word processing documents or text files, use the .htm suffix at the end of your file names instead of .doc or .txt; for example, save your file as "mypage.htm." It is especially important for all you Macintosh users out there to remember this because you probably are not accustomed to adding suffixes to your document names. Because your Web pages will be served to Macintosh, Windows, DOS, and UNIX users alike, you might as well begin using the eight-character-file-name three-character-suffix DOS naming conventions now, even though you don't have to, and probably don't want to.

Among the ingredients that your Web page recipes will use are:

■ **Formatting tags:** *Every element in your home page must be defined with HTML markup tags. Otherwise, your browser won't know how to display your home page. In general, every time you change any of the formatting of your text, you must add opening and closing tags. HTML has tags for headers, paragraphs, bulleted lists, numbered lists, block quotes, and more.*

For example, the following HTML entry with formatting tags would appear in your browser as shown in Figure 1.13.

<HTML>

The <HTML> tag at the top tells the browser to view this as an HTML document.

<HEAD>
<TITLE>Our Home Page</TITLE>
</HEAD>

The <TITLE>...</TITLE> tags tell the browser to display the name of your home page on the title bar at the top of the screen.

It's considered good practice to wrap all header information like titles within the <HEAD> . . . </HEAD> tags. These tags do nothing more than block out the header information so that it's easy to figure out what parts are in the header, in the same manner that <BODY> . . . </BODY> blocks out your body section.

<H1>This is a Header</H1>

The <H1>...</H1> tags tell the browser to display this line of text in the larger, bolder type appropriate to a headline. HTML lets you use several levels of headings—H1, H2, and so on.

<BODY>
This is regular body text. Most browsers will display it in regular, 12-point, Times Roman type. But many browsers let you set a preference for the font you would like to use when viewing Web pages
</BODY>

The <BODY>...</BODY> is a "wrapper" tag that surrounds the body part of your document, and differentiates it from the header or footer. If you don't put the </BODY> tag at the end of your document, a browser will assume that it should be there.

</HTML>

Don't forget to close your HTML document.

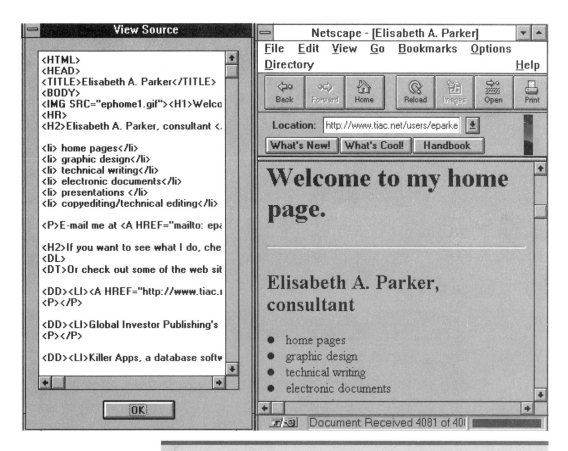

Figure 1.13 All elements of your Web page must be defined with the appropriate tags so it will display correctly.

■ *Hypertext links*: Books and magazines have tables of contents and indexes for topics addressed in the publication. Web pages are organized with hypertext links. Instead of turning pages, you simply click on a link to jump to where you want to go. You can either link to specified areas within a single HTML document, to other HTML documents in your folder, or to other people's home pages.

You can specify links by adding

<A HREF="Place to be linked to">...</A>

to your document anchor tags. We will learn how to add links in Chapter 4, "Some Sample Dishes."

■ **Graphics:** *You can add images to your Web pages by specifying the source of the image. The browser will then know to display an image. Typically, inline images in Web documents are .JPG or .GIF files. Both of these file types are cross-platform file formats.*

To point to an image file that will be displayed by your browser, you use an image tag, for example:

<IMG SRC="...">

The contents in the parentheses represent a file and its path. We will further discuss working with images in Chapter 4, "Some Sample Dishes," and Chapter 5, "Sample Meals."

NOTE

Inline .GIF and .JPG images will display as part of your HTML document. Other file formats can only be displayed by either downloading them with the browser, or viewing them in a graphics application or an external viewing helper application. We will further discuss helper applications in Chapter 2, "Gathering your Web Page Ingredients."

■ **Downloadable files:** *You can also offer sounds, movies, computer games, portable document files, and public do-main software on your Web site. However, these types of files are generally too large to be launched directly from your Web site. Instead, you can reduce their file size using a compression utility like WinZip (Windows) or StuffIt (Macintosh), and add links to these files so your visitors can download them by clicking on the appropriate link.*

Now that you have some idea of the range of items that you can put on your home page, let's learn how to use search engines to retrieve content from the World Wide Web.

○ MOVING AROUND THE WEB

The Web is more than dynamic, it is an organic beast. Don't be surprised if some of the URLs we give you no longer work (how rude! $%&*&!), or messages come up telling you that Web pages have moved to a new location (that's better!). Worse yet is the fact that the Web is huge; finding information is (or can be) like looking for a needle in a haystack. More often, it is like looking for hundreds of needles in a field of haystacks.

Fortunately, the Web boasts several sites devoted entirely to cataloging Web pages and maintaining searchable databases so you can look up topics by keyword. These types of Web sites are called search engines, and you will find them easy to use. All you have to do is enter your keyword in the query window and click on the Submit button or hit your Enter key. When your search is finished, a list of matches will appear. Since each search engine uses a different method for gathering and sorting information, you may want to use several of them when searching your topics.

Here are some of the better known search engines:

■ **Lycos** (http://www.lycos.com): The Lycos site, as shown in Figure 1.14, maintained by Carnegie Mellon University, has over two million listings of URLs and brief descriptions of the sites. When you enter your search, Lycos lists the results in order of relevance—measured by how often your keyword appears in a Web page's introductory paragraph. Of course, this method of determining relevance depends greatly on how well a Webmaster can write an introductory paragraph.

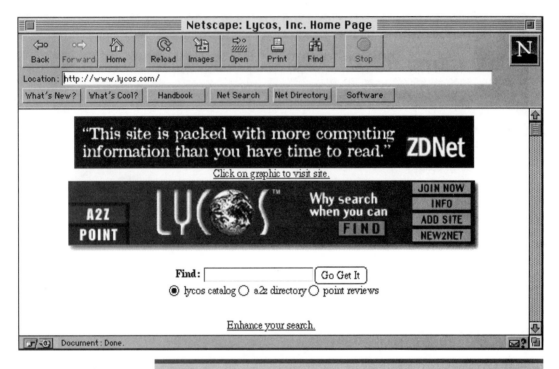

Figure 1.14 The Lycos catalog of the Internet.

- **WebCrawler** *(http://webcrawler.com): WebCrawler, as shown in Figure 1.15, is programmed to search the Web and automatically index Web pages for inclusion in its giant database. Like Lycos, the WebCrawler lists your matches in order of relevance. Recently, WebCrawler was purchased by America Online; however, it is still (and hopefully always will be) available on the Internet.*

WebCrawler and Lycos build their indices by having an automated software program go out and visit sites on the Internet. The robot (as it's called) reads the HTML documents at a Web site and indexes the important words it finds. Yahoo (described be-low) creates a directory listing by manual entries into a database.

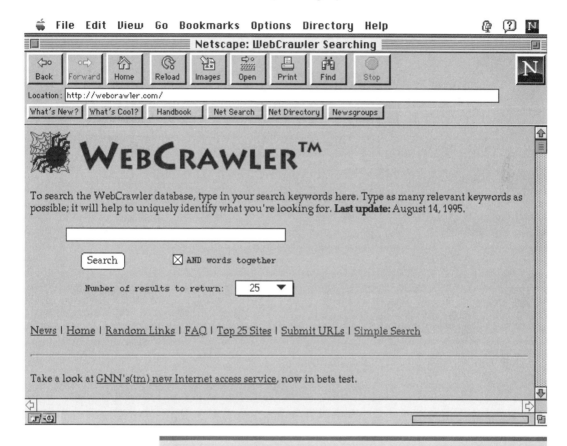

Figure 1.15 The WebCrawler.

■ *Yahoo (http://www.yahoo.com): Yahoo seems to be every-one's favorite directory service these days. (It certainly is Barrie's.) It's easy to use, and has fun graphics and more than 50,000 Web sites cataloged on their server. Yahoo lets you search by keyword for matches by title, URL, and com-ments, as shown in Figure 1.16. When the search is com-plete, a list of titles will appear in the Yahoo Search*

Window. The administrators, two Stanford University graduates, are continuously adding new listings. Plus, you can fill out an on-line form to tell them about your new Web site.

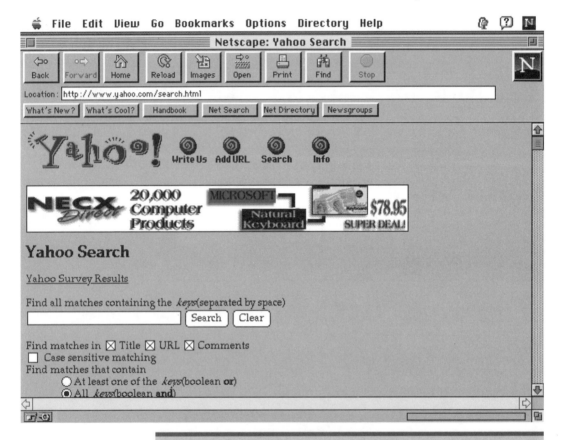

Figure 1.16 The Yahoo search page. (Text and artwork copyright ©1996 by YAHOO!, Inc. All rights reserved. YAHOO! and the YAHOO! logo are trademarks of YAHOO!, Inc.)

What we particularly like about Yahoo is its flexibility. In addition to its ability to do different types of searches, Yahoo organizes its database by topic listings. Therefore, you can search for topics like Art, Business, Computers, Economy, Education, and so on. Unlike searching a database, Yahoo has the feel of searching a good on-line encyclopedia.

Every search engine or directory service contains its own set of information organized in its own way. You shouldn't limit your search to the three services mentioned above. There are many more to be tried, and each always seems to yield something of value. In a serious search of the Internet, try the listings mentioned below.

- ■ *Other search engines: If you don't find enough information on the topic you're looking for, try EINet Galaxy (http://www.einet.net/) and the CUI W3 Catalog (http://cuiw-ww.unige.ch/w3catalog). These sites also have many listings and serve as a good jumping-off point to other search engines. You can also search for "search engines" using one of the tools we've mentioned to get a list of what's out there.*

○ COOL WEB SITES

To gain inspiration for creating your own Web pages, you should check out what's already out there. Since most browsers let you check the source document, these sites will give you many new ideas to try. Here are some places that we have enjoyed visiting:

- ■ *Fox Broadcasting (http://www.eden.com/users/my-html/fox.html): This site offers television listings, news about Fox and its stars, and links to Web sites related to popular shows such as Beverly Hills 90210, Mighty Morphin Power Rangers, Melrose Place, and The Simpsons.*

- ■ *Netscape: What's Cool? (http://home.mcom.com/escapes/whats_cool.html): Start your 'Net surfing expedition at Netscape's "What's Cool" page. Since Netscape specializes in Web browser products and software, they should know what's hip. Here, you will find links to fun, useful, and new places on the Web. This page also links you back to the Netscape main home page, where you can find out about their latest products.*

- **GNN Home Page** *(http://nearnet.gnn.com/gnn/gnn/): Global Network Navigator's home page also offers an array of interesting links. From here, you can get to the Whole Internet Catalog, NCSA Mosaic, Net News, Best of the Net, and more. And, of course, you can also see a catalog of GNN products, which you can order on-line.*

- **Kodak Digital Images** *(http://www.kodak.com/digitalImages/digitalImages.shtml): Kodak offers an impressive array of photographs, ranging from tourist attractions from around the world to impressive landscapes. Feel free to download some of your favorites.*

- **Hot Wired** *(http://www.hotwired.com): Now you can get really wired. This is the electronic version of Wired magazine, a slick publication covering trends, happenings, and personalities in the cyber-community. Naturally, they have one of the most impressive home pages on the 'Net.*

- **Dan's News** *(http://www.emi.net/boynton/dan.html): This electronic newsstand offers links to on-line versions of newspapers across the globe, including the New York Post, Chicago Tribune, International Express, and more. Although viewing publications on-line isn't always the most ideal way to read them, it's a great way to access information on a particular current events topic.*

- **Bartlett's Familiar Quotations** *(http://www.columbia.edu/acis/bartleby/bartlett): Stumped because you can't remember who said "Early to bed, early to rise, makes a man healthy, wealthy and wise..."? (Ben Franklin said it in Poor Richard's Almanac.) Instead of driving out to your local library, simply log on to the Bartlett's Familiar Quotations* *site, as shown in Figure 1.17, and use their keyword-searchable index. Researching has never been easier.*

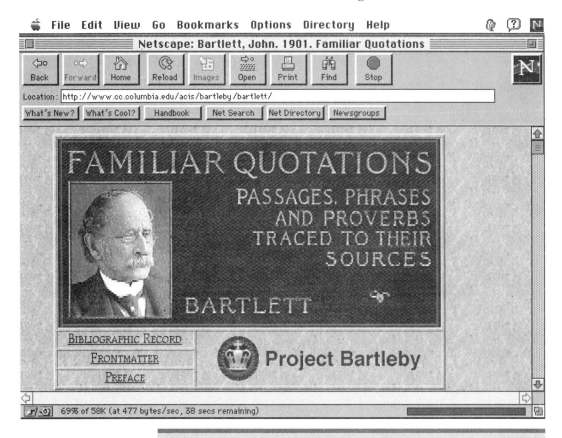

Figure 1.17 Bartlett's Familiar Quotations.

■ **ESPNET** (*http://espnet.sportszone.com*): *Sports fans can check out ESPN's Web site, which publishes feature stories, photographs, statistics, and sports news about teams and athletes from around the globe.*

■ **The Louvre** (*http://www.cnam.fr/louvre/*): *Can't afford that trip to Paris? Take a tour of the Louvre from your own home. The French Ministry of Culture's Louvre Web site offers images of some of the world's most celebrated works of art, along with explanatory text.*

■ **The White House** *(http://www.whitehouse.gov): The White House home page (shown in Figure 1.18) lets you e-mail the president, jump to other U.S. government sites such as the U.S. Senate, browse important historical documents such as the Constitution, and even see pictures of the first family.*

Figure 1.18 White House home page.

As you look at these sites in your Web browser, note some of the effects: how the pages were set up, how images were used, the use of type, and so on. You might also want to look at the underlying HTML descriptions as a challenge for the future. As you learn more about HTML, you will be able to use what you see in other Web pages to help you build your own Web pages. Now that we've taken a look at what's out there, we can move on to the next chapter.

○ ARE YOU WEBBED UP?

We assume that since you bought this book, you already have an Internet hookup with access to the World Wide Web. But in case you haven't, we'll pause a moment to address this issue. To put your home pages on the Web, you'll need the following:

■ **PPP/SLIP Internet Account:** *Remember how we mentioned Point-to-Point and Serial Line Internet Protocols? You need to make sure that your Internet provider offers those services.*

The large national services like America Online, Delphi, and CompuServe all have Web browsers up and running. However, you might get a better deal with a smaller, local Internet provider. Many of them offer space on their Web server to post your Web pages, and all the software you need (free of extra charge) just for signing up! The smaller providers also often offer a flat rate (our service charges us $29 per month for 100 hours of log-on time) instead of charging you for each hour you're hooked up. And you'll probably need a lot of hours when you're first getting started.

■ **TCP/IP Software:** *You also need Internet software for your computer so that it will know how to manage your communications applications. When you subscribe to a service, they should provide you with a suite of appropriate software and directions on how to use them.*

For example, TIAC (our service) provides us with WinSock (connection software), Eudora (mail software), Netscape Navigatory Personal Edition, and some other utilities for Windows. For Macintosh users, TIAC provides Config PPP, Eudora, Fetch, Netscape, and others in their Macintosh versions. An FTP site maintained by TIAC keeps updated versions of these software suites for users to download.

- **Modem:** *Many of the graphics on the World Wide Web take a long time to download for viewing. You need a modem that can handle at least 14.4 kilobits per second (Kbps) of data. Trust us; don't even bother trying to surf the 'net with anything slower than a 14.4 modem. Hayes, Practical Peripherals, Telebit, US Robotics, Supra, and Courier are some of the many good modem manufacturers.*

TIP

Buy a 28.8 Kbps modem. You'll not only save frustration, you'll save money over time.

- **Color monitor:** *Although you can browse the Web with a black-and-white monitor, you need a color display to enjoy Web pages to their fullest.*

- **More RAM:** *No matter how much random access memory you have, you always need more, and you should have at least 8 MB. Your Web browser has to perform several functions at once: maintain the connection, process data, and display graphics and text. This can be demanding on your system.*

- **Web-related applications:** *If you get serious about cruising the Web and creating home pages, you might find yourself needing some more applications. Your Internet provider should offer access to an array of freeware and shareware programs to perform various Web-related functions, such as viewing and reformatting downloaded files,* *converting graphics to .GIF files, and editing hypertext documents. We will further discuss helper applications in Chapter 2.*

○ SUMMARY

In this chapter, we learned about the history of the Web, how Web browsers and HTML work, and using search engines to find topics. In addition, we took a look at what other people are putting forth and what the Web has to offer. Now we will move on to Chapter 2, "Gathering Your Web Page Ingredients."

chapter 2

THIS CHAPTER WILL COVER THE FOLLOWING:

- What HTML is and how it works.
- How to use our scripts.
- How to work with text and graphics.
- How to set up links.
- Helper applications for working with content that your browser can't use.

GATHERING YOUR WEB PAGE INGREDIENTS

Before we start cooking, let's gather your Web page ingredients. In this chapter you'll get a basic understanding of HTML. In particular, you'll need to know how links work and how to use helper applications.

○ WHAT IS HTML?

Hypertext Markup Language is a formatting system for text. As we mentioned, HTML is a subset of the Standard General Markup Language developed by the United States Military as a standard for document interchange. These standards let one computer talk to another computer; or, more precisely, let one computer read another computer's files. It is this inherent cross-platform compatibility that made HTML attractive to the original developers of the World Wide Web at the CERN High Energy Physics Lab in Geneva. All of this capability existed in the language before the World Wide Web was conceived.

HTML is codified by an international standards committee. The current level of HTML is Level 2.0 (adopted in Spring

1995). There is a specification called Level 3.0 (also called HT-ML+) that adds some additional features like text handling, tables and equations, better control over page setup, enhanced lists, and so on. Level 3.0 is circulating for comment, and will be adopted in early 1996.

Today, an organization called the World Wide Web Consortium, or W3C, based out of the Massachusetts Institute of Technology in Cambridge, MA, exists to direct new technology standards for the Web. Since most of the work to date existed before this standards committee, HTML usage on the Web remains nonstandard.

For example, the developers of Netscape, many of whom were developers of the original Web browser, Mosaic, decided to add their own formatting tags. They were dissatisfied with the slow pace of the development of the HTML standard. These so-called Netscape Enhancements to HTML are ignored or improperly displayed in other browsers, and have led to many service providers offering mirrored sites with and without Netscape-only features. You can think of Netscape's feature set as being a superset of HTML Level 2.0.

This book is a gentle reader for working with HTML, but there are a host of books that are dedicated to creating HTML documents at various levels. Of these books, you might want to investigate the following titles:

> ***HTML for Fun and Profit*** *by Mary S. Morris, 1995, Prentice Hall PTR, Englewood Cliffs, NJ.*

> ***Special Edition Using HTML*** *by Tom Savola, 1995, Que Corporation, Indianapolis, IN.*

> ***Creating Cool Web Pages with HTML*** *by Dave Taylor, 1995, PC Press, Indianapolis, IN.*

> ***HTML Publishing on the Internet*** *by Brent Heslop and Larry Budnick, 1995, Ventana Press, Chapel Hill, NC.*

HTML for Dummies *by Ed Tittel and Carl de Cordova, 1995, Dummies Press, San Mateo, CA.*

Teach Yourself HTML Web Publishing in a Week *by Laura Leman, 1994, Sams Publishing, Indianapolis, IN.*

HTML Manual of Style *by Larry Aronson, 1994, Ziff Davis Press, New York.*

Of these books, most are language guides and tutorials. Only Dave Taylor's book overlaps some with this book, but is less project-based. One book you might want to take a look at is the last book on this list, *HTML Manual of Style*, which will provide you with some rules for designing attractive Web pages.

There is also just a ton of resources on learning HTML online on the World Wide Web itself. If you do a search for this topic, it will reveal to you the following online tutorials that you might want to investigate:

Learn HTML—*Learn HTML, using HTML.edit, a software program that is installed on all the Macintosh computers and the World Wide Web browser Netscape. Both contain instructions. Found at http://salazar.aa.psu.edu/courses/art122w/LearningHTML.html.*

Learn to Publish—*Learning HTML. A quick reference or beginner's guide found at http://wwwhost.cc.utexas.edu/learn/pub/html.html.*

HTML Learning Nexus—*Here you'll find links to sites for learning HTML on any platform, and at any level of ability. The Learning Nexus, shown in Figure 2.1, is found at http://www.netins.net/showcase/lesmick/learn.html.*

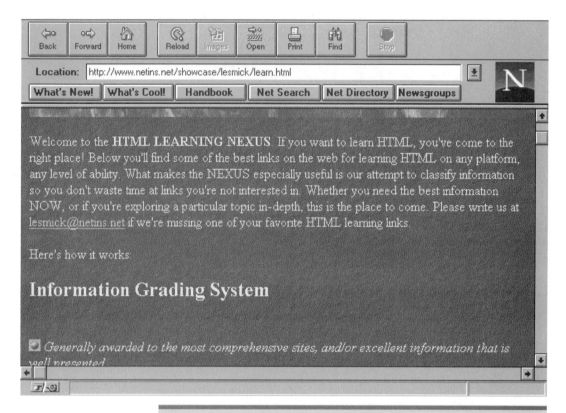

Welcome to the **HTML LEARNING NEXUS**. If you want to learn HTML, you've come to the right place! Below you'll find some of the best links on the web for learning HTML on any platform, any level of ability. What makes the NEXUS especially useful is our attempt to classify information so you don't waste time at links you're not interested in. Whether you need the best information NOW, or if you're exploring a particular topic in-depth, this is the place to come. Please write us at lesmick@netins.net if we're missing one of your favorite HTML learning links.

Here's how it works:

Information Grading System

Generally awarded to the most comprehensive sites, and/or excellent information that is well presented

Figure 2.1	The HTML Learning Nexus is a great jumping-off place for on-line tutorials to learn Web page construction.

The USNA CS Department's Beginner's Guide to Creating Web Pages—The Naval Academy's tutorial is found at http://www.scs.usna.navy.mil/users/harrison/ tutorial.html.

Writing HTML—A tutorial located at http:// hakatai.mcli.dist.maricopa.edu/tut/.

Learning HTML—A beginner's guide to HTML. Learn to write CGI forms, and about PERL, NCSA httpd Image Mapping, found at http://www.mdle.com/html.htm.

Learning HTML—This is the tutorial located at the University of Illinois Supercomputing Center. It includes a guide to learning HTML, a list of style guides, a Beginner's Guide to URLs by Marc Andreessen (one of the creators of Mosaic and the lead programmer for Netscape), and more. This tutorial is found at http://union.ncsa.uiuc.edu/ HyperNews/get/www/html/learning.html.

There are, in fact, so many tutorials on the Web dedicated to teaching you HTML that we can't list them here. Try some of these sites, and explore the pointers they contain.

HOW HTML WORKS

Let's say you're looking at a home page on the World Wide Web. You will see text, graphics, and highlighted items indicating places you can go for more information. The highlighted items are called hypertext links, and we don't need to be rocket scientists to understand how they work. In fact, nothing could be easier. When you click on the link, you will jump to another document or home page. If this new offering doesn't hold your interest, you can click on another link, or you can select the "Go Back" option to return to where you just were.

But how does your browser know what to do when you click on a link? Or where to display a graphic? Or the difference between headlines, body text, and bulleted lists? It knows because somebody entered the correct HTML codes. Have you ever created a style sheet in your word processor so you can tell the application when to display and print headers, body text, indented text, etcetera? That's exactly what you'll be doing when you use HTML. Only instead of setting style sheets, you'll be entering HTML tag commands in your word processor or text editor.

<HTML>
<TITLE>Simple Text Sample</TITLE>
<H2>For Example...</H2>
<P>For example, this is how we would enter this paragraph if we were publishing it on the World Wide Web instead of on paper. The <P> tag would tell your browser that we want this paragraph to appear as regular body text and that we want a double space between this and the next paragraph. We would then add a </P> closing tag following this text to let your browser know that this is the end of the paragraph.</P>
<P>The reason you enter tags in those funny triangular brackets is so your browser knows they are not part of the text and should not be displayed. See how the above headline and paragraph display in Figure 2.2? The header and paragraph tags tell them how to appear. Of course, if this were a real home page we would not just publish a single paragraph by itself. Otherwise, no one would want to visit it.</P>
<P>As you will see in <A HREF="Chapter4.HTM">Chapter 4, "Some Sample Dishes," </A> creating a home page is as easy as adding these types of HTML tags (if this were a real home page, you could click on the words "Chapter 4" with your mouse and jump right to it, instead of having to flip through the pages. </P>

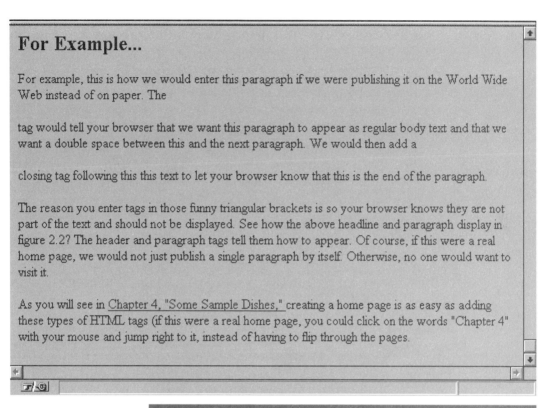

Figure 2.2   The above paragraphs as the appear in your browser.

WORKING WITH HTML AND CONTENT

Writing HTML scripts is as easy as using your word processor. You can enter your text in your word processing application, or you can even take an already existing document and turn it into an HTML script. Just save the result as a text-only file. However, it is important to remember that HTML does not handle content the same way your word processing document does. HTML is not an application, it's a markup language. HTML consists of markups—or tags—which you add to your text. These markups (like the <P> ...</P> and <H2>...</H2> tags we just introduced you to) tell your visitors' browser applications how to process your document.

NOTE

> There is one tag that can be used to recognize formatting information: the <PRE> ... </PRE> tag, for preformatted text. This tag will honor margins for its block, but shows up in a monospace typeface, and causes other problems and complications.

When working with HTML, remember the following:

- **HTML is text-only:** *You must save your scripts as text-only documents so they can be read by the Web browsers. Browsers do not recognize tabs, indents, columns, bold and italicized text, or any other formatting attributes. They only recognize formatting attributes that are entered with HTML markup tags. Do not save your file as text-only with line breaks (if your editor offers that option), just straight text-only.*

- **Web pages include images—HTML scripts don't:** *You can't insert visual elements directly into your HTML documents the way you can with word processing documents. Instead, you will enter an <IMG SRC="path/name of graphic"> tag which tells your browser to look for and display a separate graphic file in your directory.*

- **HTML is not a layout program:** *You can do lots of neat things with HTML, but fancy formatting isn't one of them. Home pages generally look like the one shown in Figure 2.3: a series of headers, body text, and bulleted or numbered lists that fit across the screen (although we will discuss using the <PRE> ... </PRE> tags, which allow you to add tables, in Chapter 5, "Some Sample Meals").*

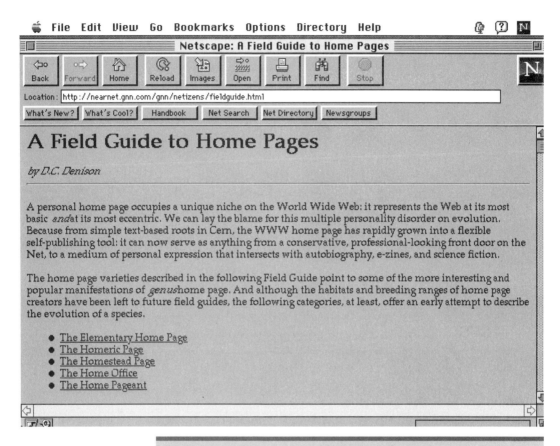

Figure 2.3   Sample home page at http://nearnet.gnn.com/gnn/
netizens/fieldguide.html.

- ■ ***Think links:*** *Remember all that strictly linear logic you learned in school (A + B = C)? Forget about it. With HTML, you can add links to create dynamic, interactive documents that let visitors jump around to other places in your document or to other locations in any order they wish.*

- ■ ***HTML is cross-platform:*** *Whether you use a Windows, Macintosh, DOS, or UNIX machine, you can cruise the World Wide Web. This explains why Web browsers can only handle text-only documents.*

> **NOTE**
>
> Due to cross-platform considerations, we have stuck with DOS naming conventions throughout the book.

The Web offers exciting opportunities to distribute and publish information. However, it is important to remember that it is a new form of media with its own set of rules and aesthetics. For example, instead of using a nice layout to guide your visitors' eyes through your document, you will use navigational links. We will further discuss organizing and formatting your HTML document in Chapter 3, "Getting Your Kitchen in Order."

GATHERING TEXT

Since we have just discussed how HTML handles content, you're probably wondering what content we're talking about. Well, we supply you with instructions, templates, and graphics, but only you can provide the content. You can put anything you want on your Web page—newsletters, memoranda, poems, the report card your child just got an A+ on, photographs with explanatory text, and more. However, all text must be formatted as HTML documents.

Here are three ways to gather your text:

- ■ **Start from scratch:** *Write whatever text you want to put on the Web the way you do when generating a document that you would print, but don't bother bolding and italicizing text, using tabs, or any of the things you normally do to format text. When you save your document as a text-only file, all formatting attributes will be stripped out. When you want to add an image, use the <IMG SRC="path/Name of image"> tag to tell the browser to find the file and display it.*

- ■ **Use an existing word processing file:** *Perhaps you have a document that has already been written, printed, and distributed, and now you want to put it up on the Web. Noth-*

ing could be easier. Open your document, save a copy of it (so you don't mess up the original), and add the appropriate markup tags. When you are finished, use the **Save As...** command in your **File** menu, and select the **Text Only** option. Figure 2.4 shows how we do this in Microsoft Word.

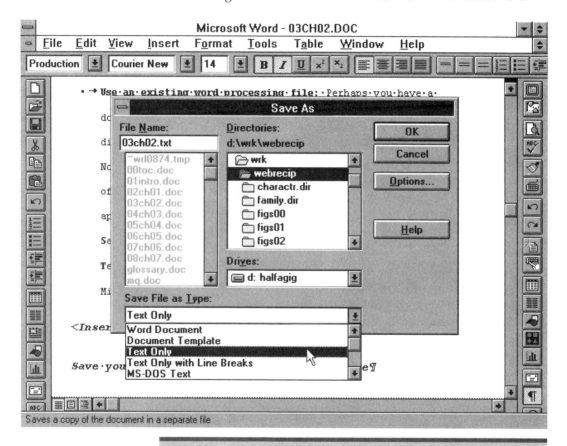

Figure 2.4   Save your HTML document as a text-only file.

■ *Use an existing file in a page layout or spreadsheet program:* Perhaps you want to put a brochure, newsletter, or financial report on-line. This gets a little more complicated because you probably laid out this information in a page layout program like QuarkXPress or Microsoft Pub-

lisher, or a spreadsheet program like Excel. Fortunately, most of these programs let you save, export, or publish individual blocks of text to your word processing program. If you have Microsoft Object Linking and Embedding (OLE) or Macintosh System 7.5's "Drag and Drop" feature, you can even copy text to your clipboard from one program and paste it into your word processing application.

But remember—HTML scripts will not support your images, tables, and charts. These must be saved individually as graphics files, which would then be converted to .GIF or .JPG formats. We will discuss converting graphics in greater detail later in this chapter.

Charts and tables can also be preformatted and published on the Web; however, all of those nice tabbing schemes and columns would have to be reentered by using your space bar—a tedious but sometimes necessary method. We will discuss using <PRE>...</PRE> preformatting markup tags further in Chapter 5, "Some Sample Meals." Tables are not the best use of the <PRE>...</PRE> tag (margins are), but some people get by creating tables this way. You should note that newly proposed extensions to HTML have table creation tags included in them.

NOTE

If you start generating lots of Web pages, you may find an HTML conversion or editing program to be very helpful.

Some of your favorite word processors (like Microsoft Word and WordPerfect) now take add-on programs that allow them to work directly with HTML and easily create tags. These programs are available on-line, and some are found on the accompanying CD-ROM. There are also lots of freeware, shareware, and commercial programs available to help you generate HTML pages in friendly environments. We will discuss these programs further in Chapter 7, "Coffee and Dessert: Learning More About the Web."

Whether you're using preexisting documents, or generating them from scratch, it is easy to serve your information on the Web.

○ HOW TO USE OUR SCRIPTS

Generating content is easy, or at least no more difficult than it was before. Learning and memorizing HTML markup tags can take a little longer. Fortunately, we have created the scripts for you. All you have to do is open up the appropriate document in the CD-ROM and either fill in our templates with your text or start cutting and pasting. For those of you who don't have a CD-ROM, Chapters 4 ("Some Sample Dishes") and 5 ("Some Sample Meals") contain sample HTML scripts, pictures of how the scripts appear on a Web browser, and detailed instructions. Since the HTML scripts are saved as text-only files and the graphics are saved as .GIF and .JPG files, you will be able to open and view them in your browser on either a Windows or Macintosh machine.

You will find the following on the CD-ROM:

■ ***Chapters 4 and 5 examples:*** *The Chapter 4 and Chapter 5 directories (Chap4.DIR and Chap5.DIR) contain the entire HTML scripts, graphics, and contents of the Web pages discussed in these chapters.*

Each home page is organized into individual directories within the chapter directories. You can use these examples, along with the graphics, for creating your own home pages. However, since Chaos Control, Margaret Weigel's Haiku page, and Byte It! are real-life publications you can find on the Web, we ask that you not use their logos. When you finish reading this book, you will be able to create a Web page like the one shown in Figure 2.5.

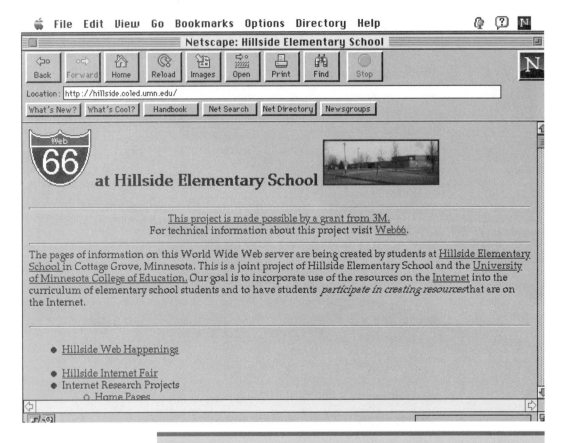

Figure 2.5   You can create a Web page like the one shown here!

■ *Sample scripts: We have also provided an array of sample scripts which you can use as templates for generating your home page. They are organized by category, and you will find each script, with an accompanying graphic or logo, in its own directory. You will find a complete list of sample scripts in Appendix C. If a sample script suits your needs, copy the folder onto your hard drive and open it in your word processor.*

- **Parts:** *You will also find templates for different HTML parts in the Parts.DIR directory on your CD-ROM. This way, entering more complex HTML elements like anchor tags, definition lists, and preformatted tables will be as easy as cutting and pasting. Don't worry if you don't yet understand the terms we just used in the last sentence. After reading Chapters 4 and 5, you will.*

- **Graphics:** *We don't want to limit you to the graphics provided in each individual script. We also offer photographs, icons, bullets, horizontal rules, logos, and other images. These are organized by directory, and you will find a complete list of them in Appendix C.*

- **Freeware:** *The CD-ROM also contains public domain web-related freeware for Windows and Macintosh users to assist in generating and viewing content. You will also find a complete list of our offerings in Appendix C.*

After copying and pasting our scripts, all you have to do is enter the text you want and the appropriate file names for your images and links. If your computer doesn't have a CD-ROM, don't worry—*The Web Page Recipe Book* still makes creating Web pages easy and fun. Chapters 4 and 5 are full of sample HTML scripts with detailed instructions, and you'll find a complete table of HTML markup tags in Appendix B.

And once you've got your home pages, other Web pages, and associated image and other content files completed, you simply either copy the files to your folder or directory on your local Web server, or upload it to your folder on your on-line service or service provider (by FTPing it), and voilà! It's cake.

○ WORKING WITH GRAPHICS

The ability to display images makes the Web a more exciting place than the rest of the Internet. However, your browser can only display .GIF and .JPG files without an external helper application. We will discuss helper applications in greater detail later in this chapter. Unless you have a graphics application, like Adobe's Photoshop, that can open .GIF and .JPG files, you will not be able to display the graphics on the CD-ROM individually; but you will still be able to view them on your Web page by opening your browser.

Actually, although Adobe Photoshop can open these graphics files, you would hardly want to use it as a "helper" application. Photoshop consumes mucho RAM, and is slow on anything but a fast computer. You are better served by using something like LViewPro as your graphics viewer.

Listed below are the types of graphics you can display on the Web:

- ***JPEG or JPG (Joint Experts Photographic Group) files:*** *This file format was created to enable the compression and display of complex graphics, such as photographs. Compression is important on the Web because images with large file sizes take forever to download to your screen. Use .JPG when adding large, detailed images to your home page. Most current versions of graphics and imaging programs like CorelDRAW and Photoshop let you save images in the .JPG format.*

- ***GIF (Graphic Interchange Format) files:*** *This is a proprietary format designed by CompuServe to enable the compression and display of images on the Web. Because .GIF compression indexes graphics into 8-bit color, they do not display with the high resolution of a .JPG image. However, the .GIF format is ideal for displaying logos, black-and-white graphics, and images with bold and simple color schemes—and saves precious disk space because the resulting files are tiny.*

There are several versions of GIF out there for you to work with. GIF 89 files are notable because they allow the display of images with transparent backgrounds, which make them appear to float on the Web page. GIF 87 files offer higher resolution and color levels up to 24-bit.

Although you can also load .TIF, Postscript, and other types of graphics files onto your Web page, you probably wouldn't want to because they take up loads of disk space, and your visitors won't be able to view them without external helper applications.

HOW DO I GET .GIF AND .JPG FILES?

For starters, you can check out our CD-ROM for a wide array of .GIF and .JPG formatted graphics that you can use. However, if you start to get serious about generating Web pages, you'll need a larger selection of graphics. You can either create graphics yourself, purchase commercially available collections of images and clip art, or download graphics from the 'Net.

You have the following options for getting graphics:

- **Do it yourself:** *If you're creatively inclined and have the right software and equipment, you can generate your own images and serve them up. You can scan photographs or create illustrations in a drawing or imaging program. Many software packages, like Photoshop and CorelDRAW, will let you save images as .GIF or .JPG files.*

- **Commercial clip art collections:** *You can order collections of line art, stock photographs, and other types of images from commercial providers, such as Planet Art (800) 200-3405, ClickART (800) 9-TMAKER, Clipables (800) 288-7595, or Image Club (800) 387-9193. Call them and request a catalog.*

Image Club even has an impressive Web site, as shown in Figure 2.6, at http://www.imageclub.com.

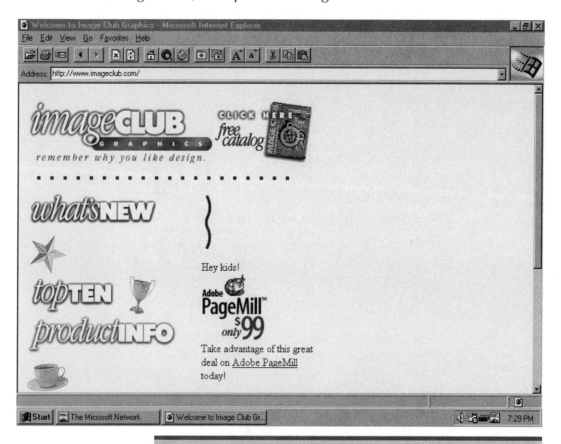

Figure 2.6   Image Club's Web site.

- **Get 'em off the 'NET:** *The Internet offers a wide selection of clip art resources which are already formatted as .GIF and .JPG formats. You can view them on the Web and download them for yourself. A good place to start your search is at the Yahoo Pictures page at http://www. yahoo.com/yahoo/computers/multimedia/pictures.*

■ **Search the Web:** *You will also find a wealth of resources by using your search engines.*

CAUTION

Avoid potential legal problems! When borrowing from the 'net, be aware that some of these images may be copyrighted, and that some of the artists request a donation in exchange for using their work.

Once you have your graphics, you will need some way of formatting them in .GIF or .JPG formats. If you've been creating your own images, you probably have commercial software that enables you to do this. If none of your programs offer options for saving images as .GIF or .JPG. files, you will need a graphics converter program. Fortunately, these are easy to find on the Web and download. Chances are, your Internet provider offers an on-line software library with these and other Web-related applications.

When you launch a converter application, you can open your graphic through the File menu and then save it to the desired format. Converters do not allow you to resize or edit your graphic, however, so you should make sure your graphic appears exactly how you want it to on your home page.

Here are your options:

■ **For Windows users:** *PaintShop Pro and Lview both let you save graphics as .GIF and .JPG files. Another popular program is giftool.exe. For creating transparent .GIF 89 files, you can use giftrans.exe.*

You can find these utilities by searching for them on the Internet, or by searching for them in the software libraries of your favorite on-line services like AOL or CompuServe.

TIP

Try the Yahoo page at http://www.yahoo.com/
Computers_and_Internet/Internet/World_Wide_Web/Browsers/
Helper_Applications/ for a jump to places where you can
download various helper applications.

■ ***For Mac users:*** *Gif Converter lets you save graphics as .GIF files. Graphic Converter lets you save graphics as either .GIF files or .JPG files. To create transparent .GIF 89 files, you'll need a program called Transparency.*

○ LINKS

Since people can't turn pages on the Internet, we need links for navigating Web pages. Links are not only an exciting feature on the Web, they are the primary tool for organizing the content on your home page and referring your visitors to more information. When you define a link by entering an Anchor markup tag, you are telling the browser to jump to the link's target when the link is pressed or activated. In order for links to work, you must have a place to start from and a target to jump to. The <A HREF="address or location"> Link </A> tags perform the functions of:

1. Displaying the text differently from the surrounding text (usually by showing it in a different color or by underlining it), as shown in Figure 2.7, so your visitors know it's a link.

2. Giving the browser an address or location to jump to.

Figure 2.7 Your visitors don't see the Anchor tags, but they know it's a link.

We are particularly fond of browsers that help the user figure out a link easily. Netscape changes the arrow cursor to a hand whenever it is over a link. The location of the linked item appears at the very bottom of the screen. If the link is a pointer (underlined text), a visit to that site changes the color of the link for a certain period of days. This is right neighborly behavior.

You can create the following types of links:

■ ***Internal links to locations in the same document:*** *You can help people navigate your document with internal links. You do this by setting up jump targets with*

<A NAME="...">...</A> anchor tags, and then creating the links. Naming sections of your document gives them an address to jump to.

This construct helps your viewers by letting them navigate quickly to sections of a document without having to scroll about. When you use this form of jump, you can have very long documents without a major penalty for your viewers.

■ ***External links to other documents in your directory:*** *If you prefer working with several shorter documents instead of one lengthy document, you can jump your visitors to other files in your directory. They'll never know they've left your main home page. The address will consist of the document name.*

You don't need to specify the entire URL because browser applications recognize relative file names (*i.e.,* where items in the same or neighboring directories are relative to the main document). One construct you often see is an alphabet jump map. This can take the form of an alphabet, where each letter points to a listing of topics starting with that letter.

■ ***External links to other locations:*** *You can refer people to other Web pages for additional information on relevant topics or fun places to go. To do this, you must specify the complete URL address so the browser knows what document to find.*

If this all seems confusing to you, you'll get a better idea when we work with links and anchor tags in Chapter 4, "Some Sample Dishes."

○ MORE ABOUT URLS

If there's no roadmap of the Internet, how does your browser know where to look for everything? Humans can be nomads with no particular home address, but every entity on the Internet must have an address. However, instead of looking for the name, street address, city, state, zip construct like your mail deliverer does, your browser looks for the type of file server, name of file server, directory name, and document name.

The most general components of a URL includes the many services that are found on the Internet: HTML Web pages and servers, Gopher servers and documents, UseNet news, and FTP archives. Broken down, it would be:

```
service :// host name: port / directory and path
```

Service is the transfer protocol that is used to move information from the server to the client (you and your browser, ... walking down the avenue, ...). The host name is an address to the server or host computer that contains the information you seek. Ports are channels that can be used to send or receive information. When port information is left out of an address, it is because the default value for the port is used. When a non-default value is used, the port value needs to be specified.

Don't forget, most URLs for servers are case-insensitive. However, document references can be (but are not always) case-sensitive, and particular services (like Gopher) use case structures. You should enter URLs into your browser and your Web pages exactly as you find them in their sources. Even simple things like the final "/" can make a big difference.

One thing all URLs have in common is that none of them allow space characters. That's why you see an underscore character in many URLs. In order to use a space character in an address, you must substitute the hexadecimal equivalent in your address preceded by a percentage sign. Therefore, you might use the following as an address: www.killer%20apps.com. Other hexadecimal equivalents you might be interested in are tab, %09; percent, %25; enter, %0A; and line feed, %0D.

WEB URLS

By looking at a URL, you can tell what Internet application you need to find it, what kind of service it is, who runs the server, and what type of file it is. The http service stands for Hyper-

Text Transport Protocol, which is how Web documents are viewed and transferred. A browser reads an "http://…" address as an HTML Web document.

A Web document looks like this:

```
http://name of server/directory/file name.
```

In a typical address, www.killerapps.com, the com is called a zone, killerapps is a domain or host, and www is a server of the computer on the network. Since domains on the World Wide Web are registered, they point to the computer that contains the domain information. Therefore, you don't need more specific information about the server name than the appropriate domain and zone. Rarely do you see port addresses in Web addresses (like :8080, etc.), although they do crop up from time to time.

The file name is optional. If you don't specify a file name, a default file is loaded from that directory. Many times that document is called "default.html," "index.html," "Welcome.html," or some other file name. This default file points to all of the other documents at that site.

FTP AND TELNET URLS

Another example of accessing a different yet equally important service on the Internet is FTP. File Transfer Protocol document names look like this:

```
ftp://name of server/directory/filename
```

A sample FTP site might have an address like ftp://ftp.ibm.com/pub/. Here the server or host is ftp.ibm.com, and the address includes the pub for "public" directory. When you use an Internet browser to view an FTP site, you see a listing of directories and files in the browser window. When you double-click on a folder your browser is smart enough to open that folder, and when you click on a file on an FTP site your browser downloads it using the FTP protocol.

There are many, many file servers that use the FTP protocol; many more, in fact, than there are Web servers. In order to get into these servers, you can connect to most of them using an anonymous FTP session. When you connect, the server will ask you for a password and your e-mail address. It is considered good citizenship to enter your e-mail address as your password, and the word "anonymous" as your username. Anonymous access is usually limited to one or selected folders (or directories) on the FTP server. Most often the /PUBLIC folder is accessible.

TIP

When you are given an FTP site, particularly when the /PUB directory is specified, you can almost be certain that anonymous FTP is allowed.

FTP servers can be configured so that they also allow non-anonymous access. In fact, many FTP servers allow both anonymous and non-anonymous access of different folders or directories. In this instance, when you log onto the server you enter your account and password, which determine your level of access.

Telnet is similar to FTP, in that you log onto the host computer for access to folders and files. When you log onto a Telnet computer, it is just as if you were connected to that computer over a local area network. The URLs for Telnet servers and documents offer little new. A typical address might be: "telnet://kill-erapps.com." When you use a Web browser to access a Telnet site, your browser will most likely need a helper application to interact with the remote computer.

GOPHER URLS

Gopher servers are another form of Internet service, developed out of work at the University of Minnesota (whose mascot is the Golden Gopher). When you view Gopher servers in your browser, they appear almost like FTP sites. However, Gopher servers are cross-referenced through a master index, and so share some of the hypertext attributes of Web servers. Gopher

73

menu items don't necessarily correspond to the internal names for folders and documents in Gopher-space.

Gopher servers are organized as a hierarchical menu system of text and file archives, just like your computer directory file (an inverted tree structure). Since the Gopher system spans many computers, this listing is quite large. My sense of it is that the Web has greatly eclipsed what you can find on Gopher servers, and FTP is much larger still.

When you connect to a Gopher host, you go to the top of the tree for that Gopher menu. The top of the tree is the narrowest part of the file structure. A Gopher URL contains a single character prefix that indicates the item type: 0 for files, and 1 for folders or directories. Therefore, a typical Gopher URL might look like the following:

```
gopher://KillerApps.software.com:80/1/Database
```

Gopher addresses are more likely to use upper and lower case letters, and their exact usage is important. Here the number :80 refers to the port, and 1 refers to the database folder.

USENET URLS

A UseNet newsgroup contains a text listing of text messages exchanged among users. A typical server would have a URL that looks like this:

```
alt.barney.die.die.die
```

A very strange address indeed! Aside from the many bizarre Newsgroups that are out there, notice that the address doesn't specify a server. When configuring your browser, a setup dialog box allows you to enter the host that you use to access the UseNet system. Therefore, you do not enter any server or paths—your server contains that information already. All you do is reference the server and newsgroup name.

If you are building a URL for a newsgroup into your document, you simply follow the word "news:" with the name of the newsgroup. The address "news:foxpro.support" would be a valid address.

A UseNet host is a news server that your Internet provider maintains. What is on that server depends on what your service provider decides to reference. Most services reference quite a large number of UseNet groups. On AOL in June 1995 there were 7500 newsgroups. In December 1994, IBM's Web server stored 14,000 newsgroup references. There are very few public access UseNet servers on the Internet.

E-MAIL URLS

Strange as it seems, you can also specify URLs for electronic addresses for mail you want to send. In Internet parlence, these are referred to as mailto: addresses. Any valid e-mail address can be translated into a mailto: by (you guessed it!) prefixing the address with mailto:. Therefore, my mailto: address would be "mailto:basman@killerapps.com." Notice that there are no spaces in a mailto: address, as in any other valid URL address.

Each browser handles mailto:s in a different way. Mailto:s are the key to electronic forms, and are described in detail in this book.

○ USING HELPER APPLICATIONS

Your browser can display text and graphics, which account for most of what you'll find on the World Wide Web. But many Web sites also have other offerings, including sounds, video clips, and portable document formats (PDFs), which greatly add to the fun of using the Web. These files, unlike text and graphics, cannot be opened directly through your browser yet; instead, you download the files and launch them with a helper application.

Helper applications are small programs that enable you to open files even if you don't have the application in which they were created. Many browsers let you register your helper applications (see Figure 2.8) so that when the file is finished downloading, the helper launches automatically. Each browser has a slightly different method for registering a helper application, so check your browser's documentation or on-line help system for instructions.

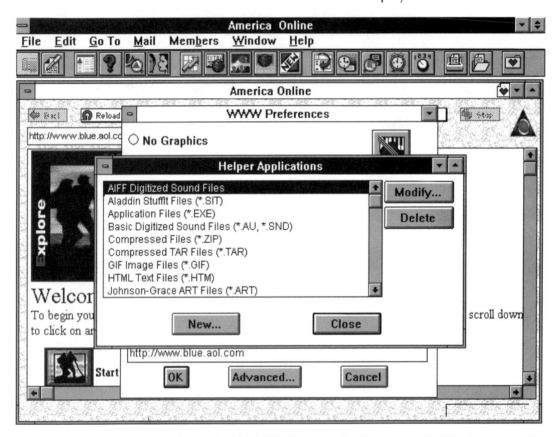

Figure 2.8   Adding a helper application to the America Online Web browser.

The 'Net abounds with freeware and shareware Web helpers, so happy downloading!

Here is some information on some of the files you'll come across and the applications you'll need to open them:

■ ***Sound:*** *Sound clips are fun—and the Web offers everything from silly beeps and animal noises to samples from recording artists' CDs. Sound files come in the .au, .aiff,*

.wav, and .mp2 formats. You will also increasingly come across .mpeg sound files, although that file format is generally used for video files.

If you use Windows, the Waveform Hold and Modify (WHAM) program converts common sound formats. You can get it at: file://ftp.ncsa.uiuc.edu/Mosaic/Windows/Viewers/wham.zip.

WAVAny (ftp.netcom.com/pub/neisus/wvany.zip) is also a good bet. If you use a Macintosh, the freeware application SoundApp is a good bet. You can get it at ftp://sumx-aim.stanford.edu/info-mac/snd/util/sound-app-131.hqx.

TIP

When looking for fun multimedia stuff to download, a good place to start is the Multimedia page at http://Sunsite.sut.ac.jp/multimed/multimed.html.

- **Video files:** *Video files are also really neat. Most files will be formatted as either .AVI, .MPG/.MPEG, or QuickTime .MOV files. Since .MPG videos are cross-platform-compatible, this is becoming the most popular format.*

You can use MPEGplay to play .MPEG videos. For you Macintosh users out there, a QuickTime movie player that contains MPEG codecs (compression/decompression routines) comes with your system software. Windows users can get Quicktime for Windows, for which a player from Apple exists. These and other helper applications can be found at ftp://ftp.ncsa.uiuc.edu/Web/Mosaic.

- **Portable Document Format (PDF) files:** *PDF files are relatively new, but you'll find more and more of them on the Web as time goes on. They have the potential to revolutionize the Web because they allow for rich-content material to be incorporated directly into documents.*

PDF files are created with Acrobat (a commercial program by Adobe Systems, Inc.) as well as with other programs like Farallon's Replica. Acrobat "prints" newsletters, brochures, and other

77

publications generated in page layout, illustration, and wordprocessing programs to PDF files. The resulting PDF files can be
viewed on Windows, Macintosh, DOS, and UNIX platforms—
with all graphics, formatting, and layout intact—regardless of
what platform or application the documents were created in. All
you need to view these files is the Acrobat Reader, a freeware
application you can download from the Adobe Acrobat Web site
at http://www.adobe.com/Acrobat/. An example of this is shown
in Figure 2.9. The Adobe site also offers links to a spectacular array of .PDF files available on the Web for downloading. Acrobat
is noted for its high quality and extensibility, but it's slow.

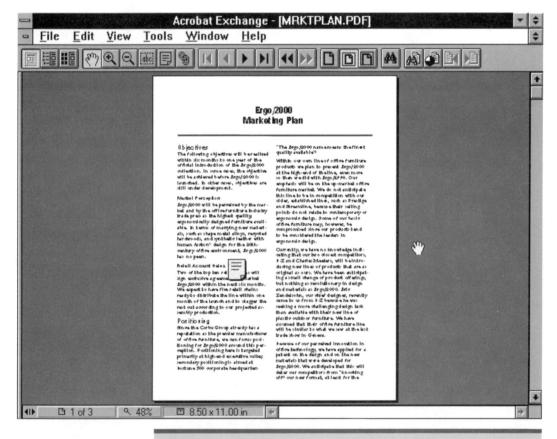

Figure 2.9   A PDF file viewed with the Acrobat Reader.

Now that you have everything you need for generating and perusing Web pages, let's move on to Chapter 3, "Getting Your Kitchen in Order."

○ SUMMARY

In this chapter, we gathered our ingredients so we can begin creating Web pages. We introduced you to HTML, explained how to use the scripts we've provided on the CD-ROM, and overviewed different types of Web content. By now, you should have some idea of what creating a Web page entails. Chapter 3 will give you some tips on how to organize and present your Web page so you can serve it up with style.

THIS CHAPTER WILL COVER THE FOLLOWING:

- WRITING YOUR PAGE'S CONTENT
- ORGANIZING YOUR WEB PAGE
- HOW TO PRESENT INFORMATION
- WEBBING UP YOUR BUSINESS
- SOME DO'S AND DON'TS
- HOW WE TESTED OUR WEB PAGES

GETTING YOUR KITCHEN IN ORDER

○ THE LOOK AND FEEL OF YOUR HOME PAGE

Just because HTML doesn't support fancy layouts doesn't mean that you shouldn't pay attention to the look and feel of your home page. You can make an impression and create a mood through well-chosen graphics, and by paying attention to how you organize your information. Remember that you're working in an entirely new media with its own aesthetic, form, and function. A good Web site has more in common with a presentation than it does with a book.

By creating an outline, storyboards, and jump maps, adding a few appropriate graphics, and following a few of the tips you'll learn about in this chapter, generating an attractive Web page will come easily to you.

○ STEP 1: WRITE YOUR DOCUMENT

Like any other undertaking, it helps to have a plan. Once you've decided what type of information you want to put on the Web, you'll need to outline your ideas, and to write and refine your text. Your organization of the document that will serve as the basis for your Web page needs to present information in a logical, ordered, and structured manner because the amount of material which can appear on a computer screen is limited. The best Web pages use white space well; they almost have a sparse look to them. Every word counts!

To begin writing your Web page, follow these steps:

- **Choose your main topic:** *Choosing a subject or subjects to address may seem too obvious to mention, but making this choice will determine how your page is organized and who visits you. Committing to a main topic doesn't mean you have to limit yourself.*

- **Choose your subtopics well:** *The low cost of disk space makes it tempting to bury your audience in information; and to some degree, you can—but only if you organize your sub-topics well.*

The issues here are that you only have one computer screen to work with at a time. Also, if you are providing hypertext links, you have given the viewer control over the sequence in which they access the information. To make best use of these two features, you need strong topic development and logical sequencing. Think of your subtopics in terms of "data chunking."

For example, if you put up a Web page dedicated to publishing your poetry, you can also add information about local and national poetry-related events, biographies of favorite poets, a form so other Web poets can submit to your page, links to poetry-related sites, and more. Find a way to organize these subtopics—with an outline, a jump map, or both.

Stick to a single theme and related topics when designing your Web page.

And although you could (it's your home page), you probably wouldn't want to link to the National Football League home using a special *Neat Links That Have Nothing to Do with Poetry* category. Doing so is the Web page equivalent of the "Ransom Note" desktop published document you can create by using too many fonts. Such a Web page would qualify for Mirsky's Worst of the Web list at http://turnpike.net/metro/mirsky/Worst.html.

- ■ ***Create an outline:*** *Organization is crucial to generating successful Web pages. Outline your thoughts the same way you would if you were writing a report. You should also note which graphics (if any) you would like to have appear near which items of text.*

- ■ ***Write your copy:*** *Good writing is always important, especially on the Web, where fickle 'Net surfers can jump to another, more potentially exciting location with a click of their mice. Remember that despite all of the Web's fancy features, the content's the main thing people look for.*

Keep your sentences concise, lively and informative. Be sparse! Make each word count.

- ■ ***Revise and refine:*** *After you've written your outline, take a breather; then go back and begin the revision process. If you can, get a friend or colleague to review your work and make comments.*

- **Proofread and run your spell checker:** *You will always want to avoid putting anything on your Web page that distracts from your content—spelling and grammatical errors distract from your message!*

Now that you've written some compelling copy that looks great on paper, you can begin working towards making it look great on your Web page.

○ STEP 2: ORGANIZE YOUR WEB PAGE

Unlike writing a report or copy that appears in print, writing Web pages requires a second step in the outlining process. It is critically important to remember that your visitors will read your copy on a computer screen. A writer organizes documents by section. A graphic designer organizes documents by guiding the reader's eye visually. As a Web page "content provider" you will have to do both.

To organize your Web page, do the following:

- **Think presentation:** *A presentation consists of a speech accompanied by visual aids with graphics and summaries of points made. Of course, you won't be giving a talk; but thinking along the lines of a presentation can help you put forth information in a way that's easy on the eye. This is what your visitors need to easily scan your page, see what you have to offer, and quickly find the information they want.*

TIP

Bulleted lists are easy to read—use them to list what's on your page, and offer items on your list as links to different topics. Chapter 4 teaches you how to use lists on your Web pages.

■ ***Sketch out a storyboard:*** *People in ad agencies do this when generating ideas for commercials, so why shouldn't you? After all, a home page is like an ad. A storyboard looks almost like a comic strip, only you would draw the panels in the rectangular shape of most computer screens. You can then sketch out how you want each screenful of information to appear; an example is shown in Figure 3.1.*

Storyboarding your Web pages will give you an idea of how much text and graphics fits on a single computer screen, and how it will appear to your visitor. You can certainly use any competent drawing program to storyboard your pages, but there are also special storyboarding programs you can buy for this purpose.

Figure 3.1 Example of a storyboard.

85

- **_Create a jump map:_** _Your visitors should never have to scroll to find an item on your home page. Make it easy for them to jump from place to place by creating a "jump map" of properly placed links._

And remember to always give your visitors somewhere central and familiar to go, even if that is only the option to return to your home page. Many sites use navigational buttons to guide the reader around at their site.

Figure 3.2 shows you an example of a home page that uses a jump map, the Apple Computer home page. You can not only jump to various places, but there is a toolbar at the bottom of the page that lets you navigate about from wherever you are. You can call up on-line help from anywhere (a good thing!), return to an index, find out what's new, and go to a form that lets you e-mail feedback to Apple. This page hides a tremendously rich and complex site, and represents a very good interface design that you can learn from.

Did you notice the Apple at the far left of the toolbar? That image is a pointer back to the home page from anywhere in the system.

Each panel can represent either a separate HTML document in your directory (an external link), a different screen in your main document (an internal link), or combinations of the two.

Figure 3.2 The Apple Computer home page shows good interface design. (Home Page Device ©1995 Apple Computer, Inc. used with permission. All rights reserved.)

■ ***Design for text-only viewers:*** *Some of your viewers will not be able to view graphics or, because of the speed of their modems or their own impatience, won't want to. You must accommodate text-only displays.*

You can design for text-only viewers in one of two ways: either design your pages so that one set of pages contains images, or duplicate the function of your images in text format. In Figure 3.3, you see how the navigation toolbar you saw earlier in the Apple home page is duplicated in a set of text pointers on another page in the Apple Web site. Even if a user cannot see your images, they can see and use the text pointers.

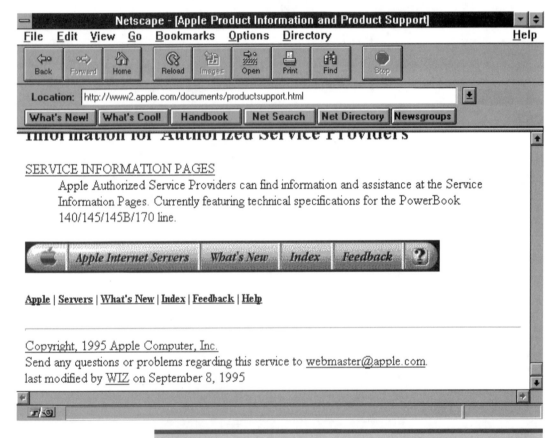

Figure 3.3   Notice how the toolbar is duplicated by a set of text pointers on this Web page.

Now that you have your basic organizational scheme down, let's work on refining your layout.

○ STEP 3: MAKE A SPLASH

First impressions count, so it is important to make your Web page look inviting. You don't have to use splashy images or be a graphics whiz to do this. Some home pages offer few or no images at all. However, a home page should be formatted in a way that clearly communicates what you have to offer and makes your visitors want to see more. Often, you have no more than a couple of seconds to make your point on the screen.

You can make your home page more inviting by following these guidelines:

- ■ *Catch people's eye: Your main page is what your visitors see first, so hook them in right away. Boldly proclaim the name of your page with either a catchy logo or a header, describe what they'll find in a catchy, concise paragraph, and give them a list of links.*

- ■ *Set a tone: Do you want your page to come across as humorous, professional, cutting-edge, eclectic, a combination of these, or none of these? You can use your copy, graphics, and overall look to convey an impression that will draw like-minded people to your page.*

For example, when you look at the Capitol Steps home page (http://pfm.het.brown.edu/people/mende/steps/index.html#washington) shown in Figure 3.4, you immediately know that the subject is politics. A quick glance at the bulleted list items tells you that the material consists of humor and satire.

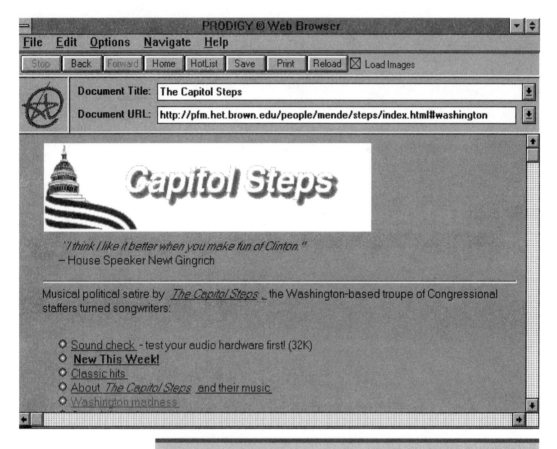

Figure 3.4   Capitol Steps home page.

■ **Format your page:** *Use headers, paragraphs, and list for-mats to differentiate content types. Each screen should have a header with its current topic. Use body text or paragraphs and bulleted or numbered lists, and give your* *page appropriate white space. Don't make your page hard to look at, with large amounts of body text and too many headlines.*

■ ***Use graphics judiciously:*** *Graphics can look impressive, but make sure they enhance the content of your page rather than distract from them. Images should illustrate your copy, provide visual cues regarding your content, establish your home page's identity, or tell your visitors what to do next.*

Many people (even wizened Web veterans) cringe when they have to wait for extensive image files to be transferred to view a page. These graybeards even turn off their graphics so it doesn't distract from the surfer experience. To help these people and the rest of us, many Web page designers use a format called interlaced GIF.

An interlaced GIF image is displayed with one set of alternate lines at a time so the image builds in. The image starts out fuzzy, and then clarifies as more of the data file is transferred over. With interlaced GIF, viewers can get an idea whether the page is what they want to see, and move on if it isn't. Figure 3.5 shows you an example of an interlaced image in the middle of its transfer. You can learn more about this graphic format and method of image display by viewing the Web page at: http://www.prenhall.com/divisions/ptr/yourdon.

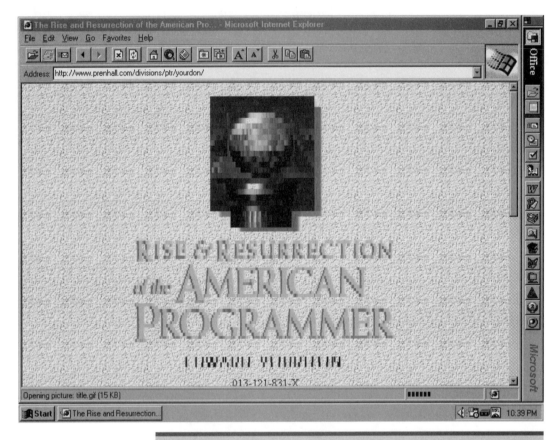

Figure 3.5   Interleaved GIF images can save time and frustration.

○ WEBBING UP FOR BUSINESS?

If you're putting up a Web page for your business, that's great. Whether you run a growing company or work as an independent consultant, the Web is a great place to promote your company and offer services to your customers. However, you should be aware of a few issues:

■ ***Netiquette:*** *Be aware that most people on the Internet find blatant advertising and self-promotion offensive. These* *folks consider the Web as a global community consisting of responsible members who "give back to the 'net."*

However, there's no reason why you can't let people know about your products or services and serve up other offerings that your visitors will find interesting, fun, and useful. Create links to related resources on the Web. Maintain an updated list of cool places to go. Donate some of your Web space to nonprofit organizations and offer links to them. Hold contests and games. Create an interactive newsletter about trends and happenings in your industry.

For example, Macromedia, the publisher of graphics and animation software including Freehand and Director, has a home page(http:// www.macromedia.com/) shown in Figure 3.6, that offers tips and tricks, subscriptions to a newsletter, updates, and other resources for the computer graphics community, along with company information.

- **Security:** *The Internet abounds with hackers and cyberthieves. Yes, you can create electronic order forms on the Web. But unless you have the resources to ensure security, don't invite potential customers to enter their credit card numbers, social security numbers, or other confidential information. Instead, use forms to let repeat customers place orders with purchase order numbers, enable visitors to request brochures, request feedback, and take customer and visitor surveys.*

- **Can you handle it?:** *If your Web page gets popular, can you and your Internet provider handle it? Some services charge you if large amounts of data pass through your Web page. If that's the case, would increased traffic on your Web page result directly or indirectly in sufficient profit for investing in a higher level of services or setting up your own server? If hundreds of people started filling out your forms, would you or your employees be able to process them? You need to think these issues through before deciding what to offer on your Web page and how heavily you want to promote it.*

Figure 3.6 Macromedia Director home page.

○ DO'S AND DON'TS

■ *Do add links to and from your sections so your visitors can find things easily.*

■ *Do create Web pages that stand on their own without depending on previous or following pages.*

■ *Do organize your Web page by topic.*

- *Do be nice to visitors without graphical browsers and use the <ALT="..."> attribute (described in the next chapter) for your graphical links.*

- *Do format header, text, and bulleted/numbered list material consistently throughout your work.*

- *Do make a splash with your main home page by immediately hooking them into your content.*

- *Do use graphics to enhance your content.*

- *Do break up large amounts of text so it's easier to read.*

- *Don't use too many formatting attributes. Pages with too many headers and too much bold or italic text look cluttered.*

- *Don't distract your visitors with too many graphics.*

- *Don't use large images on your opening screen. Use thumbnails that point to the full-sized image instead.*

Lots of people use large images anyway, and they often look impressive, but visitors often get impatient with waiting for large images to download and move on.

Some sites use what are called image maps. Image maps are Web pages that contain graphics in place of pointers. Building image maps into a Web page is somewhat dependent on the server you are going to use, but well worth the trouble. A typical example of an image map is a clickable alphabet used in an on-line help system. This book outlines the process for creating image maps in Chapter 7, "Creating Clickable Image Maps."

- *Don't leave your visitors stranded—always offer links.*

- *Don't use too many horizontal rules.*

- *Don't link to unrelated information.*

- *Don't include multimedia content without telling visitors what size the files are and how long they will take to download. Video and sound files take up immense amounts of disk space; more important, they take way too long to download! Also tell your viewer what format the files are in.*

NOTE

How We Tested Our Web Pages: We tested the Web pages you're about to work with in a variety of graphical browsers. However, we do address the issue of offering alternatives to graphics and graphical links in Chapter 5, "Some Sample Meals." We also checked and double-checked the links, and viewed them on both Macintosh and Windows machines. In special cases, such as using Netscape extensions (Chapter 4, "Some Sample Dishes"), where HTML code may not work consistently, we make note of that.

As final steps, it is considered good form to always check the integrity of your links. Since Web sites and pages come and go, what works one day might not work the next. Therefore, when you set up your Web site, check your links by testing them. Every so often, test them again. If you have lots of links in your site, there are programs that will actually test your links for you.

As people build their Web sites, many folks post pages or sections of documents that contain "Under Construction" notices or icons. These constructs are to be eschewed. Try and build up your Web pages without using these dummy notices. One way to avoid them is to build a site in modules, and substitute an updated single index document when you add the next module.

○ SUMMARY

This chapter gives you some food for thought while generating content, and organizing and formatting your Web pages. You need not be a graphic maven or techno wizard to whip up some cool Web pages. If you stick with our basic guidelines, you can create inviting home pages that people enjoy visiting. Now let's cook up some of our own Web recipes in Chapter 4, "Some Sample Dishes."

P A R T 2

Start Cooking!

NOTE

To view the examples of the Web pages you are reading about in Netscape, open the browser and use the "Open File" command on the File menu to view the various pages on the CD-ROM. Then select the "Source Document" command on the View menu to view the HTML code. The Microsoft Internet Explorer uses the "Open" command on the File menu and the "Source" command on the View menu in the same manner. In Mosaic, the commands are "Open Local" and "View Source." and both are located on the File menu.

THIS CHAPTER WILL COVER THE FOLLOWING:

- Working with body text, line breaks, paragraphs, lists, and text styles
- Creating outlines with header tags and horizontal rules
- Using Netscape extensions
- Displaying foreign text and special characters
- Creating internal links for navigating long documents and external links for jumping to other documents
- Creating external links to other web sites
- Working with graphics and adding graphical links

Some Sample Dishes

Now that we've taken a grand tour of the World Wide Web, you're probably eager to start creating your own home page and associated Web pages. This chapter gives you everything you need. Here, you will find sections covering everything from simple letters to complex documents with graphics and forms. The text gives you the scripts, and explains how to use them and why. The progression in this chapter is from simple page elements to more complex ones, so you can build up your knowledge one construct at a time.

This chapter consists of two page spreads. On the left-hand side, you will see the Web page you are about to create. The scripts and explanatory notes on where and how to use the features will appear on the right side. You can follow along entering our recipes to learn about the various tags and Web page components. Or, if you like you can find the completed pages in the CHAPTER4.DIR folder of the CD-ROM. Coupled with the PARTS.DIR, you will find many of the elements you need to build exciting home pages.

And remember that creating your own web page is a lot like cooking: once you get the hang of it, you can add your own variations. We are simply offering you building blocks and examples of how you can use the World Wide Web to publish your information. Substitute your own text and graphics for the ones we provide. After all, it's YOUR home page.

○ USING THE CD-ROM WITH THIS CHAPTER

If you look at the CD-ROM, you'll find the examples in this chapter along with an array of sample text ingredients, graphics, and HTML documents so you can cut and paste a wondrous Web page.

The elements of this chapter are contained in the following folders or directories:

■ **PARTS.DIR:** *Use the documents in this directory to cut and paste together your own personal home page. Here you will find Web page elements, including scripts for bulleted lists, graphical links, and more. All you have to do is enter the names of your own documents and graphics, and voilà! an instant Web page.*

- **GIZMO.DIR:** *Gizmos, Ltd. is the fictitious company we have created to show what businesses can do with their home pages. All of the Gizmos, Ltd. sample material discussed in this chapter can be found in this directory.*

- **POETRY.DIR:** *Margaret Weigel has kindly donated material from her Haiku Page (http://www.mit.edu:8001/people/maweigel/MA.html) so that we can learn how to work with text styles and use Netscape's HTML extensions.*

- **FAMILY.DIR:** *This directory gives you scripts, graphics, and everything you need for creating a home page for your family. This folder even includes Mom, Dad, Brother, Sister, and Baby icons for different nationalities (Caucasian, African American, Asian American, and Latin American). To display the appropriate icons, just change the names of these graphics.*

As we've told you before, remember that when you make changes to our templates, you must save your document as a text-only file. Otherwise, your browser won't be able to read it. Also, Web browsers are case-sensitive! This means that when entering file names in your text, you make sure that the upper and lower case letters match the file name exactly. Otherwise, your browser won't know where to look for the file.

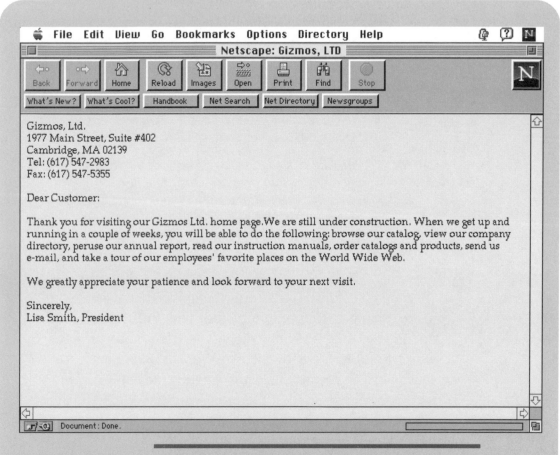

Figure 4.1   Putting a letter on the Web.

○ PUTTING A LETTER ON THE WEB: WORKING WITH PARAGRAPHS AND LINE BREAKS (LETTER1.HTM)

This recipe teaches you about the following Web page elements:

- *Opening and closing <HTML>…</HTML> document tags*

- *Defining a header section in your document with the <HEAD>…</HEAD> tags*

- *Creating titles with the <TITLE>…</TITLE> tags*

- *Defining the body section in your document with the <BODY>…</BODY> tags*

- *Marking paragraphs of text with the <P>…</P> tags*

- *Separating paragraphs with a line break using the <BR> tag*

Ingredients:

- *<HTML>… </HTML> Tags: Every web document must open with <HTML> and close with </HTML>. <HTML> tags signify the beginning and end of an HTML file and let your readers' computers know that they should handle it as HTML.*

105

If you fail to place a closing </HTML> tag at the end of your file, your browser will still recognize the document as an HTML format because it reaches the end-of-file marker. Since there is nothing after the </HTML> tag, nothing can go wrong. Still, it's considered good form to close the document with this end-of-document tag.

- *<HEAD> ... </HEAD>: It's good form to enclose your title and other header elements within <HEAD> ... </HEAD> tags.*

These tags are section markers (or wrappers), and they make it easier for other folks who view your Web pages source text to recognize your header section. If you are that person, as you may be at a later date, you will appreciate seeing them. Just like the <BODY> ... </BODY> tags, your Web pages can often function without these tags, but it isn't recommended.

- *<TITLE>...</TITLE> Tags: Before beginning to work on your Web Page, give it a title by entering <TITLE>Document Name</Title> . Your document's name will then appear on the Title bar of your browser application.*

- *<BODY>...</BODY> Tags: Use the <BODY> tags for marking the body section of your document.*

- *
 Tag: Enter <BR> to create a forced line break in your text.*

>
 does not require a closing tag.

- *<P>...</P> Tags: To add space between your paragraphs or between lines of text, use the paragraph tags.*

- *Chap4.DIR/GIZMO.DIR/Letter1.DOC: This document contains all the text discussed in the sample letter below.*

Now, let's get started on putting our first document on the web.

Don't forget to tell your browser this is an HTML document.

<HTML>

Notice how the title of your document appears on the title bar on top of Figure 4.1?

<HEAD>
<TITLE>Gizmos, LTD</TITLE>
</HEAD>

You can break up the lines in your body text using the <BR> tag. Think of <BR> as a carriage return. You will also notice that we don't need to add the </BODY> closing tag until we reach the end of the document.

You can also find the above two elements in "01HTML.DOC" in the PARTS directory.

<BODY>
Gizmos, Ltd.
1977 Main Street, Suite #402
Cambridge, MA 02139
Tel: (617) 547-2983
Fax: (617) 547-5355

You can add a double space between paragraphs by entering a <P> tag where you want the new paragraph to begin. You can also find body text and paragraphs with the above-mentioned tags in "02TEXT.DOC" in the PARTS directory.

<P>Dear Customer:

<P>Thank you for visiting our Gizmos Ltd. home page. We are still under construction. When we get up and running in a couple of weeks, you will be able to do the following: browse our catalog, view our company directory, peruse our annual report, read our instruction manuals, order catalogs and products, send us e-mail, and take a tour of our employees' favorite places on the World Wide Web.

<P>We greatly appreciate your patience and look forward to your next visit.</P>

You do not have to add a closing tag until the end of the last paragraph before a new text format (in this case, body text).

Sincerely,
Lisa Smith, President</P>

The body tags mark out the lines above as being the "body" section of your Web page.

</BODY>
</HTML>

Don't forget to add the closing tags to your document.

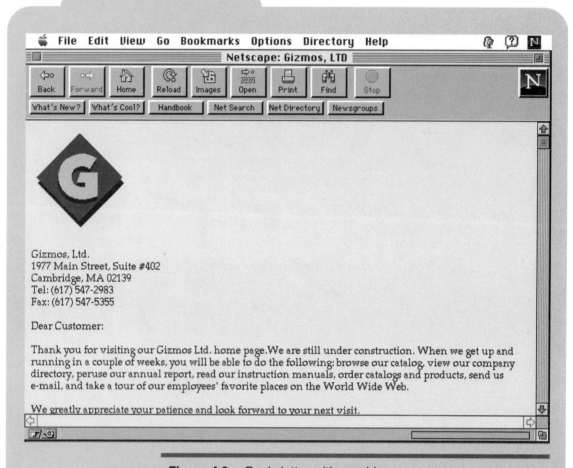

Figure 4.2 Basic letter with graphic.

○ ADDING AN IMAGE

Images really make your Web page come alive. Adding an image teaches you about the following Web page elements:

■ *The image tag <IMG SRC= "...">*

■ *Locating an image file of the appropriate type (.GIF or .JPG) at the location pointed to in the image tag.*

Now, let's jazz up your letter by adding a graphic. We will keep things simple for the time being, and discuss working with images in more detail later in this chapter. This letter will have the same text as the last one, except that a graphic will be added. It results in Figure 4.2

Ingredients:

■ *<IMG SRC= "..."> Tag: The image source tag tells your browser where to look for the graphic and where to place it on your page.*

■ ***Chap.DIR/Gizmo.DIR/Letter2.DOC:*** *This letter is exactly the same as the previous one, except that an image source tag has been added.*

■ ***Chapter4.DIR/Gizmo.DIR/Gizmo.GIF:*** *This logo was created in a graphics application and converted to a .GIF file for displaying on the World Wide Web. You can also display graphics with the .JPG suffix.*

<HTML>
<HEAD>
<TITLE>Gizmos, LTD</TITLE>
</HEAD>

Where you type the image source tag in your document is where, in relation to the text, your graphic will appear. Your visitor's browser then searches your folder for the graphic and displays it on your page. Just as the line break tag doesn't require a closing tag, the image source tag requires none.

<BODY>
<IMG SRC="Gizmo.GIF">

> Your graphic's name must be placed in quotes.

<P></P>

We have added two paragraph tags here to leave space between the logo and the text below.

Gizmos, Ltd.
1977 Main Street, Suite #402
Cambridge, MA 02139
Tel: (617) 547-2983
Fax: (617) 547-5355

<P>Dear Customer:</P>

<P>Thank you for visiting our Gizmos Ltd. home page. We are still under construction. When we get up and running in a couple of weeks, you will be able to do the following: browse our catalog, view our company directory, peruse our annual report, read our instruction manuals, order catalogs and products, send us e-mail, and take a tour of our employees' favorite places on the World Wide Web.

<P>We greatly appreciate your patience and look forward to your next visit.</P>

Sincerely,
Lisa Smith, President</P>
</BODY>
</HTML>

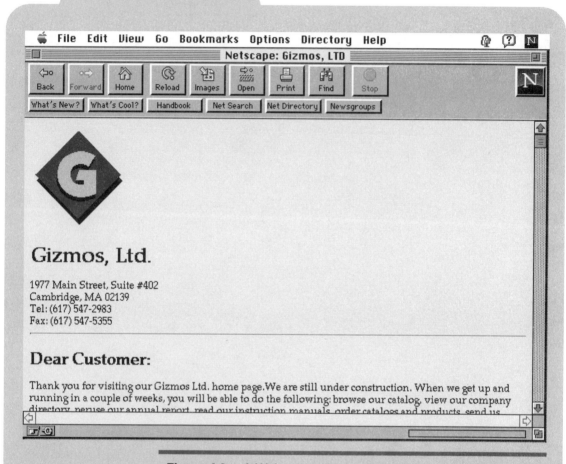

Figure 4.3　A Web page with header and horizontal rule.

○ WORKING WITH HEADER TAGS AND HORIZONTAL RULE

HTML lets you create different levels of header paragraphs, and separate your text with horizontal lines of various thickness (called rules). With this example, you learn about:

■ *The various header tags <H1>...</H1> through <H5>...</H5> that format your heading paragraphs.*

■ *The <HR> tag which creates a horizontal line on your Web page.*

Now your page is starting to look better. But it could still use a little more formatting. Here, we will continue building on the same letter and add a couple of header tags and a horizontal rule. The result appears in Figure 4.3.

Ingredients:

■ *<H1>...</H1> tags: You can enter header tags to display bigger, bolder text. The <H1> tag indicates the largest, highest-level heading.*

■ *<H2>...</H2> tags: The <H2> tag is the second largest heading. Most browsers also support <H3> and <H4> headings, which descend in size.*

■ *<HR> tag: This tag draws a thin horizontal line across your Web page.*

■ ***Chap4.DIR/Gizmo.DIR/Headers.DOC:** This is the same letter we have been working on all along, only we will now add headers and a horizontal rule. You can also find tags for heading elements and horizontal rules in "03Head.DOC" in the Parts directory.*

```
<HTML>
<HEAD>
<TITLE>Gizmos, LTD</TITLE>
</HEAD>

<BODY>
<IMG SRC= "Gizmo.GIF">
<P></P>
```

Now your company name will jump out at your visitors.

```
<H1>Gizmos, Ltd.</H1>
```

```
1977 Main Street, Suite #402<BR>
Cambridge, MA 02139<BR>
Tel: (617) 547-2983<BR>
Fax: (617) 547-5355<BR>
```

See how the horizontal rule creates a line across the screen? Horizontal rules are useful for dividing one section of your document from another, but use them sparingly. Too many rules will clutter up your Web page.

<HR>

<H2>Dear Customer:</H2>

<P>Thank you for visiting our Gizmos Ltd. home page. We are still under construction. When we get up and running in a couple of weeks, you will be able to do the following: browse our catalog, view our company directory, peruse our annual report, read our instruction manuals, order catalogs and products, send us e-mail, and take a tour of our employees' favorite places on the World Wide Web.

<P>We greatly appreciate your patience and look forward to your next visit.</P>

Sincerely,
Lisa Smith, President
</BODY>
</HTML>

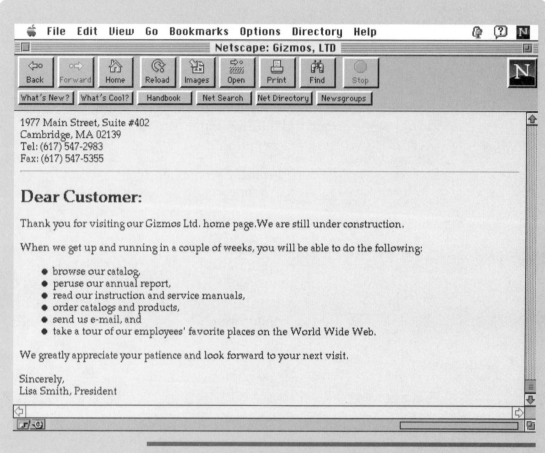

Figure 4.4 A Web page with items in an unordered list.

○ CREATING AN OUTLINE: WORKING WITH UNORDERED TAGS AND BULLETED LISTS

Lists are an important Web page ingredient that lets you present a lot of related information in logical way. In this recipe you learn how to create an unordered list:

■ *An unordered list must be surrounded by the <UL>…</UL> "wrapper tags" that indicate a numbered list follows.*

■ *Bulleted items on the list are created by surrounding the items with the <LI>…</LI> tags.*

HTML is great for creating lists, which is why Webmasters and Webmistresses often use it for that purpose. The bulleted list format (called an unordered list in HTML-speak) makes it easier for readers to scan for important information and find out what your site has to offer. Figure 4.4 shows you our letter with a bulleted list.

Lists are also an ideal way to present hypertext links to other sections of your document and to other Web sites. We will discuss adding links a little later in this chapter.

Ingredients:

■ *<UL> … </UL> tags: UL stands for unordered list, meaning that items are bulleted rather than listed in numerical order.*

■ *<LI> tag: Each item within the unordered list must be preceded with the List tag. Items will appear with a bullet next to them.*

■ ***Chap4.DIR/Gizmo.DIR/Listul.HTM:*** *This script shows you how to separate text items into an unordered list with bulleted items.*

```
<HTML>
<HEAD>
<TITLE>Headers</TITLE>
</HEAD>

<BODY>
<IMG SRC= "Gizmo.GIF">
<P></P>
<H1>Gizmos, Ltd.</H1>

1977 Main Street, Suite #402<BR>
Cambridge, MA 02139<BR>
Tel: (617) 547-2983<BR>
Fax: (617) 547-5355<BR>
<HR>
<H2>Dear Customer:</H2>

<P>Thank you for visiting our Gizmos Ltd. home page. We
are still under construction.

<P>When we get up and running in a couple of weeks, you
will be able to do the following: </P>
```

We will now break up the items listed in this paragraph and create a list. The <UL> tag tells the browser to display the following items in the Unordered List format with bullets next to them.

NOTE

The unordered list format indents the text by a standard amount. We will learn how to create lists with varying indents when we work with definition lists (aka glossary lists) later in this chapter.

<UL>

Add the List tags before new items in your list. You will notice that because list items exist within the <UL> definition, you do not have to add closing tags after each item.

<LI>browse our catalog,
<LI>peruse our annual report,
<LI>read our instruction and service manuals,
<LI>order catalogs and products,
<LI>send us e-mail, and
<LI>take a tour of our employees' favorite places on the World Wide Web.
</UL>

Make sure to add the closing tag when you're finished adding items to your list.

<P>We greatly appreciate your patience and look forward to your next visit.</P>

Sincerely,
Lisa Smith, President

</BODY>
</HTML>

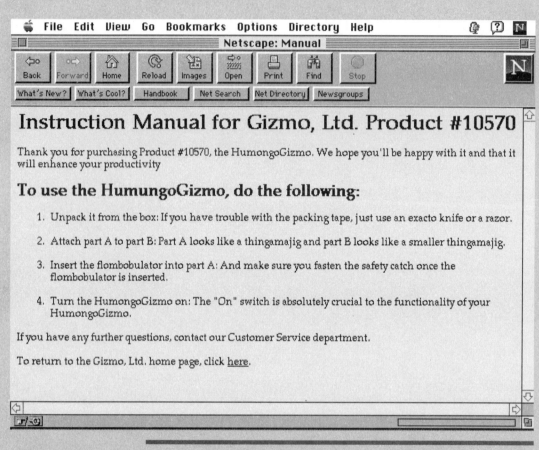

Figure 4.5 A Web page with items in an ordered list.

○ AN ON-LINE INSTRUCTION MANUAL: WORKING WITH NUMBERED LISTS

Numbered lists are a great way of telling people how to perform a task or indicating a level or order of importance. You will learn about the following ordered list components:

- *An ordered list is surrounded by the <OL>...</OL> "wrapper tags" that indicate a numbered list follows.*

- *Numbered items on the ordered list are created by surrounding the items with the <LI>...</LI> tags.*

- *Numbered items on the ordered list are created by surrounding the items with the <LI>...</LI> tags.*

You also learn in this recipe how to create a hypertext link in your document:

- *The anchor tag <A>...</A> points to a location in your document, or a location in another file that your reader is taken to when they click on the underlined text in the Web page.*

In some situations, such as when you are giving your visitors instructions, you will want to have numbered lists instead of bulleted lists. Next, we create a simple instruction manual so you can see how numbered lists work in HTML documents. This new document is shown in Figure 4.5.

Ingredients:

- *<OL> ... </OL> Tags: OL stands for ordered list. Items appearing in lists with the <OL> ... </OL> tags will have numbers instead of bullets next to them.*

- *<LI> Tag: Add List tags the same way you did in the last document.*

- ***Chap4.DIR/Gizmo.DIR/Listol.doc:*** *Tell your customers how to use one of Gizmo, Ltd.'s products.*

Don't forget—since we're starting a new document instead of building on an old one, you need to begin with an <HTML> tag and add a new title.

<HTML>
<HEAD>
<TITLE>Manual</TITLE>
</HEAD>

Remember that adding header tags makes it easier for your reader to know what your Web page is about.

<BODY>
<H1>Instruction Manual for Gizmo, Ltd. Product #10570</H1>

<P>Thank you for purchasing Product #10570, the HumongoGizmo. We hope you'll be happy with it and that it will enhance your productivity.</P>

<H2>To use the HumongoGizmo, do the following:</H2>

You will notice that ordered list tags work the same way as unordered list tags, only the items in the list are numbered instead of bulleted.

<u>\<OL\></u>
<u>\<LI\>Unpack it from the box:</u>
<u>If you have trouble with the packing tape, just use an exacto</u>
<u>knife or a razor.</u>

We have added paragraph opening and closing tags because the list items take up more than one line. Adding space between the items make the text easier to read.

<u>\<BR\></u>
<u>\<BR\></u>

The two line breaks place two blank lines in your page. You could also achieve the same effect with a single line containing the following: \<P\>\</P\>. Since these tags separate paragraphs into separate regions, you get two line breaks from a single line of this type. But two lines of \<BR\> is conceptually easier and cleaner.

<u>\<LI\>Attach part A to part B:</u>
<u>Part A looks like a thingamajig and part B looks like a</u>
<u>smaller thingamajig.</u>
<u>\<BR\></u>
<u>\<BR\></u>

<u>\<LI\>Insert the flombobulator into part A:</u>
<u>And make sure you fasten the safety catch once the flom-</u>
<u>bobulator is inserted.</u>
<u>\<BR\></u>
<u>\<BR\></u>

In the lines below, you may notice that the first line of the <LI> tag ends with a space and a carriage return. Your browser ignores the carriage return and places the next line on the same line as the previous one.

HTML ignores extra spaces between words or single letters. The ISO-Latin-1 nonbreaking space can be used to add extra space between the letters. See "Foreign Text and Special Characters" later in this chapter for more details.

<LI>Turn the HumongoGizmo on:
The "On" switch is absolutely crucial to the functionality of your HumongoGizmo.

End your ordered list with a closing tag.

</OL>

<P>If you have any further questions, contact our Customer Service department.</P>

We snuck anchor tags in here because we will eventually link this instruction manual to the final Gizmo, Ltd. home page we create. We will discuss anchor tags and hypertext links later in this chapter. For the time being, go ahead and sneak a peak at the Gizmo, Ltd. home page with your Web browser.

You will find it by using the Open File command to open "Chap4.DIR/GIZMO.DIR/Gizmo.HTM."

<P>To return to the Gizmo, Ltd. home page, click <A> HREF="Gizmo.HTM">here</A>.

In the above hypertext link, we've explicitly put a "click here" in the link. That's the way the link functions, of course, but it is considered bad form to be so explicit. You want your links to be natural, and "click here" not only wastes space, but it is clumsy and unnecessary. It should be obvious in your browser that you've created a link due to colored text, underlining, or whatever your browser uses to mark links. A better link would read: <A HREF = " ... ">Return to Gizmo Ltd. Homepage</A>

</BODY>
</HTML>

Always add your closing tags at the end of your document.

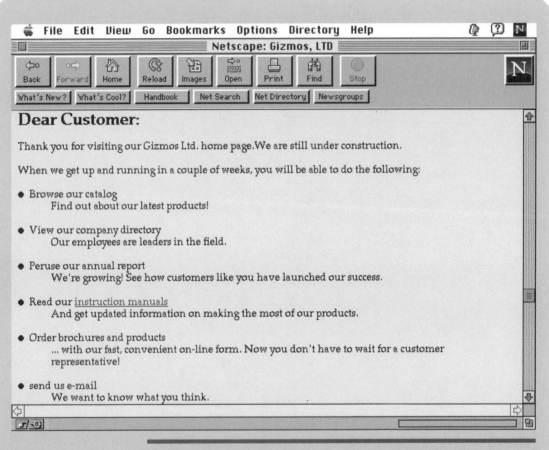

Figure 4.6 A Web page with items in a definition list.

○ WHAT'S ON THE MENU? WORKING WITH DEFINITION LISTS

HTML offers you the ability to create hierarchical lists of information, by indenting paragraphs to create lists within lists. This recipe teaches you about the following lists:

- *A definition list is surrounded by the <DL>...</DL> "wrapper tags" that indicate a multilevel list follows.*

- *The first level paragraph of a definition list is indicated with the <DT> tag.*

- *The second level indented paragraph of a definition list is indicated with the <DD> tag.*

- *You also learn how to mix in bulleted and numbered paragraphs in a definition list in this recipe.*

The definition list format let you create lists with indented text following each item, or lists within lists. This is useful in situations where you have listings under different categories, or when having indented explanatory notes would make each list item easier to understand. Figure 4.6 shows you our example using definition lists.

If you want to create your own lists, you will find the elements for unordered lists, ordered lists, and definition lists in **04LISTS.DOC** in the **Parts** directory.

Ingredients:

- *<DL>...</DL>: DL stands for definition list. All definition lists must begin with the <DL> tag, and must end with the </DL> closing tag.*

- *<DT>: The DT tag stands for definition term, and is used for each main item on the list. Definition term text will appear flush left on the screen.*

129

■ *<DD>: The DD tag stands for definition description, and is used to either indent text under a definition term, or list items underneath a definition term.*

The above three components are the only ones defined as part of a definition list. You can easily add bullets to individual entries on the list by having lines like the following:

<DT><LI>Browse our catalog

You get a bullet in the above entry when it is embedded in a <DL> because HTML assumes that you wanted to use a <UL> before the entry. However, <DT><LI> is not a standard part of a definition list.

■ ***Chap4.DIR/GIZMO.DIR/Listdl.HTM:*** *Now we will return to the Gizmos LTD home page we've been working on, and add indented text to the list items you have already entered.*

<HTML>
<HEAD>
<TITLE>Gizmos, LTD</TITLE>
</HEAD>

<BODY>
<IMG SRC= "Gizmo.GIF">
<P></P>
<H1>Gizmos, Ltd.</H1>
<BODY>
1977 Main Street, Suite #402
Cambridge, MA 02139
Tel: (617) 547-2983
Fax: (617) 547-5355
<HR>
<H2>Dear Customer:</H2>

<P>Thank you for visiting our Gizmos Ltd. home page. We are still under construction.

<P>When we get up and running in a couple of weeks, you will be able to do the following:</P>

Begin your definition list by adding the <DL> tag. If you have left commas after each item from back when we listed these items in a paragraph, you should remove the commas now.

<DL>

Add the <DT> tag to the left of the <LI> tag you have already entered. This item is your definition term.

<DT><LI>Browse our catalog

Add the <DD> tag and enter your explanatory text. This item is your definition description. Like the <LI> tags, you do not have to close your <DD> and <DD> tags.

<DD>Find out about our latest products!
<P></P>

<DT><LI>View our company directory
<DD>Our employees are leaders in the field.

Remember how we added these paragraph tags to insert space between list items a couple of examples ago? We don't want additional space between the definition terms and definition descriptions, however, because we want to show that these items go together.

<P></P>

<DT><LI>Peruse our annual report
<DD>We're growing! See how customers like you have launched our success.
<P></P>

The anchor tags link the instruction manual to the final Gizmo, LTD home page. We should also link to the instruction manual to this page. We will further discuss Anchor Tags later in more detail in a moment.

<DT><LI>Read our <A HREF= "Listol.HTM"> instruction manuals</A>
<DD>And get updated information on making the most of our products.
<P></P>

<DT><LI>Order brochures and products
<DD>... with our fast, convenient on-line form. Now you don't have to wait for a customer representative!
<P></P>

<DT><LI>Send us e-mail

<DD>We want to know what you think.
 <P></P>

<DT><LI>Take a tour of our employees' favorite places on the World Wide Web.
<DD>We work hard, but we like to have fun too. And our employees have found great sites to check out on the 'Net.

When you are done adding items to your definition list, enter the closing tag.

</DL>

<P>We hope you enjoy our home page.</P>

Sincerely,
Lisa Smith, President
</BODY>
</HTML>

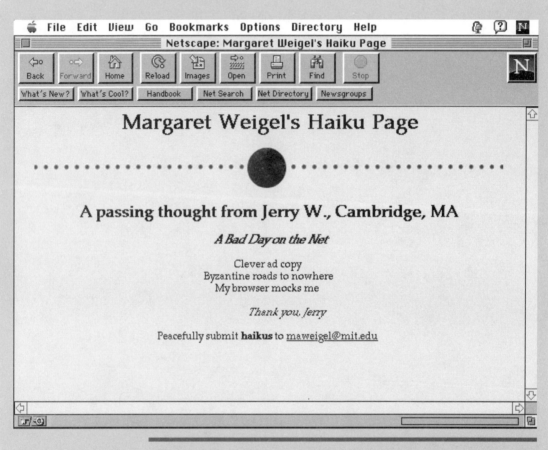

Figure 4.7 A Web page with formatted text.

○ YOUR FIRST POEM ON THE WEB (WORKING WITH TEXT STYLES)

Text can be formatted in a Web page so that it stands out. This recipe teaches you how to do the following things:

■ *Bold text using the <B>...</B> tags.*

■ *Italicize text using the <I>...</I> tags.*

■ *Underline text using the <U>...</U> tags.*

■ *Center justify text using the <CENTER>...</CENTER> tags.*

■ *Create a block of text using the <BLOCKQUOTE>... </BLOCKQUOTE> tags.*

Although HTML's text formatting capabilities are still limited, most browsers do recognize text that has been bolded, centered, italicized, and underlined with the appropriate tags. You can also indent text in a block quote format. These options enable you to design more interesting and readable home pages, as shown in the example created here and shown in Figure 4.7.

NOTE

Many of the improvements in HTML Level 3.0 (HTML+) and the Netscape extensions are in this area of improved text formatting.

Ingredients:

■ *<B>...</B> tags: You can add emphasis to items in your paragraphs by **bolding** them.*

■ *<I>...</I> tags: You can indicate titles of publications, movies, and recordings or add variety to your headers by italicizing them.*

- *<U>...</U> tags: You can also underline text; however, many browsers, including earlier versions of Netscape, do not always recognize underlined text.*

Use underlined text in Web pages sparingly. Not only do many browsers not recognize underlining, but underlined text clashes with links, which are also underlined. When not used properly, underlined text will appear to your viewers as if it is a nonfunctional link. Both aspects of this problem are unfortunate.

- *<BLOCKQUOTE>...</BLOCKQUOTE> tags: You can indent text without having to create a definition list. The block quote element can be used to set apart long quotations, credit written work, or emphasize a paragraph.*

- *<CENTER>...<CENTER> tags: Many browsers also recognize text that has been centered with the appropriate tags. This allows you to add variety to your page layout.*

- *<H3>...</H3> tags: Although we have already discussed headers, we have not yet used the level 3 header. <H3> is ideal for documents with many headers because the smaller size makes your document less cluttered-looking than if you used larger headers.*

- ***Chap4.DIR/Poetry.DIR/Poetry.HTM:*** *This sample from Margaret Weigel shows how you can use text formatting features. You can check out her live (and lively) home page, which features interesting graphics and links, at*

http://www.mit.edu:8001/people/maweigel/MA.html.
You can also piece together text formatting elements for
your own home page by cutting and pasting them from
Chap4.DIR/Parts.DIR/05FORMAT.DOC.

- ***Chap4.DIR/Poetry.DIR/Line.GIF:*** *Margaret got tired of*
  that boring old horizontal rule and created her own divid-
  ing line with a graphics application.

```
<HTML>
<HEAD>
<TITLE>Margaret Weigel's Haiku Page</TITLE>
</HEAD>

<BODY>
```

Poetry looks ideal when you center the text. Many, though
not all, browsers are capable of displaying centered text.

```
<CENTER>
<H1>Margaret Weigel's Haiku Page</H1>
<P>
```

Even the simplest graphics can add interest to your Web
page.

```
<IMG SRC = "Line.GIF">
<P>
<H2>A passing thought from Jerry W., Cambridge, MA
</H2>
```

Titles should generally be italicized.

<H3><I>A Bad Day on the Net</I></H3>

Margaret thought the poem would look better with a space between the title and the piece. Therefore, another <P> tag was inserted. Had Margaret wanted additional space, the line <P></P> could have been inserted. That line would have been read by most browsers as two blank lines, one before and one after the empty paragraph it encloses.

<P>

Clever ad copy
Byzantine roads to nowhere
My browser mocks me
<P>

We can set the poem's author credit apart by indenting it with the Block Quote tag.

<BLOCKQUOTE><I>Thank you, Jerry</I></BLOCKQUOTE>

If you're on-line right now, this anchor tag will let you send e-mail to the creator of this page. We will further discuss the "Mail To" anchor tag in Chapter 5. With the right browser, you may even be able to see where the word "haikus" is underlined. No matter what, you will notice that the word is bold.

```
<P>Peacefully submit <B><U>haikus</U></B> to <A
HREF="mail to: maweigel@mit.edu">maweigel@mit.edu
</a>
</P>
```

In this example, all of the text, including the headings, was centered. Now that the page is complete, you need to close the <CENTER> tag with its partner, </CENTER>.

```
</CENTER>
</BODY>
</HTML>
```

Figure 4.8   A Netscape-enhanced Web page.

○ YOUR SECOND POEM ON THE WEB: EXPLORING NETSCAPE EXTENSIONS

Netscape extensions offer you additional text formatting options that you will find useful. This recipe explores the most popular extensions, including:

- *Adding backgrounds (pictures and patterns) to your pages using the <BODY BACKGROUND= "..."> tag.*

- *Including blinking text items with the <BLINK>... </BLINK> tags.*

- *Changing font sizes on the fly with the <FONT SIZE= "...">...</FONT> tags.*

If you're already hooked up to the World Wide Web, chances are you (and much of your audience) have access to the Netscape browser. Netscape is the most popular browser (with an estimated 85% market share) because it is easy to use and offers an array of extensions to regular ol' HTML. Netscape version 1.1 enables users to view fancy backgrounds, custom-sized text, and blinking boxes. Even if you don't have Netscape 1.1 or later, you can add these features to your home page; you just won't be able to see them for yourself in other browsers.

We will now explore how we can use Netscape's HTML extensions to create truly impressive home pages.

Ingredients:

- *<BODY background="...">*

- *<BLINK>...</BLINK>*

- *<FONT SIZE="+ or - number">...</FONT>*

- ***Chap4.DIR/Poetry.DIR/Poetry2.HTM:*** *To create your own Netscape-enhanced page, cut and paste the elements from **Chap4.DIR/Parts.DIR/06NETSC1.DOC**.*

141

■ ***Chap4.DIR/Poetry.DIR/Blueston.JPG:*** *The Blueston.JPG file is a patterned graphic element, which will fill your Web page as a background. Patterned backgrounds make a nice alternative to that normal, dull gray we keep seeing.*

```
<HTML>
<HEAD>
<TITLE>Margaret Weigel's Haiku Page</TITLE>
</HEAD>
```

Add your background with the <BODY> tag at the *beginning* of your HTML document; otherwise, Netscape will not display it.

```
<BODY>
<BODY background="Bluestone.JPG">
<CENTER>
<H1>Margaret Weigel's Haiku Page</H1>
<P>
```

You can create a blinking box around text you wish to emphasize using the <BLINK>...</BLINK> tags. Beware of overusing the Blink feature, however; too much blinking text can be hard on your visitor's eyes.

```
<H2>This site is best savored with <BLINK>Netscape
Version 1.1</BLINK></H2>
<P>
<IMG SRC = "Line.Gif">
<P>
```

The font size feature lets you increase the size of all text proportionally by the increments you specify. You can also specify smaller font sizes. Netscape defaults to 12-point body text. The font size correction is fully dependent on the browser you use, and has nothing to do with any particular browser default setting. It is a relative correction.

All text that follows this font size entry will be two sizes bigger.

<FONT SIZE="+2">
<P>A passing thought from Jerry W., Cambridge, MA

Without a closing tag, the Web page continues to use Font Size +2 until we instruct it otherwise. We will now increase the size of the poem's title by entering a larger font size. Since we have added a closing tag at the end of this line, the following text will revert to the previous setting of +2.

<P><FONT SIZE="+3"><I>A Bad Day on the Net</I>
</FONT>

Clever ad copy
Byzantine roads to nowhere
My browser mocks me
<P><blockquote><I>Thank you, Jerry</I></blockquote>
</P>
Peacefully submit <B><U>haikus</U></B> to
<A HREF="mail to: maweigel@mit.edu">mawei-
gel@mit.edu
</a>

Let's close out the change in font size from above so that all of our tags are balanced.

</FONT>
</P>
</CENTER>
</BODY>
</HTML>

Figure 4.8 shows you the results of your efforts with Netscape extensions.

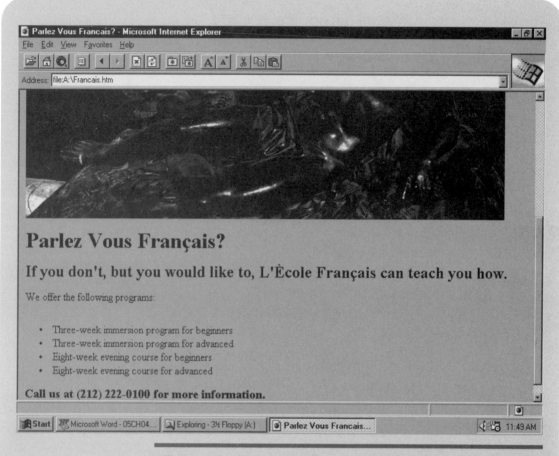

Figure 4.9   A Web page with special characters.

○ FOREIGN TEXT AND SPECIAL CHARACTERS

Many special characters, accented vowels, ligatures, and symbols are not standard text. However, using the ISO-Latin-1 codes allows you to use them in your text. In the following recipe you learn about:

- *Entering character entities using the "&…;" character strings.*

- *Entering numeric strings using the "&#…;" character strings.*

- *A listing of the more common character and numeric entities in use.*

What can you do if you're a stickler for detail and need to add an accented word, such as "résumé," to your web page? Since Web browsers can only read plain-text formats, special characters often don't display correctly. Fortunately, the International Standards Organization has set up a standard language called ISO-Latin-1 for representing special characters.

NOTE

The ISO codes of foreign text and special characters are, as our technical reviewer stresses, boring. Unless you have a need for this information, you might want to pass this section by until required.

Instead of entering the special character itself, you represent it with either a numeric entity or a character entity, which can be explained as follows:

- **_Character entities:_** _These are character strings represented by "&...;"—The ampersand tells the browser that you are starting a character string; the semicolon tells the browser that you are ending the character string. For example, to display the accented letter "ƒ" you would enter "È"._

- **_Numeric entities:_** _These are numerical strings represented by "&#...;"—Once again, the ampersand symbol tells the browser that you are starting a numerical string, and the semicolon tells the browser that you are ending the numerical string. For example, to display an inverted exclamation point "¡" you would enter "="._

NOTE

When creating HTML documents in your word proces-sor, turn off the "Smart Quotes" option in the Preferences dialog box (or whatever setting you use to make your quotation and apostrophe marks look curly). Curly quotation marks are special typographer's characters, and your browser will not display them correctly.

Special Characters and Their Numeric or Character Entities

% (percent sign)	&#37;	© (copyright):	&#169;
± (plus or minus sign)	&#177;	£ (pound sterling):	&#163;
¡ (inverted exclamation point)	&#161;	° (degree sign):	&#176;
¿ (inverted question mark)	&#191;	§ (section sign):	&#167;
¶ (paragraph mark)	¶"	$ (dollar sign):	&#36;
® (registered trademark)	&#174;	¢ (cent sign):	&#162;

How to Handle Accented Characters

À (A grave accent, uppercase)	&Agrave;	à (a grave accent, lowercase)	&agrave;
Á (A acute accent, uppercase)	&Aacute;	á (a acute accent, lowercase)	&aacute;
Â (A circumflex accent, uppercase)	&Acirc;	â (a circumflex accent, lowercase)	&acirc;
Ã (A tilde accent, uppercase)	&Atilde;	ã (a tilde accent, lowercase)	&atilde;
Ä (A umlaut mark, uppercase)	&Auml;	ä (a umlaut mark, lowercase)	&auml;
Å (A ring mark, uppercase)	&Aring;	å (a ring mark, lowercase)	&aring;
Æ (A ligature, uppercase)	&AElig;	æ (a ligature, lowercase)	&aelig;
Ç (C cedilla, uppercase)	&Ccedil;	ç (c cedilla, lowercase)	&ccedil;
È (E grave accent, uppercase)	&Egrave;	è (e grave accent, lowercase)	&egrave;
É (E acute accent, uppercase)	&Eacute;	é (e acute accent, lowercase)	&eacute;
Ê (A cicumflex, uppercase)	&Eacute;	ê (e circumflex, lowercase)	&ecirc;
Ë (E umlaut mark, uppercase)	&Euml;	ë (e umlaut mark, lowercase)	&euml;
Ì (I grave accent, uppercase)	&Igrave;	ï (i umlaut mark, lowercase)	&iuml;
Í (I acute accent, uppercase)	&Iacute;	ì (i grave accent, lowercase)	&igrave;
Î (I circumflex, uppercase)	&Icirc;	í (i acute accent, lowercase)	&iacute;
Ï (I umlaut mark, uppercase)	&Iuml;	î (i circumflex, lowercase)	&icirc;
Ñ (N tilde accent, uppercase)	&Ntilde;	ñ (n tilde accent, lowercase)	&ntilde;
Ò (O grave accent, uppercase)	&Ograve;	ò (o grave accent, lowercase)	&ograve;
Ó (O acute accent, uppercase)	&Oacute;	ó (o acute accent, lowercase)	&oacute;
Ô (O circumflex, uppercase)	&Ocirc;	ô (o circumflex, lowercase)	&ocirc;
Õ (O tilde, uppercase)	&Otilde;	õ (o tilde, lowercase)	&otilde;
Ö (O umlaut mark, uppercase)	&Ouml;	ö (o umlaut mark, lowercase)	&ouml;
Ø (O slash mark, uppercase)	&Oslash;	ø (o slash mark, lowercase)	&oslash;
Ù (U grave accent, uppercase)	&Ugrave;	ù (u grave accent, lowercase)	&ugrave;
Ú (U acute accent, uppercase)	&Uacute;	ú (u acute accent, lowercase)	&uacute;
Û (U circumflex, uppercase)	&Ucirc;	û (u circumflex, lowercase)	&ucirc;
Ü (U umlaut mark, uppercase)	&Uuml;	ü (u umlaut mark, lowercase)	&uuml;
		ÿ (y umlaut mark, lowercase)	&yuml;

ISO-Latin-1 will become clearer to you as you continue reading through this section. Unfortunately, even the International Standards Organization has its limitations, and displaying special characters is dicey at best. For example, we have found that Netscape 1.1 often displays numeric entities incorrectly, and the text-only Lynx browser often displays blank spaces where special characters should be. Many Webmasters and Webmistresses avoid this problem altogether by not even attempting to represent special characters.

We will now create a Web page with special characters, shown in Figure 4.9.

Ingredients:

- *"ç" (ç) ISO-Latin-1 character entity: To represent the accented letter "ç", insert this character entity instead of the c with a cedilla in the word "Français".*

- *"&Egrave" (É) ISO-Latin-1 character entity: To represent the accented letter "É", insert this character entity instead of the E with an accent grave in the word "École".*

- ***Chap4.DIR/Charactr.DIR/Francais.HTM:*** *We can use this document to practice using special characters in our text. Unfortunately, we can't promise this will work because different browsers display ISO-Latin-1 numeric and character entities inconsistently.*

- ***Chap4.DIR/Charactr.DIR/France.JPG:*** *Even if our experiment doesn't work with your browser, at least you can enjoy viewing an attractive image!*

```
<HTML>
<HEAD>
<Title>Parlez Vous Francais?</Title>
</HEAD>
```

This photograph of the Palace at Versailles, and other images from international cities, can be downloaded from the Kodak site (http://www.kodak.com/digitalImages/samples/cityPlaces.shtml).

```
<BODY>
<IMG SRC="France.JPG">
<H1>Parlez Vous Fran&ccedil;ais?</H1>
```

See how we entered the character entities in place of the actual accented letters? The words should display correctly in your browser application.

```
<H2>If you don't, but you would like to, the
L'&Egrave;cole Fran&ccedil;ais can teach you how.</H2>
<P>We offer the following programs:</P>
<UL>
<LI>Three-week immersion program for beginners
<LI>Three-week immersion program for advanced
<LI>Eight-week evening course for beginners
<LI>Eight-week evening course for advanced
</UL>
<H3>Call us at (212) 222-0100 for more information.</P>

</BODY>

</HTML>
```

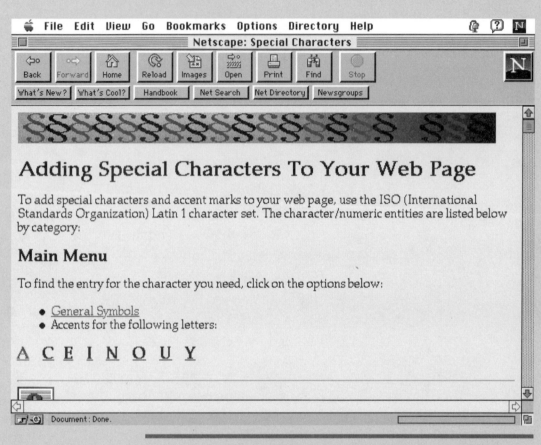

Figure 4.10 The main menu of a long document with links to other sections.

○ ANCHOR TAGS 101: USING INTERNAL LINKS FOR HANDLING LONG DOCUMENT

In the following recipe you create a long document listing special symbols. You also learn to work further with the anchor tag to create jumps or hypertext links in a document. In the following recipe you learn about:

- *More ISO codes representations.*

- *Using the anchor tag <A HREF="#...">text or graphic </A> to link to text or a graphic in another location in your document.*

- *Using the anchor tag <A NAME="#...">text or graphic </A> to link to a file in another location.*

So far, we have only worked with short documents. Longer documents are best constructed with hypertext links so that your visitors don't have to scroll endlessly down your Web page. Creating hypertext links is done with anchor tags. These tags are referred to as anchors because they specify the locations of the links and the location to which your visitors will jump.

Since we have just been discussing ISO-Latin-1 character and numeric entities for representing accents and special characters, let's create the document shown in Figure 4.10, which lists these entries for easy reference.

Ingredients:

- *ISO-Latin-1 character and numeric entities: We will continue working with representing special characters.*

- *<A HREF="#...">Linked text or graphic</A> anchor tags: These tags let you create a link from the specified text or graphic to another location within your HTML document.*

Your visitors will know that a link is present because either the text or the border around the graphic will be highlighted.

■ *<"A NAME="...">text or image</A> anchor tags: In order to link to sections of a document, we must specify areas to link to by anchoring the area with a name. When your visitors click on the links you specify, they will jump to the exact area where you placed the <"A NAME="..."> anchor.*

■ **Chap4.DIR/Charactr.DIR/Charac.HTM:** *Watch out—It's going to be a long, bumpy ride.*

■ **Assorted graphics in the Chap4.DIR/Charactr.DIR** *directory: Adding visual appeal to a lengthy document never hurts.*

<HTML>
<HEAD>
<TITLE>Special Characters</TITLE>
</HEAD>

Feel free to ignore the <BASEFONT> tag if you don't have Netscape 1.1. We only used it so that the figure display of this Web page would be more readable.

<BODY>
<BASEFONT SIZE=+1>
<IMG SRC="Charactr.GIF">
<H1>Adding Special Characters To Your Web Page</H1>
<P>To add special characters and accent marks to your web page, use the ISO (International Standards Organization) Latin 1 character set. The character/numeric entities are listed below by category:</P>

We named the Main Menu so we can add links for visitors to jump back to it.

<u>\<H2>\<A NAME="MENU">Main Menu\</A>\</H2></u>
<u>\<P>To find the entry for the character you need, click on</u>
<u>the options below:\</P></u>

We added a hypertext link to the words "General Symbols" so visitors can jump to that section without scrolling. If you are viewing this in your browser application, you will notice that the linked text is either highlighted, underlined, or both.

<u>\<UL>\<LI>\<A HREF="#SYMBOL">General Symbols\</A></u>
<u>\<LI>Accents for the following letters:</u>
<u>\</UL></u>

As you learned earlier, HTML does not acknowledge the presence of extra spaces between words or single letters. The ISO-Latin-1 " " (nonbreaking space) comes in handy here for adding an extra space between the letters.

We will now link each of these letters to the corresponding sections. Entering a # sign before the section anchor name is very important. If you forget to enter the # sign, your browser will search for another document within your folder and give you an error message.

<u>\<H2>\<A HREF="#A">A\</A>   \<A HREF="#C">C</u>
<u>\</A> \<A HREF="#E">E\</A> </u>
<u>\<A HREF="#I">I\</A>   \<A HREF="#N">N\</A></u>
<u> \<A HREF="#O">O\</A>   \<A</u>
<u>HREF="#U">U\</A>   \<A HREF="#Y">Y\</A>\</H2></u>

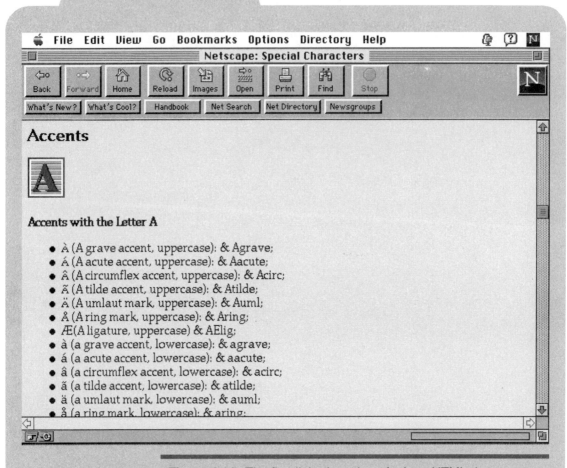

Figure 4.11 The first linked section of a long HTML document.

<HR>

Remember that each section must be anchored with a name so that the linked text you created will have a specified place to which to jump. We decided to anchor the links to the graphics instead of the text. The result is shown in Figure 4.11.

<A NAME="SYMBOL"><IMG SRC="AMP.GIF"></A>
<H3>General Symbols</H3>
<UL>
<LI>& (ampersand) & amp;
<LI>% (percent sign): & #37;
<LI>± (plus or minus sign): & #177;
<LI>¡ (inverted exclamation point): & #161;
<LI>¿ (inverted question mark): & #191;
<LI>¶ (paragraph mark): & #182;
<LI>®(registered trademark): & #174;
<LI>©(copyright): & #169;
<LI>£ (pound sterling): & #163;
<LI>° (degree sign): & #176;
<LI>§(section sign): & #167;
<LI>$ (dollar sign): & #36;
<LI>¢ (cent sign): ¢
<LI>space: (to add an extra space) & nbsp;
</UL>
<HR>
<H2>Accents</H2>
<A NAME="A"><IMG SRC="A.GIF"></A>
<H3>Accents with the Letter A</H3>
<UL>

You have probably noticed that the character and numerical entities entered at the end of each line have a space following the ampersand. We typed it in that way so that visitors can look up what character or numerical strings they should use to represent special characters, rather than the special characters themselves (which are displayed at the beginning of each line).

```
<LI>&Agrave; (A grave accent, uppercase): & Agrave;
<LI>&Aacute; (A acute accent, uppercase): & Aacute;
<LI>&Acirc; (A circumflex accent, uppercase): & Acirc;
<LI>&Atilde; (A tilde accent, uppercase): & Atilde;
<LI>&Auml;  (A umlaut mark, uppercase): & Auml;
<LI>&Aring; (A ring mark, uppercase): & Aring;
<LI>&AElig;(A ligature, uppercase) & AElig;
<LI>&agrave; (a grave accent, lowercase): & agrave;
<LI>&aacute; (a acute accent, lowercase): & aacute;
<LI>&acirc; (a circumflex accent, lowercase): & acirc;
<LI>&atilde; (a tilde accent, lowercase): & atilde;
<LI>&auml; (a umlaut mark, lowercase): & auml;
<LI>&aring; (a ring mark, lowercase): & aring;
<LI>&aelig; (a ligature, lowercase): & aelig;
</UL>
<P>Return to <A HREF="#MENU"> Main Menu</A>.</P>
```

Links to other locations in your files or to locations in your files or to locations in other files in your directories are among the most commonly used constructs in web page design. As your web site develops, you need to take special care that the locations referenced still exsist. Small changes, like changing a file or folder name, are enough to cause your jump to drop out. Be especially cautious and aware of these links, and always test your pages to see that they still function correctly.

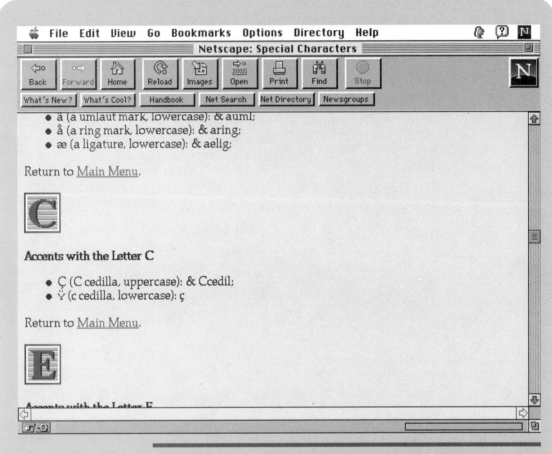

Figure 4.12 The second linked section of a long HTML document.

```
<A NAME="C"><IMG SRC="C.GIF"></A>
<H3>Accents with the Letter C</H3>
<UL>
<LI>&Ccedil; (C cedilla, uppercase): & Ccedil;
<LI>   (c cedilla, lowercase): &ccedil;
</UL>
```

Remember to always create a link so that your visitors can return to the main part of your Web page. Figures 4.12 through 4.14 show you the second, third, and fourth sections of this long linked document.

```
<P>Return to <A HREF="#MENU"> Main Menu</A>.</P>
```

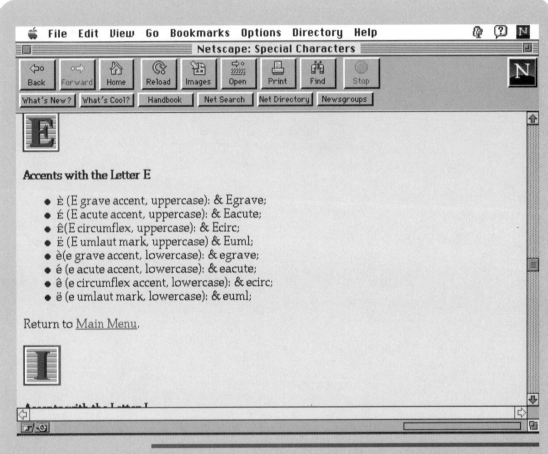

Figure 4.13 The third linked section of a long HTML document.

Don't forget that HTML is case-sensitive. You need to enter section names and links in your anchor tags consistently so that the upper and lower case letters match each other; otherwise, your links may not work. This also goes for naming graphics indicated in <IMG SRC="..."> tags.

<A NAME="E"><IMG SRC="E.GIF"></A>
<H3>Accents with the Letter E</H3>
<UL>

ISO-Latin-1 character strings are also case-sensitive. Otherwise, your browser wouldn't know whether to display upper or lower case accented letters.

<LI>È (E grave accent, uppercase): & Egrave;
<LI>É (E acute accent, uppercase): & Eacute;
<LI>Ê(E circumflex, uppercase): & Ecirc;
<LI>Ë (E umlaut mark, uppercase) & Euml;
<LI>è(e grave accent, lowercase): & egrave;
<LI>é (e acute accent, lowercase): & eacute;
<LI>ê (e circumflex accent, lowercase): & ecirc;
<LI>ë (e umlaut mark, lowercase): & euml;
</UL>
<P>Return to <A HREF="#MENU"> Main Menu</A>.</P>

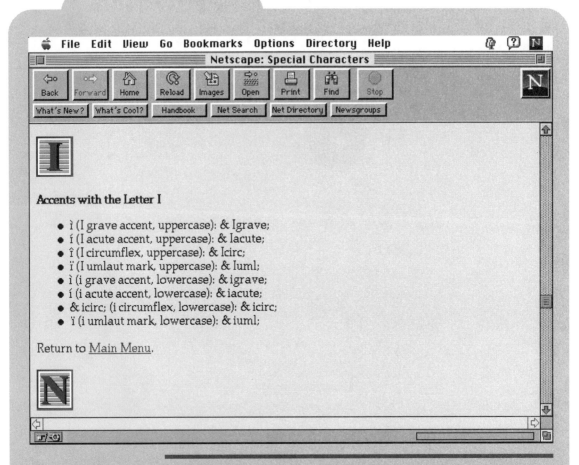

Figure 4.14 The fourth and fifth linked sections of a long HTML document.

```
<A NAME="I"><IMG SRC="I.GIF"></A>
<H3>Accents with the Letter I</H3>
<UL>
<LI>&Igrave; (I grave accent, uppercase): & Igrave;
<LI>&Iacute; (I acute accent, uppercase): & Iacute;
<LI>&Icirc; (I circumflex, uppercase): & Icirc;
<LI>&Iuml; (I umlaut mark, uppercase): & Iuml;
<LI>&igrave; (i grave accent, lowercase): & igrave;
<LI>&iacute; (i acute accent, lowercase): & iacute;
<LI>& icirc; (i circumflex, lowercase): & icirc;
<LI> &iuml; (i umlaut mark, lowercase): & iuml;
</UL>
```

Remember that the "#" mark is important.

```
<P>Return to <A HREF="#MENU"> Main Menu</A>.</P>
<A NAME="N"><IMG SRC="N.GIF"></A>
<H3>Accents with the Letter N</H3>
<UL>
<LI>&Ntilde; (N tilde, uppercase): & Ntilde;
<LI>&ntilde; (n tilde, lowercase): & ntilde;
</UL>
<P>Return to <A HREF="#MENU"> Main Menu</A>.</P>
```

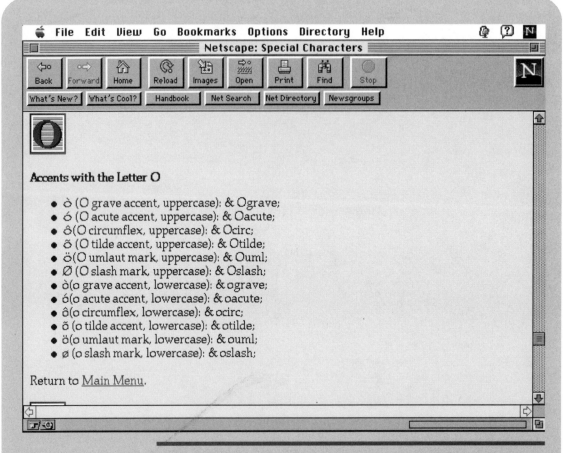

Figure 4.15 The sixth linked section of a long HTML document.

Finally, Figure 4.15 shows you the sixth linked section of this long document we have been working on.

```
<A NAME="O"><IMG SRC="O.GIF"></A>
<H3>Accents with the Letter O</H3>
<UL>
<LI>&Ograve; (O grave accent, uppercase):  & Ograve;
<LI>&Oacute; (O acute accent, uppercase): & Oacute;
<LI>&Ocirc;(O circumflex, uppercase): & Ocirc;
<LI>&Otilde; (O tilde, uppercase): & Otilde;
<LI>&Ouml;(O umlaut mark, uppercase): & Ouml;
<LI>&Oslash; (O slash mark, uppercase): & Oslash;
<LI>&ograve;(o grave accent, lowercase): & ograve;
<LI>&oacute;(o acute accent, lowercase): & oacute;
<LI>&ocirc;(o circumflex, lowercase): & ocirc;
<LI>&otilde; (o tilde, lowercase): & otilde;
<LI>&ouml;(o umlaut mark, lowercase): & ouml;
<LI>&oslash; (o slash mark, lowercase): & oslash;
</UL>
<P>Return to <A HREF="#MENU"> Main Menu</A>.</P>
```

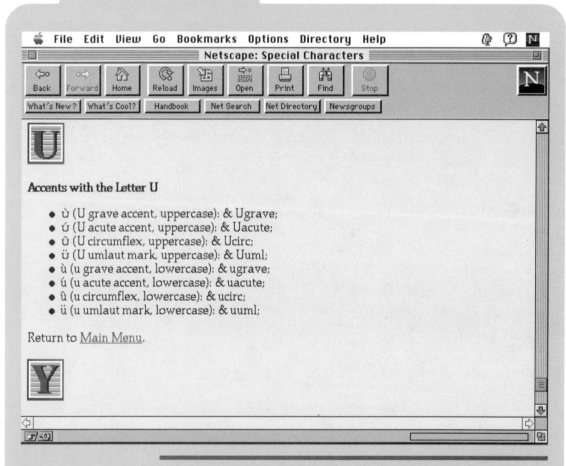

Figure 4.16 The seventh and eighth linked sections of a long HTML document.

```
<A NAME="U"><IMG SRC="U.GIF"></A>
<H3>Accents with the Letter U</H3>
<UL>
<LI>&Ugrave; (U grave accent, uppercase): & Ugrave;
<LI>&Uacute; (U acute accent, uppercase): & Uacute;
<LI>&Ucirc; (U circumflex, uppercase): & Ucirc;
<LI>&Uuml; (U umlaut mark, uppercase): & Uuml;
<LI>&ugrave; (u grave accent, lowercase): & ugrave;
<LI>&uacute; (u acute accent, lowercase): & uacute;
<LI>&ucirc; (u circumflex, lowercase): & ucirc;
<LI>&uuml; (u umlaut mark, lowercase): & uuml;
</UL>
<P>Return to <A HREF="#MENU"> Main Menu</A>.</P>
<A NAME="Y"><IMG SRC="Y.GIF"></A>
<H3>Accents with the Letter Y</H3>
<UL>
<LI>&yuml; (y umlaut mark, lowercase): & yuml;
</UL>
<P>Return to <A HREF="#MENU"> Main Menu</A>.</P>
</HTML>
```

The section of HTML code above results in the seventh and eighth linked sections shown in Figure 4.16.

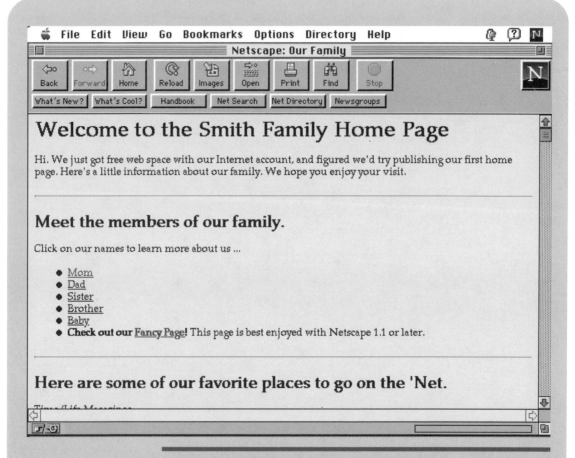

○ YOUR FAMILY HOME PAGE: USING EXTERNAL LINKS WITHIN A DIRECTORY

The following recipe sets up a collection of hypertext linked documents that are the essence of a Web site. You use the anchor tag to link to other documents on your Web page's server, or to pages on any location on the World Wide Web. Here you learn about:

■ *Using the anchor tag <A HREF="Name.HTM">Linked Item</A> to link to text or a graphic files in another location.*

■ *Using the anchor tag <A HREF="http"//website.location.htm>Linked Items</A> to link to a file anywhere on the WWW.*

Whew! The last document was a lot of work. Now we will create a brand new home page and learn how to work with external anchor tags so you can link to multiple documents within your directory. To create links in your new document, you can also cut and paste elements from **Chap4.DIR/Parts.DIR/08LINKS.DOC**.

Ingredients:

■ *<A HREF="Name.HTM"> Linked Item </A> tags: Use these anchor tags to link text and graphics to other documents in your folder. This lets you quickly add material to your Web pages without having to cut and paste an entire file into your original HTML document.*

■ *<A HREF="http"//website.location.htm">Linked Item </A> tags: You can link to other Web sites in the same way as described above. Simply enter the correct URL instead of a document name.*

■ ***Chap4.DIR/Family.DIR/Family.HTM:*** *The following script offers a template for creating a home page with your* *family. First, we will create the main page. Each member of the family can then create their own documents.*

■ *Secondary documents: You will also find the following linked documents in the* **Family** *directory on your CD-ROM:* **Mom.HTM, Dad.HTM, Sis.HTM, Bro.HTM,** *and* **Baby.HTM**. *For the sake of saving space, we will only take a look at the* **FAMILY.HTM** *file, the result of which is shown in Figure 4.17.*

Feel free to view these documents in your browser application to see how the links work. You will also find links to the **Family2.HTM** "fancy page," which we will work on later in this chapter.

```
<HTML>

<HEAD>
<TITLE>Our Family</TITLE>
</HEAD>

<BODY>
<H1>Welcome to the Smith Family Home Page</H1>
<P>Hi. We just got free web space with our Internet
account, and figured we'd try publishing our first home
page. Here's a little information about our family. We hope
you enjoy your visit.</P>
<HR>
<H2>Meet the members of our family.</H2>
<P>Click on our names to learn more about us ...
<UL>
<LI><A HREF="Mom.HTM">Mom</A>
<LI><A HREF="Dad.HTM">Dad</A>
<LI><A HREF="Sis.HTM">Sister</A>
<LI><A HREF="Bro.HTM">Brother</A>
<LI><A HREF="Baby.HTM">Baby</A>
```

See how easy it is to work with external links? We don't even have to go through the document to add section names or enter that pesky # mark!

<LI><B>Check out our <A HREF="Family2.HTM">Fancy Page</A>!</B> This page is best enjoyed with Netscape 1.1 or later.

The thorough Webmaster offers options for both text-only and graphical browsers.

All of the documents listed below are in the FAMILY directory on your CD-ROM. You have probably noticed that the anchor tags listed below work almost exactly the same way as in the last document we created.

</UL>
<HR>

You can also add links to documents in a separate directory:

- *To link to a document in another subdirectory within the same main directory, enter <A HREF="../Name.DIR/File Name.HTM">Linked Item</A>.*

- *To link to a document in a different directory entirely, enter <"A HREF="/Name.DIR/Name.DIR/File Name.HTM">Linked Item</A>.*

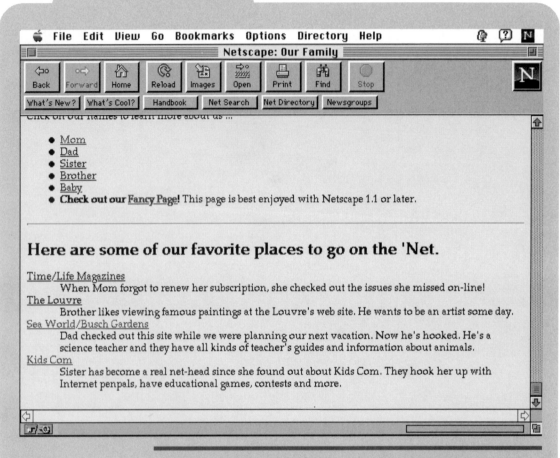

Figure 4.18 A Web page with external links to other Web sites.

○ OUR FAVORITE PLACES: ENTERING EXTERNAL LINKS TO OTHER WEB SITES

Now that you know about anchor tags, and how to use them to point to locations anywhere on the World Wide Web, this recipe lets you create a jump page of references to favorite sites. Here you learn about:

- *Using anchor tags to create a jump page.*

- *Some of the different syntax used in the anchor tag for various Web sites.*

We will now continue with the second part of the page we were just working on, but with external links to other Web sites, resulting in Figure 4.18. As you can see, creating external links to other places on the World Wide Web is merely an extension of techniques you've already learned.

<H2>Here are some of our favorite places to go on the 'Net.</H2>

The definition list format is ideal for listing and describing other Web sites.

<DL>

When entering the locations of other Web sites, you must enter the URL exactly or else the link will not work.

<DT><A HREF= "http://pathfinder.com">
Time/Life Magazines</A>
<DD>When Mom forgot to renew her subscription, she checked out the issues she missed on-line!
<DT><A HREF= "http://www.cnam.fr/louvre">The Louvre/A>
<DD>Brother likes viewing famous paintings at the Louvre's web site. He wants to be an artist some day.
<DT><A HREF="http://www.bev.net/education/SeaWorld/homepage.html"> Sea World/Busch Gardens</A>
<DD>Dad checked out this site while we were planning our next vacation. Now he's hooked. He's a science teacher and they have all kinds of teacher's guides and information about animals.
<DT><A HREF="http://www.kidscom.com/">
 Kids Com</A>
<DD>Sister has become a real net-head since she found out about Kids Com. They hook her up with Internet pen-pals, have educational games, contests and more.

These Web sites really exist! Check them out.

</DL>
</HTML>

Depending on your purpose, links to other web sites can be either a major or minor component of your design. Don't neglect the opportunity to "trade" links with other sites to publicize your own web page. Many active sites offer to cross-link to other sites through agreements made by e-mail. The increased traffic benefits both sites, making each more interesting.

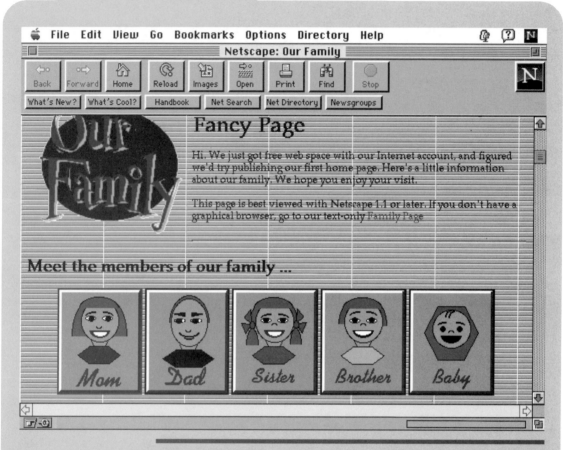

Figure 4.19 A Web page featuring graphical links.

○ TAKING A PEEK AT AN EXTERNALLY LINKED DOCUMENT

We have created documents for each member of the family, but for the sake of time and space we will only discuss Mom's page here (**Chap4.DIR/Family.DIR/Mom.HTM**) You can open the other linked texts in the **Family** directory on your CD-ROM and explore them on your own.

```
<HTML>

<HEAD>
<TITLE>Mom's Page</TITLE>
</HEAD>

<BODY>
<H1>Mom's Page</H1>
<P> Hello. I haven't put anything on this page yet, but come back soon. </P>
<P>Here are links to the rest of the family</P>
<UL>
<LI><A HREF="Dad.HTM">Dad</A>
<LI><A HREF="Sis.HTM">Sister</A>
<LI><A HREF="Bro.HTM">Brother</A>
<LI><A HREF="Baby.HTM">Baby</A>
```

Don't leave your visitors stranded! Always offer them a variety of places to go and a link back to the main home page.

<LI>Back to the<A HREF="Family.HTM">Smith Family Home page</A>
<LI><B>Back to the <A HREF="Family2.HTM">Fancy Page</A>!</B> This page is best enjoyed with Netscape 1.1 or later.

</UL>

</HTML>

○ MY FANCY FAMILY PAGE: WORKING WITH IMAGES

In the following recipe you use images in various ways. Here you learn how to:

- *Use the image tag and an anchor tag to link to text or graphic files, as you have seen previously.*

- *Add the ALIGN=LEFT; ALIGN=TOP; ALIGN=MIDDLE; and ALIGN=BOTTOM clauses to the anchor tags to align your graphic images on your Web pages.*

- *Use the HSPACE="number of pixels"/VSPACE="number of pixels" clauses to place a border of white space around an image and its surrounding text.*

Images make Web pages more fun to look at. We have already added images to some of our HTML documents, but there's more to adding images than meets the eye. You can align your graphics in different ways to add interest to your page layout, and even create graphical links. Check out Figure 4.19 to see the results of your work here.

Ingredients:

- *<IMG SRC="Graphic Name.GIF"> tag: The image placement tag tells your browser what image you wish to display.*

- *<A HREF="Document Name.HTM"><IMG SRC="Graphic Name.GIF"></A> tags: You can create graphical links the same way you added text links in the previous document. In this example, the linked items consist graphics instead of text, which is why you will find the <IMG SRC=...> tag in between the <A HREF...> anchor tags.*

- *ALIGN=LEFT entry: You have a variety of options for placing and aligning your graphics. To indicate an alignment option, enter the command after the document name in the <A HREF=...> tag as follows: <A HREF="Document Name.HTM" ALIGN=LEFT>...</A>.*

- *ALIGN=TOP, ALIGN=MIDDLE, ALIGN=BOTTOM entries: You can add visual interest to your paragraphs by inserting small images within your text. We will see examples of how these options affect how the graphics line up with the text in the examples shown in the following script.*

- *HSPACE="number of pixels"/VSPACE="number of pixels" setting: You can enter a number indicating how much horizontal or vertical space you wish to leave between your image and the surrounding text.*

- ***Chap4.DIR/Family.DIR/Family2.HTM:** This is the "Fancy Page" we referred to when we added links to the **Family1.HTM** script. We also added Netscape enhancements here, but you can enjoy the graphics we have created even if you don't use Netscape version 1.1 or later.*

- **Chap4.DIR/Family.DIR/Family.GIF:** *We use the **Family.GIF** graphic to demonstrate how using the ALIGN LEFT option effects the way the graphic interacts with the text.*

- *Family icons: The family icons are located in the **Family** directory on your CD-ROM, and are named "Momcauc.GIF," "Dadcauc.GIF," "Siscauc.GIF," "Brocauc.GIF," and "Babycauc.GIF." These will serve as examples for creating graphical links.*

NOTE

The icons used here are for a Caucasian American family. You will also find icons for African American ("Momafri.GIF," etc.), Asian American ("Momais.GIF," etc.), and Latin American ("Momlat.GIF," etc.) families in the Family directory on the CD-ROM. To appropriately reflect the ethnic backgrounds of your family members, simply rename the graphics.

- *Pet and house graphics: We have also included **House.GIF**, **Cat.GIF**, and **Dog.GIF** in the **Family** directory on the CD-ROM to show how the ALIGN-TOP, ALIGN-MIDDLE, and ALIGN-BOTTOM options effect the way the graphics interact with the text.*

- **Chap4.DIR/Family.DIR/BG1.JPG:** *If you have Netscape version 1.1, you will see a new background.*

```
<HTML>

<HEAD>
<TITLE>Our Family</TITLE>
</HEAD>

<BODY>
<BODY Background="BG1.JPG">
```

When you use the "ALIGN=LEFT" option, the graphic will float to the left, and the text will line up along the right.

<IMG SRC="Family.GIF" ALIGN=Left>
<H1>Welcome to the Smith Family Fancy Page</H1>
<P>Hi. We just got free web space with our Internet account, and figured we'd try publishing our first home page. Here's a little information about our family. We hope you enjoy your visit.</P>
<P>This page is best viewed with Netscape 1.1 or later. If you don't have a graphical browser, go to our text-only <A HREF="Family.HTM">Family Page</A></P>
<HR>
<H2>Meet the members of our family ...</H2>

We have replaced the bulleted lists and text links from the previous page with graphical links. In addition, we added Paragraph and Center tags to leave space between the graphics and surrounding lines of text, and to make the icons look nicer.

<P><Center><A HREF="Mom.HTM"><IMG SRC="Momcauc.GIF"></A>
<A HREF="Dad.HTM" ALIGN=RIGHT><IMG SRC="Dadcauc.GIF""></A>
<A HREF="Sis.HTM"><IMG SRC="Siscauc.GIF"></A>
<A HREF="Bro.HTM"><IMG SRC="Brocauc.GIF"></A>
<A HREF="Baby.HTM"><IMG SRC="Babycauc.GIF">
</A></CENTER>
</P>

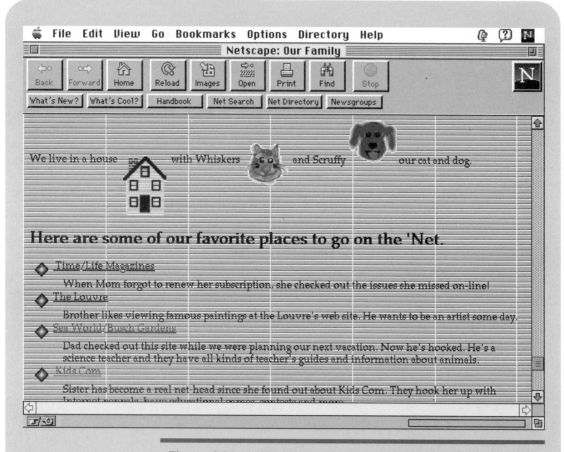

Figure 4.20 A Web page using graphic alignment options and graphical bullets.

The "ALIGN=TOP" option aligns your graphic with the top of the text in the current line. The "ALIGN=MIDDLE" option aligns your graphic with the middle of the text in the current line. The "ALIGN=BOTTOM" option aligns your graphic with the bottom of the text in the current line. Let's work with these tags in the next section of code, the result of which appears in Figure 4.20.

```
<P>We live in a house <IMG SRC="House.GIF"
ALIGN=Top> with Whiskers <IMG SRC="Cat.GIF"
ALIGN=Middle> and Scruffy <IMG SRC="Dog.GIF"
ALIGN=Bottom> our cat and dog.</P>

<H2>Here are some of our favorite places to go on the
'Net.</H2>
We replaced the <LI> tags from the first Family home page
with graphics! Using small icons as bullets can make lists
look more interesting.
<DL>
<DT><IMG SRC="Bullet.GIF" ALIGN=AbsMiddle
HSPACE="4"><A HREF= "http://www.timeinc.com/path-
finder/">
Time/Life Magazines</A>
<DD>When Mom forgot to renew her subscription, she
checked out the issues she missed on-line!
```

We also used the "ALIGN=AbsMiddle" option to align the middle of the bullets with the middle of the text line, and allowed four pixels of horizontal space between the bullet and the following text.

```
<DT><IMG SRC="Bullet.GIF" ALIGN=AbsMiddle
HSPACE="4"><A HREF= "http://www.cnam.fr/louvre">The
Louvre</A>
<DD>Brother likes viewing famous paintings at the Lou-
vre's web site. He wants to be an artist some day.
<DT><IMG SRC="Bullet.GIF" ALIGN=AbsMiddle
HSPACE="4"><A HREF="http://www.bev.net/education/
SeaWorld/homepage.html">Sea World/Busch Gardens</A>
<DD>Dad checked out this site while we were planning
our next vacation. Now he's hooked. He's a science
teacher and they have all kinds of teacher's guides and
information about animals.
<DT><IMG SRC="Bullet.GIF" ALIGN=AbsMiddle
HSPACE="4"><A HREF="http://www.kidscom.com/">
 Kids Com</A>
<DD>Sister has become a real net-head since she found
out about Kids Com. They hook her up with Internet pen-
pals, have educational games, contests and more.
</DL>

</BODY>
</HTML>
```

○ A COMPLETE LIST OF IMAGE TAGS

ALIGNMENT OPTIONS

- *<IMG SRC="Name">: Aligns your image on the left side of your screen and with the baseline of the next line of text.*

- *<IMG SRC="Name" ALIGN=Left>: Floats your image to the left side of your screen, with the following text lining up along the right side of the image.*

- *<IMG SRC="Name" ALIGN=Right>: Floats your image to the right side of the screen, with the following text lining up along the left side of the image.*

- *<IMG SRC="Name" ALIGN=Top>: Aligns the image with the top of the tallest item in the following line.*

- *<IMG SRC="Name" ALIGN=Bottom>: Aligns the image with the baseline of the following text.*

- *<IMG SRC="Name" ALIGN=Baseline>: This entry yields the same results as ALIGN=Bottom.*

- *<IMG SRC="Name" ALIGN=Middle> : Aligns the middle of the image with the baseline of the following text.*

- *<IMG SRC="Name" ALIGN=TextTop>: Aligns the image with the tallest letters of the following text.*

- *<IMG SRC="Name" ALIGN=AbsMiddle>: Aligns the middle of the image with the middle of the text in the following line.*

- *<IMG SRC="Name" ALIGN=AbsBottom>: Aligns the bottom of the image with the bottom of the following text.Ê*

BOUNDARY OPTIONS

- *<IMG SRC="Name" VSpace="number of pixels">: Add vertical space to keep your image from butting up against other elements in your page by entering a numeric value representing a number of pixels.*

- *<IMG SRC="Name" HSpace="number of pixels">: Add horizontal space to keep your image from butting up against other elements in your page by entering a numeric value representing a number of pixels.*

- *<IMG SRC="Name" Border ="number of pixels">: Control the thickness of the border surrounding your graphic. When you leave this option unspecified, the border generally defaults to three pixels.*

- *<IMG SRC="Name" Width ="number of pixels" Height ="number of pixels">: You can make your images display more quickly by specifying their measurements (in pixels).*

○ SUMMARY

Congratulations! When you picked up this book, you didn't even know how to create a simple HTML document, and now you've just put together several kinds of Web pages with exciting images and graphical links to multiple documents. So pat yourself on the back. In this chapter, you learned how to put a basic document on the web, use header tags, work with lists, and format text styles. You then went on to add internal, external, and graphical links. Finally, you learned a bit about displaying graphic images in your Web pages.

In Chapter 5, we will go on to cook up some exciting sample meals with photographs, interactive forms, multimedia files, and more. Topics discussed will include electronic résumés, an on-line magazine, a photo album, a company catalog, and more.

chapter 5

HERE ARE SOME OF THE WEB PAGES YOU WILL LEARN TO CREATE:

- INTERACTIVE FORMS THAT LET YOU RECEIVE INFORMATION LIKE BUSINESS ORDERS OR MAIL.

- PAGES CONTAINING MULTIMEDIA CONTENT

- AN ELECTRONIC PHOTO ALBUM

- A CORPORATE HOME PAGE THAT YOU CAN USE TO SOLICIT BUSINESS

- AN INVENTORY TABLE USING <PRE> </PRE> TAGS

- TEXT ALTERNATIVES TO GRAPHICAL LINKS FOR VIEWERS NOT USING GRAPHICAL BROWSERS

- AN ON-LINE ELECTRONIC MAGAZINE, AKA A 'ZINE

SOME SAMPLE MEALS

In the first part of this chapter, we will learn about some of the more advanced functions of HTML, including adding sounds, movies, and animation to your Web page, generating interactive forms, and offering text alternatives for images so that visitors with text-only browsers will know where your graphics are placed.

The second part of this chapter gives you samplings of a few complete HTML scripts. Parts of these scripts will serve as the source of many of the 50 templates that you will find on the CD-ROM. Rather than giving the scripts in line-by-line detail, the templates are in block diagram format with notes. On the left page, you will find a picture of the Web page as it appears in your browser. The right page contains notes describing how the home pages were constructed, and pointing out any special features of which you should take note.

○ INTERACTIVE FORMS 101

The following recipe lets you create a page with a button that opens a pop-up form. In this recipe you learn to use:

■ *The anchor tags "MAIL TO: yourusername@site.com" clause to provide a button that opens a form that your readers can fill in.*

One of the greatest things (we think) about publishing on the World Wide Web is that your readers can interact with you instantaneously. HTML supports the creation of forms, with which you can let your visitors give you feedback or submit orders to your business. The potential of the Web for business has not been lost on the commercial community.

Perhaps the easiest interactive form to create is an e-mail form, so let's look at an example like the one you see in Figure 5.1. To create what is called a Mail To: field, all you have to do is enter the following line in your HTML document:

<A HREF= "MAIL TO: yourusername@site.com">Send e-mail!</A>

When your visitors click on your e-mail link, an e-mail form with your address and your visitor's return address will appear ready for sending. Nothing could be easier. In the next few sections, we will use *Chaos Control*'s HTML scripts for examples of how to create forms and add multimedia files to our home pages. *Chaos Control* is a state-of-the-art electronic 'zine on the Web, and it features music write-ups, exciting graphics, multimedia files for downloading, and more.

```
┌──────────────────────────────────────────────────────────────────┐
│ ▣ ▥▥▥▥▥▥▥▥▥▥▥▥ Send Mail/Post News ▥▥▥▥▥▥▥▥▥▥▥▥ ▣ │
├──────────────────────────────────────────────────────────────────┤
│     From: "Elisabeth A. Parker" <eparker@tiac.net>    ┌─────────┐  │
│                                                       │  Send   │  │
│  Mail to: rsgour@aol.com                              └─────────┘  │
│                                                                    │
│  Post to:                                                          │
│                                                    ┌──────────────┐│
│  Subject:                                          │Quote Document││
│                                                    └──────────────┘│
│Attachment:                                         ┌──────────────┐│
│                                                    │  Attach...   ││
│                                                    └──────────────┘│
```

Figure 5.1   When you click on a "Mail To" link, an e-mail form
             will appear.

NOTE

You can enjoy the magazine used as an example here on either a Windows or Macintosh computer. However, you need a Macintosh with System 7.0 or later containing HyperCard (or its player) to launch the multimedia files.

Ingredients:

- **<A HREF= "MAIL TO: ..."</A>:** *You can link visitors to your electronic mail box the same way you have been linking them to other documents and Web sites throughout the last chapter.*

- **Chap5.DIR/Chaos.DIR/Chaos.HTM:** *Chaos Control , a multimedia electronic magazine devoted to music, offers excellent examples of how to generate forms and add multimedia to your pages. Published by Bob Gourley of New York, NY, you can find the actual 'zine in all its kinetic glory at http://www.ids.net/~chaos/chaos.html.*

<HTML>
<HEAD>
<TITLE>Chaos Control</TITLE>
<HEAD>

Notice the ALT="..." command within the image tag below. This was added so that those with nongraphical browsers have something to look at. We will discuss the issue of offering alternatives to visitors using nongraphical browsers later in this chapter. For the time being, you can see how the page would display with a graphical browser in Figure 5.2.

<IMG ALIGN=TOP SRC="chaoslog.gif"
ALT="CHAOS CONTROL">

Let's now add a Netscape extension to create a horizontal rule five pixels high, and adjust the font size up two units from its default setting. Remember, not all browsers will be able to display Netscape extensions, so you might want to note it on your Web page. For example, many sites say something like "Netscape enhanced site."

<hr size=5><font size =+2>
<p>
<H1>Welcome to Chaos Control!</H1>
<p>
 Chaos Control is an interactive electronic magazine focusing on industrial, gothic, techno, and experimental music. The main form is an interactive Macintosh HyperCard stack, but all past and <A HREF="current.HTM">current</A> articles can also be read on-line. In addition, you can download other music-related interactive files from this site. You can also read some <A HREF="reviews.HTM">reviews</A> on-line, and because so many people asked for it, a <A HREF="PTV-disc.HTM">Psychic TV discography</A>.

This HTML document continues on from here, as you can observe by opening up the CHAOS.HTM document in the CHAP5.DIR directory.

When you use the "Mail To" anchor an e-mail form like the one shown in Figure 5.1 will pop up when your visitors click on it.

In addition, you can <A HREF="mailto:rsgour@aol.com"> email</A> Chaos Control directly from this page and see a list of other interesting Internet sites, as shown in Figure 5.2.

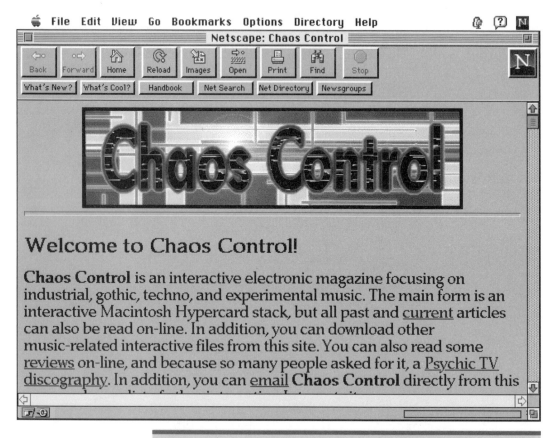

Figure 5.2   First screen of Chaos control, using the "Mail To" command.

○ GENERATING INTERACTIVE FORMS

This recipe lets you create form fields that readers can fill in, and which return the information to you via your e-mail. In this recipe you use:

■ *The form wrapper tags <FORM>...</FORM> indicates the enclosed information is an on-line form.*

- *The <FORM METHOD=POST" ACTION= "MAIL TO:...> indicates how the information in an on-line form should be handled.*

- *The <INPUT TYPE=> tag creates checkboxes, image buttons, or radio buttons on your form that perform the transfer of information — depending upon the TYPE attribute specified.*

- *The SUBMIT/RESET attributes of an Input button set the type of action that button performs.*

- *The <VALUE= "..."> tag creates a button that sends the value mentioned in the tag as information to you in the form.*

- *The <TEXT AREA>...</TEXT AREA> tags set the amount of space a field on your form has for your readers to fill in.*

The savvy Webmonster also wants to find out who their visitors are, what people like about the Web site, and what people would like to see more of. *Chaos Control* solicits input from visitors by asking them to sign a Guestbook, which consists of an interactive form. Your visitors' answers will come to you in the form of e-mail. Generating interactive forms seems complicated at first, but gets easier once you get the hang of it.

Ingredients:

- ***<FORM>...</FORM> tags:*** *Specify that the information within these tags will be processed as on-line forms. You cannot nest forms within forms, but you can have multiple forms within a document.*

- ***<FORM METHOD="POST" ACTION= "MAIL TO:...">:*** *Tells the server what to do with your form. In most cases, you would want the information sent to your e-mail box.*

- **<INPUT> tag:** *There are two types of <INPUT> tags: <IN-PUT TYPE>, which specifies what will appear on the form (i.e., submit and reset buttons), and <INPUT NAME>, which indicates the field in which your visitor will enter their text string.*

- **<TEXT AREA>...</TEXT AREA> tags:** *Specify the amount of space you will leave for your visitors to fill in.*

- **SUBMIT/RESET attributes:** *This lets your visitors either submit the form to your e-mail box or clear the form.*

Now, lets take a look at the first section of *Chaos Control*'s guestbook form, shown in Figure 5.3 . In this part of the form, we will be using the <INPUT NAME> element, which asks visitors to enter information in specified fields. The HTML document continues on from above.

…

The <FORM> … </FORM> tag set blocks out the beginning and end of a form, just as <HEADER> … </HEADER> and <BODY> … </BODY> server as wrappers for those parts of an HTML document.

<FORM>

Here's another Netscape extension, the horizontal rule five pixels high.

<hr size=5><p>
<blockquote><H1>Please sign the guest book!!!!!!!!!
</A>:</H1>
<p>
Tell the server to forward your visitors' input to your electronic mail box.

In the line below is a somewhat nonstandard usage of the ACTION clause, as our technical editor suggests we mention. Normally the ACTION clause points to a URL, or more commonly a CGI script or executable service on a Web server. You will want to test the following line method in your scripts before point directly to a MAILTO: address.

<form method="post"
action="mailto:rgour@world.std.com">

The text below, "Your name (optional)," appears on the computer screen. The input field specifies that this is where the visitor is supposed to enter their name, and displays 48 pixels of horizontal space for the "name" field.

<p>Your name (optional): <input name="name" size="48">

Less horizontal space is left for the e-mail address, so the fields will line up evenly on the right side (the text "Your e-mail address (optional)" takes up more horizontal space that the previous text entry).

<p>Your email address (optional): <input name="email address" size="35">

Chaos Control leaves more space in the favorite band field, because some people's favorite bands/artists could fill an entire computer screen! Since the area of this box takes up more than one line, both the rows and the columns must be specified.

<p>Your favorite bands/artists (important!!):
<textarea name="comment" rows=8 cols=60>
</textarea>...

The script continues on from here, as you see on page 199.

197

File   Edit   View   Go   Bookmarks   Options   Directory   Help

Netscape: Chaos Control

Back   Forward   Home   Reload   Images   Open   Print   Find   Stop

What's New?   What's Cool?   Handbook   Net Search   Net Directory   Newsgroups

Please sign the guest book!!!!!!!!!:

Your name (optional):

Your email address (optional):

Your favorite bands/artists (important!!):

What type of computer are you using?

Figure 5.3   First section of an interactive form.

In the second section of *Chaos Control*'s interactive form, as shown in Figure 5.4, we will explore the <INPUT TYPE="..." element. Here, visitors do not fill in their own information as they did in the previous section of the form.

Here, they choose among values already selected by the form's creator. In this case, the INPUT TYPE consists of radio buttons, which add a more professional look to your forms.

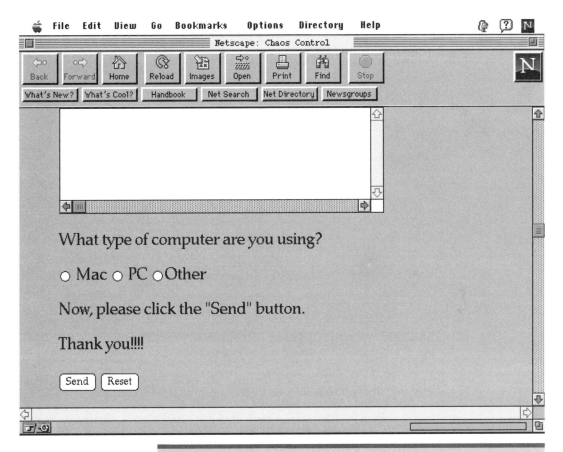

Figure 5.4   Second section of an interactive form.

> What type of computer are you using?<p>   <INPUT TYPE="radio" NAME="computer" VALUE="Mac"> Mac <INPUT TYPE="radio" NAME="computer" VALUE="PC"> PC <INPUT TYPE="radio" NAME="computer" VALUE="other">Other<p>
> Now, please click the "Send" button.
> <p>Thank you!!!!

INPUT TYPE specifies that the form should be submitted, and the VALUE entry specifies the text that appears on the button created by the INPUT TYPE. The submit action occurs when the "Send" button is selected. INPUT TYPE=RESET also offers visitors the opportunity to clear the form and not send it.

> <p align=center><INPUT TYPE="submit" VALUE="Send"> <input type=reset>

In HTML, everything has a beginning and an end. Make sure you close your form with the </FORM> tag.

> </form>
> </blockquote>

Below is the statement drawing a line of five pixels width across the screen, one of the Netscape extensions (that isn't universally accepted) described earlier.

> <hr size=5><p>

NOTE

On-line forms do have their limitations. Some of the older versions of browsers do not support forms. Incorporating new forms tags into HTML is one area where the Web is headed. As advanced tags are introduced, you may find some browsers that don't support the newer constructs.

Here are some of the values that can be added to forms:

- **<INPUT TYPE="CHECKBOX"...>:** *You can display a checkbox option for your visitors to select.*

- **<INPUT TYPE="IMAGE"...>:** *You can let visitors select a graphic or icon in your form. This tag is very rarely used in forms.*

- **<INPUT TYPE="RADIO"...>:** *You can let visitors select among items indicated by radio buttons, as shown in the example above.*

- **<INPUT TYPE="SUBMIT"...>:** *Creates a "SUBMIT" button so visitors can click on it and send you the form. Your server will know to send it to you because you entered the <FORM METHOD="POST" ACTION="MAIL TO...">" attributes at the beginning of the form.*

- **<INPUT TYPE="RESET">:** *Creates a "RESET" button so visitors can click on it and clear the form if they decide not to send it.*

- **<VALUE="...">:** *Lets you define a field. For example, <INPUT TYPE="radio" NAME="computer" VALUE="Mac"> in the script above tells your server that if someone selects this button, they are telling you they use a Macintosh.*

○ ADDING MULTIMEDIA CONTENT

Multimedia content on the Web is a developing area of technology. Some aspects of this technology are easy to use, and explored in this recipe. In this recipe you:

- *Link to sound and video files on the Web that your readers can click on and download.*

■ *Learn about the various formats and locations for multimedia plug-ins and players.*

You can add multimedia content to your Web pages the same way you have already added graphics or links to other places: by using the anchor tags to link to a multimedia file. Multimedia files can be movies, animation, sounds, and games. When your visitors click on your multimedia links, the file will then download. While some sound files can be listened to in "real time," movie files are generally too large to view without downloading them to your hard drive first.

NOTE

We expect that sound in real time is one of the features that will be added to the Web over the next eight months. Video will probably take a little longer to become standard.

During your travels on the Web, you will generally come across the following types of multimedia files:

■ **Sound:** *Sound files are generally formatted with the following extensions: .au, .aiff, .wav, and mp2 (MPEG audio). The .au format offers the only cross-platform solution; however, the most commonly used formats are .wav (Windows) and .aiff (Macintosh). The MPEG audio format is also gaining in popularity.*

There are so many new developments in the area of sound on the Internet that we can only highlight some of the more important of them. One company, RealAudio has a player and encoder that has been widely adopted. You can download this software from the RealAudio home page (Figure 5.5) at http://www.realaudio.com/.

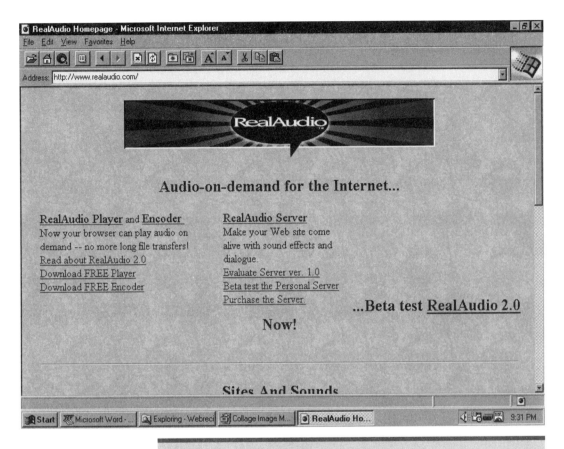

Figure 5.5   The RealAudio home page.

The RealAudio System 2.0 (Player and Encoder) provides good sound quality over 28.8 kbps modems, live broadcast capability, and other features. Future versions promise multimedia synchronization, Java integration, and more. RealAudio claims that there are more than a thousand sites using their sound format.

- ■ *Video: The most commonly used video formats are .MPEG/.MPG, which is cross-platform-compatible, and .MOV, the format used for Macintosh QuickTime videos. Also popular is the .AVI file format. At this point, the multimedia whiz kids primarily seem to prefer the Macintosh; however, this is beginning to change due to the better multimedia capabilities of Windows machines running Windows 95.*

QuickTime is cross-platform-compatible because Apple (QuickTime's developer) has released a player for Windows. Therefore, you find many multimedia CD-ROMs using QuickTime—even those released for the PC. Our tech editor notes that MPEG is probably a better choice because it is a standard and doesn't require a QuickTime player. An MPEG file can be played by a QuickTime player, as one of the codecs in QuickTime is dedicated to MPEG play/record.

New movie file formats and players are under development that let movie files be streamed out at a low bit rate. As an example of this, check out VDOLive at http://www.vdolive.com. The VDOLive home page is shown in Figure 5.6. This company offers a player (compatible with Netscape 1.x and 2.0, the Microsoft Internet Explorer, and Mosaic 1.x and 2.0) and a Netscape 2.0 plug-in for the Windows version of Netscape. It requires the use of Video for Windows for the Windows 3.1 operating system (get this at ftp://ftp.intel.com/IAL/multimedia/iv32rt.exe); Video for Windows is built into Windows 95 and Windows NT. The video file format used by VDOLive is a proprietary one.

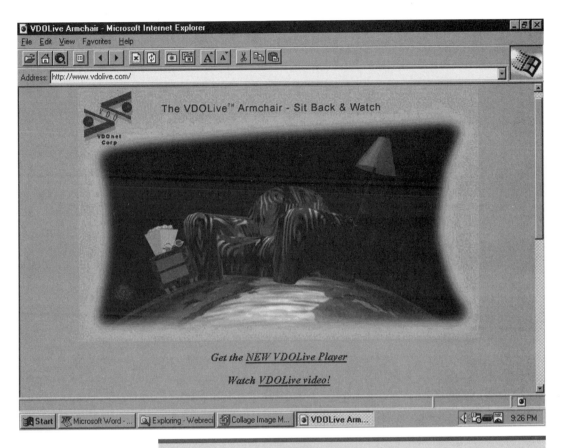

Figure 5.6   The VDOLive home page.

Current performance measurements under ideal conditions (minimal Internet traffic, no local network overhead, minimal overload on the VDOLive Server) are 2 frames/sec with a 14.4 kbps modem; up to 10 frames per second with a 28.8 kbps modem; and up to 20 frames/sec with an ISDN line. A frame rate of 32 frames/sec is standard for normal quality full-motion video.

Chaos Control offers two multimedia files for downloading in this issue. These were created in Hypercard and can be viewed on any Macintosh computer running System 7.0 or later that contains the HyperCard player. In Figure 5.7, you will see a text link to a multimedia file.

Let's continue with our script for *Chaos Control*. In the following line, a Netscape extension for a five-point horizontal rule is drawn.

    ....

<hr size=5><p>
<H1>Chaos Control update 8/2/95</H1>
<A HREF="PTVdisc.HTM">Psychic TV</A> just finished mixing their new album, "Trip Reset." Work on the LP was delayed when Genesis P-Orridge sustained injuries after being forced to jump from a second floor window during a fire at a house he was staying at.....
<A HREF="dk1.HTM">Die Krupps</A> are doing a US tour with the Young Gods..... The Boredoms have released a new album, "Chocolate Synthesizer," on Reprise Records. A Macintosh <A HREF="file: Boredoms.sea.hqx">interactive kit</A>focusing on the band can be downloaded from this site ...

Three pointers <A HREF=" ..."> point to multimedia content—particularly the last one. As you can see, you can add multimedia files the same way you would link to another HTML document or Web site. Most multimedia content (as we noted) is served up in a compressed format, which you can download and view later. For example, "Boredoms.sea.hqx" takes up 1.4 MB of disk space. This file has been compressed into a .SEA archive, Binhex file for Macintosh. It is conveniently expanded by the StuffIt expander in a drag-and-drop operation.

If you are now viewing the *Chaos Control* Web page from your browser, you will find that clicking on the link results in the browser jumping you to a page full of garbled computer programmingese (binary code). That's because you can't download something from your own workstation; if this was on the 'Net, it would work. However, if you have a Macintosh, you can view this file from **Chap5.DIR/ Chaos.DIR/Boredoms** by going to the folder and opening it directly.

A Macintosh <A HREF="Boredoms.sea.hqx">interactive kit</A> focusing on the band can be downloaded from this site…

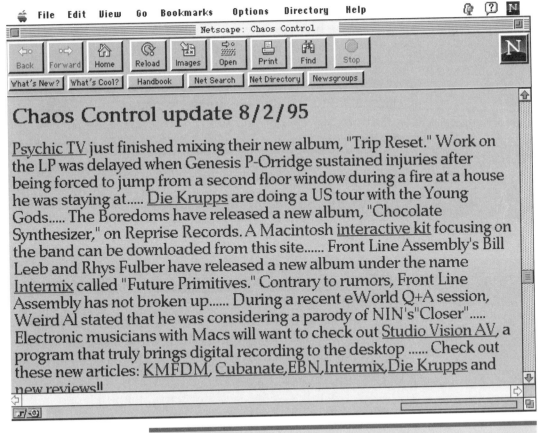

Figure 5.7 ◆ Example of linking to a multimedia file.

USING THE ALT FEATURE WITH GRAPHICAL LINKS

Not everyone has a graphical browser like Netscape. Additionally, some users with slow modem access to the Web turn off the display of graphics. In this recipe you learn how to substitute text for images, by doing the following:

- *Use the ALT= "..." clause after an IMG tag to indicate an alternative action when a graphic cannot be displayed.*

Chaos Control offers a graphical link for downloading an interactive file, as shown in Figure 5.8. But what happens if someone has a nongraphical browser? They would see only a blank space and not be able to find the link for downloading the file. "ALT" stands for "alternative," as in an alternative to the graphical link. By entering the ALT= "..." command, you can tell your visitors' browser to substitute the word "Download" for the "down.gif" graphic if it cannot display the image.

Ingredients:

- ***IMG SRC="..." ALT="..."***

Let's take a look at how this graphical link is used in the code below.

```
<H1>Chaos Control #9</H1><p>
<IMG SRC="screen9.gif">
<p>
<p>Featuring interviews with Single Gun Theory, Orbital,
Front Line Assembly, PWEI, EBN, Glorified Magnified, and
much more! It also features music samples from most of the
groups. Requires a Mac with System 7.x and Hyper-
card.<p>
<p>
```

Our Webmeister designed a nice-looking graphical link for downloading the file. However, he/she/it was also thoughtful enough to leave an alternative to visitors without graphical browsers. ALT="Download!" means that if a browser can't display the graphic, the word "Download!" will appear instead.

```
<A HREF="file:ChaosControl9(mac).sea.hqx">
<IMG SRC="down.gif" ALT="Download!"></A>
<p>
```

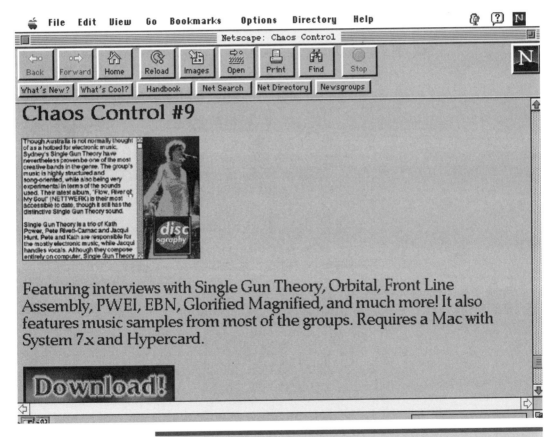

Figure 5.8 A section of a Web page featuring a link that lets you download a multimedia interactive kit.

○ COMPANY PARTS LISTING: USING <PRE> TAGS FOR CREATING TABLES

In the following recipe you see how a résumé is constructed using techniques you already know about. The elements of this résumé includes:

- *An Index file, which contains links to other pages and graphics files, is the home page.*

- *A résumé that you can use for your own, to "fill in the blanks."*

- *A set of fancy graphics that you can use to enliven your résumé.*

HTML doesn't support tabs or columns of text yet, so creating tables like the one shown below requires formatting them and entering all the spaces by hand. Feh! Furthermore, HTML doesn't even recognize the number of spaces between text—unless you add the <PRE> tags. Preformatted tags ensure that your spaces will be preserved within those tags.

NOTE

Table creation is one of the proposed improvements in HTML+, and is already supported by many HTML 3.0 browsers and Netscape. It is probably one of the more important extension or additions to the tags that are supported. One place to go to see how table creation in HTML works is found at http://www.dcn.davis.ca.us/~csandvig/ip/example.html.

Ingredients:

- **■** *<PRE>...</PRE> tags: Preformatted tags preserve the spaces entered between lines of text. As long as you keep things simple, your table should appear in your browser exactly the way it appears in your original document. By keeping things simple, we mean no tabs, bolded text, larger point sizes, or anything like that.*

- **■** ***Chap5.DIR/Gizmos2.DIR/Cat.HTM:*** *This document will become the Gizmo catalog. For the time being, we will simply create an inventory table using the <PRE>...</PRE> tags.*

<HTML>

<HEAD>
<Title>Gizmos, LTD Catalog</TITLE>
</HEAD>

<BODY>
<IMG SRC="Gizmo.GIF" ALIGN="LEFT"><H1>Gizmos, LTD. Catalog</H1>
<H2>Inventory Listing</H2>
<P>Check here for the availability of our products. Some of our models have become popular so quickly that we have fallen a little behind due to unanticipated demand. However, we should be caught up within the next couple of weeks.</P>

When you use the <PRE> tags, all the items on the page will retain the spacing attributes you have set and will appear in monospaced type, as shown in Figure 5.9.

```
<PRE>
PRODUCT          MODEL #     PRICE      AVAILABILITY
--------------------------------------------------------------
HumongoGizmo     # 10570     $599.00    Backordered
MiniGizmo        # 10571     $299.00    Available
OfficeGizmo      # 10572     $999.00    Available
HomeGizmo        # 10573     $399.00    Backordered
</PRE>
```

Don't forget to close your <PRE> tag so the rest of the page doesn't appear in monospaced type, and always give visitors a link back to the main home page.

```
<A HREF="Gizmo.HTM">Go Home!</A>

</BODY>
</HTML>
```

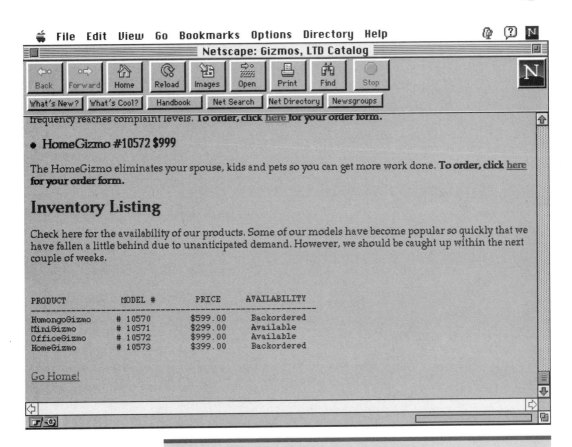

Figure 5.9   Inventory list using <PRE>tags.

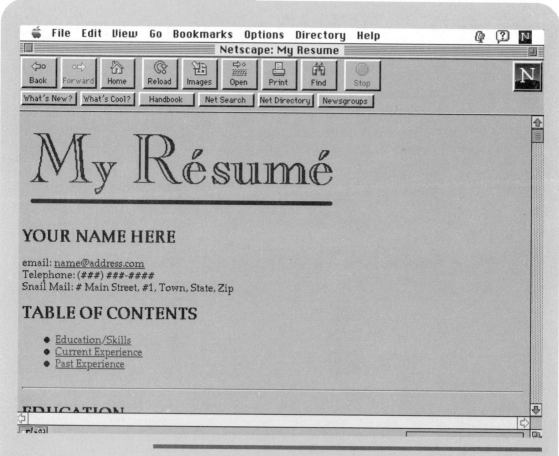

Figure 5.10 A generic résumé using the template described above.

○ POSTING YOUR ELECTRONIC RÉSUMÉ SAMPLE 1

A good use of your Web pages is to post your résumé. Elisabeth's home page, which is linked to her résumé, her clients, her friend, and her electronic magazine, Bytelt!, may be found in Chap5.DIR/Resume.DIR/Index.HTM for your perusal.

Remember, when creating a Web page, you want to give people something fun to look at, or else they'll get bored and move on. So, unless you have had a really exciting career, you probably wouldn't want your résumé to be the first thing people see. However, if visitors are interested in learning more about you and what you do, there's no harm in offering them access to more information.

Ingredients:

■ *Chap5.DIR/Resume.DIR/Index.HTM: This folder contains Elisabeth's home page.*

■ *Chap5.DIR/Resume.DIR/Resume.HTM: This offers a template for organizing and creating your own résumé for publication on the Web. This is a generic résumé that you can use as a model.*

■ *Chap5.DIR/Resume.DIR/Resume.GIF: This cool graphic says "My Résumé." Feel free to use it in your own Web page. The typeface is somewhat fancy, but if you look through the folder you will find an array of alternative "My Résumé" graphics. We hope you find one you like.*

Use the résumé template that follows to create your own home page, and leave a link to your résumé. The following example features a "mail to" link and internal document links to sections of the résumé.

```
<HTML>

<HEAD>
<TITLE>My Resume</TITLE>
</HEAD>

<BODY>
<IMG SRC="Resume.GIF">
<H2>YOUR NAME HERE</H2>
<B>email: </B>
<A HREF= "mailto:
name@address.com">name@address.com</A><BR>
<B>Telephone:</B> (###) ###-####</B><BR>
<B>Snail Mail:</B> # Main Street, #1, Town, State, Zip
<A NAME="TOC"><H2>TABLE OF CONTENTS</H2></A>
<UL>
<LI><A HREF= "#Sked">Education/Skills</A>
<LI><A HREF= "#Exp1">Current Experience</A>
<LI><A HREF= "#Exp2">Past Experience</A>
</UL>
<HR>
<A NAME="Sked"><H2>EDUCATION:</H2></A>
<P>State University, Town, MA; Degree; Month; Year</P>
```

Now, describe your education and skills, as shown in Figure 5.10.

```
<H2>SKILLS:</H2>
<UL>
<BLOCKQUOTE><LI><B>Skill #1:</B>
Description of skill<P>
<LI><B>Skill #2: </B>
Description of skill.<P>
<LI><B>Skill #3:</B>
Description of skill.<P>
<LI><B>Skill #4: </B>
Description of skill.<P>
<LI><B>Skill #5: </B>
Description of skill.</BLOCKQUOTE>
</UL>
<P><A HREF="#TOC">Back </A>to Table of Contents.
```

Here, you can use list tags to describe your education and skills. The <BLOCKQUOTE>.....</BLOCKQUOTE> tags will indent these entries.

```
<HR>
```

A horizontal rule adds a division to different sections of your résumé.

```
<H2><A NAME="Exp1">CURRENT EXPERIENCE:</A>
</H2>
```

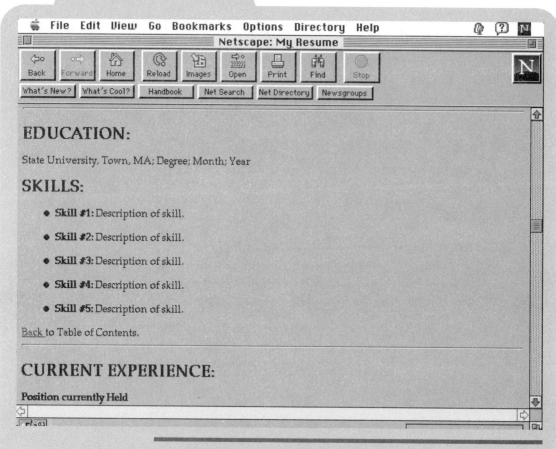

Figure 5.11 List your current experience.

Don't just list your company. Describe your job functions in detail, as shown in Figure 5.11.

<BODY><B>Position currently Held</B>
<B><I>Company Name</I>; Town, State; Date, year-Present</B>
Description of your position and what your responsibilities are. You can list them below in greater detail


```
<BLOCKQUOTE>
<UL>
<LI><B>Job Function #1:</B></A>
Projects have included the following ...<P>
<LI><B>Job Function # 2:</B></A>
Projects have included the following ...<P>
<LI><B>Job Function #3:</B></A>
Projects have included the following ...
<LI><B>Job Function #4:</B></A>
</UL>
</BLOCKQUOTE>

Projects have included the following ...
<P>
<A HREF="#TOC">Back </A>to Table of Contents.

<A NAME="Exp2"><H2>PAST EXPERIENCE</H2>
<B>Last Position Held</B><BR>
<B><I>Company Name</I>; Town, State; Date, year-
Present</B><BR>
Description of your position and what your responsibilities
are. You can list them below in greater detail<BR>
<BR>

<BLOCKQUOTE>
<UL>
<LI><B>Job Function #1:</B></A>
Projects have included the following ...<P>
<LI><B>Job Function # 2:</B></A>
Projects have included the following ...<P>
<LI><B>Job Function #3:</B></A>
Projects have included the following ...
<LI><B>Job Function #4:</B></A>
Projects have included the following ...
<P>
```

List your past experience in this section, as shown here.

```
<P>
```

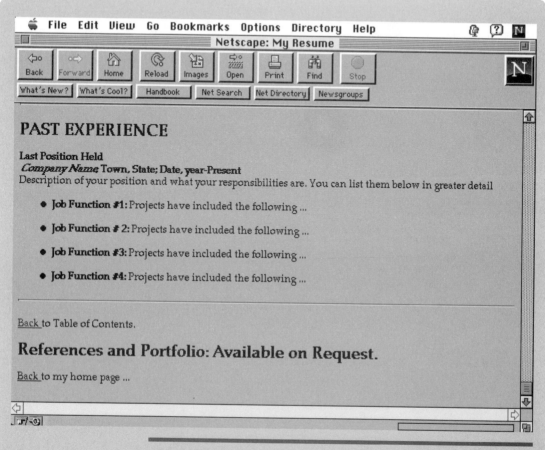

Figure 5.12 List your past experience and create your links.

Link back to the table of contents and your main home page, as shown in Figure 5.12.

<u><P></u>
<u></UL></u>
<u></BLOCKQUOTE></u>

<u><A HREF="#TOC">Back </A>to Table of Contents.</u>
<u><H2>References and Portfolio: Available on Request.</u>
<u></H2></u>
<u><P><A HREF="index.html">Back </A>to my home page ...</u>
<u></P></u>
<u></BODY></u>
<u></HTML></u>

A SECOND EXAMPLE

Ingredients:

■ ***Chap5.DIR/Madge.DIR/MWCV.HTML:*** *Elisabeth's friend, Margaret Weigel (whose haiku page you saw in the previous chapter), has a much jazzier looking résumé. Instead of using header tags, she uses images for each heading. You may want to look at this resume in your browser.*

221

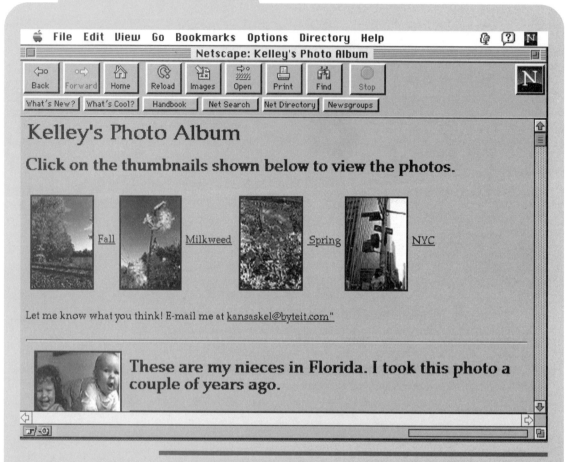

Figure 5.13 One example of how to lay out graphics on a Web page.

○ THE VIRTUAL GALLERY: AN ELECTRONIC PHOTO ALBUM BY KELLEY HURST

Here's an example of a Web page that presents a picture book of images. In this recipe you'll see how to:

■ *Create the central HTML page that points to these image files.*

■ *Create thumbnail files that users can download to view the larger complete images, thus saving download time for the central file.*

■ *Explore various alignment and spacing options to make multiple images appear attractively on your page.*

The Web's ability to display graphic images is one of its most exciting features. However, working with images can get tricky. For example, let's say you have just created a row of graphical links. This row of graphics may look wonderful when you view it with your 15-inch color monitor, but when someone views your page with a smaller monitor, one of the graphics may be forced down one line, which ruins the entire look.

Another common problem lies in graphical display. Large images may look impressive when you test them with your browser application, but visitors with slower modems than you may get so impatient with the amount of time it takes to display the image that they'll select the "Back" or "Stop" browser options and not even bother viewing your page.

When designing a Web page, you must consider the lowest common denominator: assume that some people still have 10" monitors, slow modems, and browsers other than the latest version of Netscape.

Let's take a look at Kelley's Photo Album, which offers three options for laying out pages with lots of graphics. All of the photographs shown on the following pages and located in the **Chap5.DIR/Kelley.DIR/Kelley.HTM** were taken by Kelley Hurst, a photographer and writer who lives in Somerville, MA. There are two exceptions where Kelley's friends took photographs of her.

Ingredients:

- **Chap5.DIR/Kelley.DIR/Kelley.HTM:** *Here is the HTML script for Kelley's photo album.*

- **.GIF and .JPG files:** *Kelley's directory contains an array of images. The .GIF files are thumbnail-sized versions of the larger .JPG images. Visitors will click on the thumbnails to link to the documents with the actual photos.*

- **ALT="...", ALIGN="...", and HSPACE/VSPACE="..." Values:** *Here, we will further discuss allowing alternatives to visitors with nongraphical browsers, and setting aside horizontal and vertical space around images so they do not butt up against other elements on the page.*

<HTML>

<HEAD>
<TITLE>Kelley's Photo Album</TITLE>
</HEAD>

<BODY>
<H1>Kelley's Photo Album</H1>

Remember how we named areas of our HTML scripts for linking internally within documents back in Chapter 4? We will add a link from the bottom of this Web page so people can jump back up to the top.

> <A NAME="Top"><H2>Click on the thumbnails shown below to view the photos.</H2></A>

Here, visitors can see what Kelley has to offer without having to download an enormous image.

This layout, shown in Figure 5.13, aligns text and graphics along the middle of each line. This way, you can see which photos go with which text. For those with non-graphical browsers, the thumbnail and photo title are both included within the anchor tags. We have allowed five pixels of horizontal space and ten pixels of vertical space. That way, even if somebody's computer screen is too narrow to display this entire row and a couple of photos bump down a line, they won't butt up against the elements above it.

> <P><A HREF= "Fall.HTM"><IMG SRC="01Fall.GIF" Align= MIDDLE HSPACE= "5" VSPACE="10">Fall</A>

Enter all of the following thumbnails like the one above. The thumbnail .GIF files serve as graphical links to the HTML scripts containing the actual photographs.

> <A HREF="Milkweed.HTM"><IMG SRC= "01Milkw.GIF" ALIGN=MIDDLE HSPACE="5" VSPACE="10">Milkweed </A> <A HREF="Flowers.HTM"> <IMG SRC="01flow.GIF" ALIGN=MIDDLE HSPACE=5 VSPACE="10"> Spring</A> <A HREF="2ndave.HTM"><IMG SRC= "012ndav.GIF" ALIGN=MIDDLE HSPACE="5" VSPACE="10">NYC</A> <P>Let me know what you think! E-mail me at <A HREF="MAILTO: kansaskel@byteit.com"> kansaskel@byteit.com"</A>

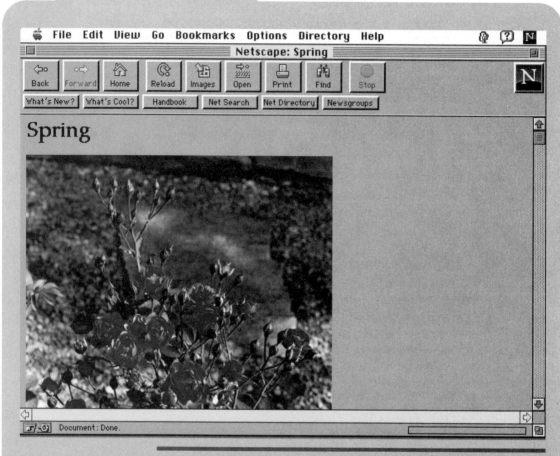

Figure 5.14 Use the thumbnails to jump to the document which displays the actual photo.

If you click on the icon with the flowers, titled "Spring," you will jump to this page, which displays the actual image, as shown in Figure 5.14. Unless you have a vertical monitor like the kind Radius makes, you will have to scroll down to view it entirely.

You will notice that we have included an "ALT" value. Those with nongraphical browsers won't see the image, but they can click on the word "Flowers" to download it and view it later.

```
<HTML>

<HEAD>
<TITLE>Spring</TITLE>
</HEAD>

<BODY>
<H1>Spring</H1>
<IMG SRC="Flowers.JPG" ALT="Flowers">
```

If you ran an actual gallery, would you lead your visitors into a room with no exit? Give them a link back to your main home page!

```
<P>This photo was taken in Gstaad.
<A HREF="Kelley.HTM">Back</A> to Kelley's page</P>

</BODY>
</HTML>
```

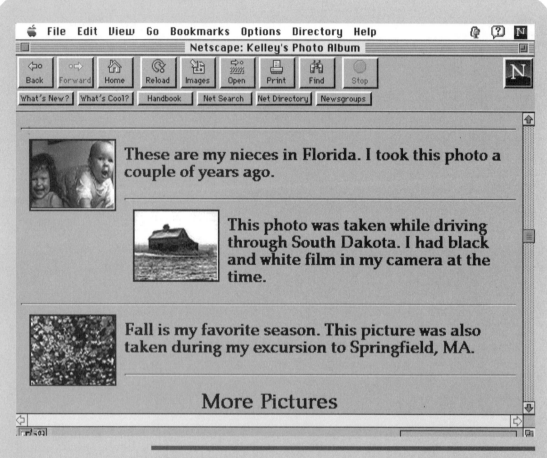

Figure 5.15 A second example of how to lay out graphics on a Web page.

Now let's go back to Kelley's main home page and check out another type of layout, as shown in Figure 5.15. Here, we will try to float the graphics along the left of your screen and have the appropriate text line up along side of it. This requires considerable tinkering with type size (for example, we use the <H2> header tag because body text does not fill enough space) and space set around the image. We also use the <HR> tag to create horizontal rules to separate each image and the accompanying lines of text.

```
<HR>
<A HREF="Kids.HTM"><IMG SRC="02kids.GIF"
ALIGN=LEFT HSPACE="10" VSPACE="5" ALT="Kids"></A>
<H2>These are my nieces in Florida. I took this photo a
couple of years ago.</H2>
<HR>
```

Yikes! This layout didn't work! The second photograph gets bumped out towards the middle of the page because the horizontal and vertical space settings of the photo above exclude it from floating to the left margin. Fortunately, we were smart enough to set aside some space around the Farm house photo. Otherwise, it would have butted up directly against the text above it, which would have looked horrible. Now it doesn't look too bad.

NOTE

Our tech editor notes that you could avoid the problem of placement by using a CLEAR BREAK (a Netscape extension). In Kelley's main page, placement relies on the default font size not being changed. Anyone who changes their default font size would trash the layout. (Hey, most people don't do this, but it pays to be safe!) Therefore, explore the use of <BR> options to set placements.

<A HREF="Farmhse.HTM"><IMG SRC="02farm.GIF" ALIGN=LEFT HSPACE= "10" VSPACE="5" ALT="Farm house"></A><H2>This photo was taken while driving through South Dakota. I had black and white film in my camera at the time.</H2>

The next photo lines up just fine, which is a coincidence. With our default font, font size, and width we needed three lines of text in order for everything to line up. However, you can't rely on this for other people's browsers. (And you can't assume that Netscape and its defaults will continue to lead the market and make these assumptions correct.) Therefore, it is better to not try to use the kind of page layout WYSIWYG ("what you see is what you get") type of methods in composing HTML documents.

CAUTION

Don't use text as a method for spacing pictures. Your assumptions might not work in other people's browsers, and may in fact look very tacky.

```
<HR>
<A HREF="Leaves.HTM"><IMG SRC="02leaves.GIF"
ALIGN=LEFT HSPACE= "10" VSPACE="5" ALT="Leaves">
</A><H2>Fall is my favorite season. This picture was also
taken during my excursion to Springfield, MA.</H2>
<HR>
```

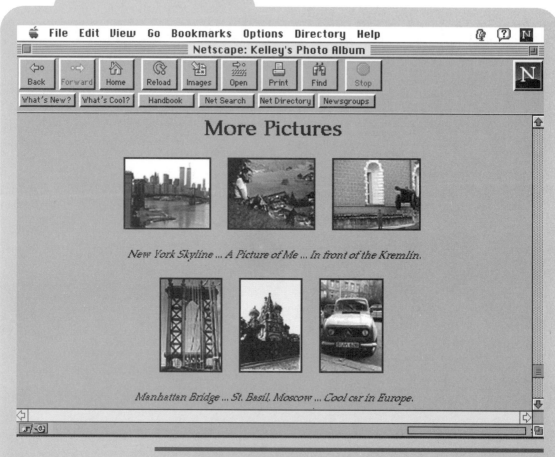

Figure 5.16 A third example of how to lay out graphics on a Web page.

Finally, the easiest way to lay out graphical links is to simply line them up on a page and include explanations or titles above or beneath them, as shown in Figure 5.16. Since no anchor tags were added to the text, we included ALT=... values in the <IMG SRC=..." tags so that those without graphical browsers will be able to find the links.

```
<CENTER>
<H1>More Pictures</H1>
<A HREF="NYSKY.HTM"><IMG SRC="02NYSKY.GIF"
HSPACE="10" VSPACE="5" ALT="NYC Skyline"></A>
<A HREF="Kelley2.HTM"><IMG SRC="02Kelley.GIF"
HSPACE="10" VSPACE="5" ALT="Kelley"></A>
<A HREF="Wall.HTM"></A><IMG SRC="02wall.GIF"
HSPACE=10 VSPACE="5" ALT="Kremlin Wall"></A>
<P>
<I>New York Skyline ... A Picture of Me ... In front of the
Kremlin.</I></P>
<P>
<A HREF="XBridge.HTM"><IMG SRC="01bridge.GIF"
HSPACE="10" VSPACE="5" ALT="Manhattan Bridge">
</A><A HREF="Stbasil.HTM"></A><IMG
SRC="01basil.GIF" HSPACE="10" VSPACE="5"
ALT="St.Basil"></A><A HREF="Car.HTM"><IMG
SRC="01voit.GIF" HSPACE=10 VSPACE="5" ALT="Cool
Car"></A>
<P>
<I>Manhattan Bridge... St. Basil, Moscow ... Cool car in
Europe.</I></P>
</Center>
```

Now, let's give our visitors a link so they can jump back to the top of your page.

```
<P>Back to <A HREF= "#Top">top of page</A></P>

</BODY>
</HTML>
```

Figure 5.17 Examples of what you can offer on your company home page.

○ A COMPANY HOME PAGE

In this example you see how an early company Web page is enlivened by adding various links and graphics to its page. In this recipe we'll explore:

- *Adding links to a page to create a more complete Web site.*

- *The use of icons on a home page to serve as links to other places and sites.*

- *More formatting and alignment options with image.*

- *Use of the ALT clause to create alternative displays for people without graphical browsers.*

- *The construction of an on-line order form.*

- *Adding an employee directory to a company's home page.*

Surprisingly, you will find many of the most creative Web pages at corporate sites. Whether you own a large company or run a small consulting firm, you can promote yourself on the World Wide Web. If people enjoy browsing your page, they'll come back and visit you again, but in order to get people to visit again, you must give back to the 'Net. Creating or visiting a corporate home page should be a mix of business and pleasure.

You should make company information available for people to look at, but you should also offer exciting graphics, links to fun places on the Web, and free goodies as well. For example, the Kodak Web site (http://www.kodak.com/digitalImages/digitalImages.shtml) lets you download an array of spectacular photographs, and the Adobe Systems Incorporated home page (http://www.adobe.com/) offers a free version of the Acrobat Reader (for viewing portable document files created with Adobe Acrobat), assorted interesting .PDF publications which you can download and view with the Acrobat Reader, and more.

Ingredients:

- **Chap5.DIR/Gizmo2.DIR/Gizmo2.HTM:** *Remember the Gizmos, Ltd. home page we began working on in Chapter 4? Now we're going to jazz it up a bit and add links.*

- **Assorted graphics:** *We have created icons for the various categories of company home page content. Feel free to use these for your own business.*

Let's begin.

<HTML>

<HEAD>
<TITLE>Gizmos, LTD</TITLE>
</HEAD>

<BODY>
<IMG SRC= "Gizmo.GIF" ALIGN=LEFT>
<H1>Gizmos, Ltd.</H1>
1977 Main Street, Suite #402
Cambridge, MA 02139
Tel: (617) 547-2983
Fax: (617) 547-5355
<HR>

The categories and links you add to your company page will depend on your business. However, most companies who are currently on the Web offer some variation of the categories shown in Figure 5.17. It is also always a good idea to link people to Web sites that address topics pertaining to your business.

```
<H2>Welcome to the Gizmos, Ltd. Home Page</H2>
<P>Now you can browse our <A HREF="Cat.HTM">cata-
log</A> and order products on-line, see our <A
HREF="Report.HTM">annual report</A>, view our
employee <A HREF="Dir.HTM">directory</A>, view our
on-line instruction <A HREF="Manual.HTM">manuals
</A>, and take a tour of our employees favorite places on
the <A HREF="Weblinks.HTM">web</A>.</P>
<H3>Choose from the following options ...</H3>
```

Once again, we use the ALT="..." value so that visitors with nongraphical browsers can link to these topics.

```
<P>
<A HREF="Cat.HTM"><IMG SRC="Cat.GIF" ALIGN=Mid-
dle HSPACE="5" VSPACE="5" ALT="Catalog"></A>
<A HREF="Report.HTM"><IMG SRC="Report.GIF"
ALIGN=Middle HSPACE="5" VSPACE="5" Alt="Annual
Report"></A>
<A HREF="Dir.HTM"><IMG SRC="Dir.GIF" ALIGN=Middle
HSPACE="5" VSPACE="5" Alt="Employee Directory"></A>
<A HREF="Manual.HTM"><IMG SRC="Manual.GIF"
ALIGN=Middle HSPACE="5" VSPACE="5" Alt="Instruction
Manual"></A>
<A HREF="Weblinks.HTM"><IMG SRC="Weblinks.GIF"
ALIGN=Middle HSPACE="5" VSPACE="5" Alt="Web
Links"></A>
<P>We hope you enjoy our home page.</P>
<BODY>Sincerely,<BR>
Lisa Smith, President

</BODY>
</HTML>
```

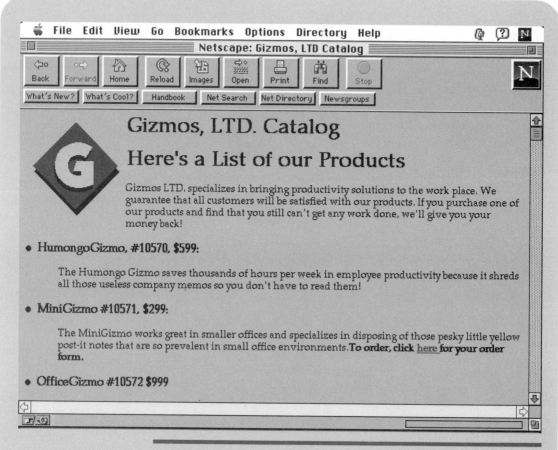

Figure 5.18 This catalog lists the products and lets you order them on-line.

COMPANY CATALOG AND ORDER FORM

An on-line company catalog, like the one shown in Figure 5.18, is a great way to promote your products. You can even add an order form. However, we must mention here that there are still security-related issues about conducting financial transactions over the Internet you need to worry about. Although Netscape and other companies offer products that can help ensure that your customers' credit card numbers and other financial information will remain private, these options are expensive, and some contend, unreliable. Avoid the necessity of putting people's credit cards on-line by only letting repeat customers enter their assigned purchase order numbers, or bill them upon delivery.

Ingredients:

■ *Chap5.DIR/Gizmo2.DIR/Cat.HTM: This document contains the company catalog and is linked to the Gizmo2 home page we just created in the last section.*

■ *Chap5.DIR/Gizmo2.DIR/Order.HTM: This is an example of an on-line order form, which is linked to the Gizmos, Ltd. Catalog home page.*

```
<HTML>

<HEAD>
<Title>Gizmos, LTD Catalog</TITLE>
</HEAD>

<BODY>
<IMG SRC="Gizmo.GIF" ALIGN="LEFT"><H1>Gizmos,
LTD. Catalog</H1>
<H1>Here's a List of our Products</H1>
<P>Gizmos LTD. specializes in bringing productivity solu-
tions to the work place. We guarantee that all customers
will be satisfied with our products. If you purchase one of
our products and find that you still can't get any work done,
we'll give you your money back!</P>
<DL>
<DT><LI><H3>HumongoGizmo, #10570, $599:</H3>
<DD>The Humongo Gizmo saves thousands of hours per
week in employee productivity because it shreds all those
useless company memos so you don't have to read them!
<P>
```

Note that in the next line we use a nonstandard <DT><LI> set of tags. You only need <DT> tags to create a definition list. When you use an <LI> tag as well, you create an implied unordered list (or bulleted list). That's OK, but you need to be aware that you are doing this.

```
<DT><LI><H3>MiniGizmo #10571, $299:</H3>
<DD>The MiniGizmo works great in smaller offices and
specializes in disposing of those pesky little yellow post-it
notes that are so prevalent in small office environ-
ments.<B>To order, click <A HREF="Order.HTM">here </
A>for your order form.</B>
```

File   Edit   View   Go   Bookmarks   Options   Directory   Help

Netscape: Order Form

Back	Forward	Home	Reload	Images	Open	Print	Find	Stop

| What's New? | What's Cool? | Handbook | Net Search | Net Directory | Newsgroups |

Order Your Gizmo Product Now!

Your name:

Your title:

Your email address:

Your company name:

Your street address:

Your City: Your State: Your Zip:

Your Daytime Phone: Your Daytime Fax:

Order your Gizmo Products

To order, Select A Product   Humongo ▼

Figure 5.19   The first part of this form solicits contact information so Gizmos, Ltd. can fulfill the order and bill the customer.

CATALOG ORDER FORM

Here is a catalog order form which is similar to the one we created earlier in this chapter. We will now review the elements of a form and explore creating pull-down lists. Ingredients:

- ■ **Chap5.DIR/Gizmo2.DIR/Order.HTM:** *This HTML script offers another example of creating a form.*

- ■ **<Select Name="..."><option>"..."<option>"..." </Select>:** *You can create a pull-down menu using the above entry.*

The above SELECT tag is really a form object, but let's work with it here so that you can add it to your repetoire. We surround it by the <FORM> ... </FORM> tag pair to block it out in our document.

Let's begin.

<HTML>

<HEAD>
<TITLE>Order Form</TITLE>
</HEAD>

<BODY>
<IMG SRC="Gizmo.GIF" ALIGN=LEFT>
<H1>Order Your Gizmo Product Now!</H1>

Remember that you must specify the form method and the action your server will perform with the information filled in by your customers.

<FORM>
<FORM METHOD="Post" ACTION="MAILTO: orders@giz-mos.com">

Have your customers enter their billing information here. You may find that you have to play around with the field sizes a bit so they line up evenly, as shown in Figure 5.19.

```
<p>Your name: <input name="name" size="48">
<p>Your title: <input name="title" size="50">
<p>Your email address: <input name="email address"
size="42">
<p>Your company name: <input name="company name"
size="61">
<p>Your street address: <input name="street address"
size="63">
<p>Your City: <input name="City" size="29">
 Your State: <input name="State" size="5"> Your Zip:
<input name="Zip" size="13">
<p>Your Daytime Phone: <input name="Daytime Phone"
size="22">
 Your Daytime Fax: <input name="Daytime Fax" size="22">
<HR>
```

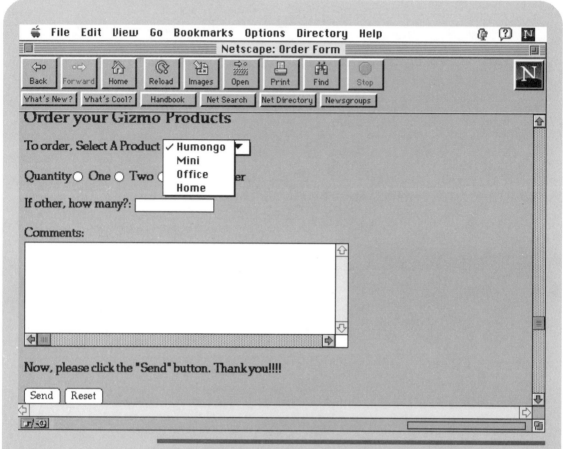

Figure 5.20 Now customers can order their products and send the form.

<H2>Order your Gizmo Products</H2>
<H3>To order, Select A Product.

Here's something new—you can create a pulldown list like the one shown in Figure 5.20! Just follow the template below and enter each option.

<Select Name="Product">
<Option>Humongo
<Option>Mini
<Option>Office
<Option>Home
</Select></P>

And now we're back to entering radio buttons and text fields.

Quantity<INPUT TYPE="radio" NAME="one" VALUE="one"> One
<INPUT TYPE="radio" NAME="two" VALUE="two"> Two
<INPUT TYPE="radio" NAME="three" VALUE="three">Three<INPUT TYPE="radio" NAME="Other" VALUE="Other">Other<p>If other, how many?: <input name="How many?" size="15">
<p>

If you wish to enter a larger text field, like the one shown in Figure 5.20, you must specify the amount of rows and columns it should take.

Comments:
<textarea name="comments" rows=8 cols=60></textarea>
<p>

Have your customers either submit or clear the information they just entered.

<H3>Now, please click the "Send" button. Thank you!!!!
</H3>
<p><INPUT TYPE="submit" VALUE="Send"> <input type=reset>
</form>

Give your customers a place to jump back to, and close your form.

<P>Return to <A HREF="Cat.HTM">Gizmo Catalog</A>
<P>Return to <A HREF="Gizmo2.HTM">Gizmo Home Page</A>
</P>

</BODY>
</HTML>

CAUTION

Don't forget that information mailed over the Internet is not generally secure. You might want to restrict the information asked for, or indicate this in a note on your form to protect your viewers.

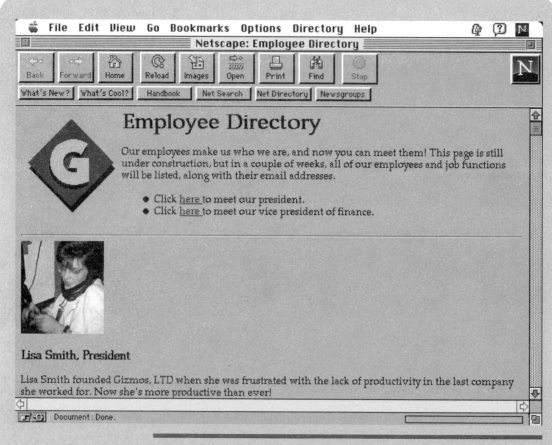

Figure 5.21 Let customers meet the people in your company.

EMPLOYEE DIRECTORY

An employee directory adds a personal touch to your company home page, and lets your customers know who they can contact in different situations. You can link customers to different departments, include photographs of key players, let customers send your employees e-mail, and give people a feel for your company.

Ingredients:

- ■ ***Chap5.DIR/Gizmos.DIR/Dir.HTM:*** *This document is linked to the main Gizmos, Ltd. home page.*

- ■ ***Pictures:*** *In the example shown in Figure 5.21, customers get to meet people in the company and view their photo.*

Let's begin.

```
<HTML>

<HEAD>
<TITLE>Employee Directory</Title>
</HEAD>

<BODY>
<IMG SRC="Gizmo.GIF" ALIGN=Left>
<H1>Employee Directory</H1>
<P>Our employees make us who we are, and now you can meet them! This page is still under construction, but in a couple of weeks, all of our employees and job functions will be listed, along with their email addresses.</P>
<P>
<UL>
```

Employee directories are an ideal example for using internal links.

```
<LI>Click <A HREF="#President">here </A>to meet our
president.
<LI>Click <A HREF="#VP Finance">here </A>to meet our
vice president of finance.
</UL>
<HR>
<IMG SRC="empl1.JPG">
<A NAME="President"><H3>Lisa Smith, President</H3>
</A>
<P>Lisa Smith founded Gizmos, LTD  when she was frus-
trated with the lack of productivity in the last company she
worked for. Now she's more productive than ever!
<BR>
<BR>
<HR>
<IMG SRC="Empl2.JPG">
<A NAME="VP FINANCE"><H3>R. Jason Peabody III, Vice
President of Finance</H3></A>
<P>R. Jason Peabody has been with the company since it
was launched in 1988. He's always hitting the golf courses
these days, because he's so productive when he works that
he hardly ever has to come into the office any more.
<P><A HREF="Gizmo2.HTM">Back to Gizmo home
page</A></P>

</BODY>
</HTML>
```

An employee database can change over time as people come and go in your company. In order to keep descriptions and photographs current, it is helpful to impose a standard file naming convention and directory or folder organization.

Figure 5.22 Logo and introductory paragraph for an electronic magazine.

○ AN ELECTRONIC MAGAZINE

Electronic magazines or e-zine offer the opportunity to create low cost widely disseminated published information. Here you'll see how to:

- *Create an e-zine with many parts and sections.*

- *Create references to other locations on the Web.*

- *Review the use of various types of lists.*

- *Learn about logical styles for adjusting text formatting on the fly.*

- *Get a brief description of Adobe's Portable Document File PDF format that offers documents with formatting and graphics that are cross-platform compatible.*

As paper and printing costs soar, electronic publishing grows increasingly attractive. Although nothing can compare with the satisfaction of actually holding a glossy magazine in your hand and perusing the pages, electronic publishing offers an unprecedented potential for direct interaction between the publisher and the reader. *Byte It!* Magazine (http://www.tiac.net/biz/byteit/index.htm) is an example of the Web's offerings, as shown in Figures 5.22–24. It currently covers the Boston scene, but plans to expand coverage to other cities and offer a travel section for people planning to visit Boston.

Ingredients:

- ***Chap5.DIR/Byteit.DIR/Index.HTM:*** *This document is linked to many sections. For the sake of brevity, we will only look at the front page and part of the music section. However, you can check the magazine out for yourself by viewing it in your browser.*

- ***Chap5.DIR/Byteit.DIR/Music.HTM:*** *Boston has a thriving music scene, and this is currently Byte It!'s biggest section. Although the book only contains an illustration of the first couple of screens, you can view the entire section in your browser.*

Let's Byte on…

<u><HTML></u>
<u><HEAD></u>
<u><TITLE>Byte It!</TITLE></u>
<u></HEAD></u>

<u><BODY></u>
<u><IMG SRC="logoweb.gif"><H1>Byte It! Magazine: What's</u>
<u>Cooking in Boston</H1></u>
<u><H3>Byte It! covers the following …</H3></u>
<u><A HREF="art.HTM">Art</A>,</u>
<u><A HREF="music.HTM">Music</A>,</u>
<u><A HREF="film.HTM">Film</A>, <A</u>
<u>HREF="plays.HTM">Performance Art</A>, <A HREF="rant-</u>
<u>ing.HTM">Random Rantings and Ravings</A>,</u>
<u><A HREF="hangout.HTM">Hangouts</A>,</u>
<u><A HREF="multi.HTM">Multimedia</A> and more! We'd</u>
<u>also like to have a literary section if anyone's interested in</u>
<u>covering books and the poetry scene.</P></u>

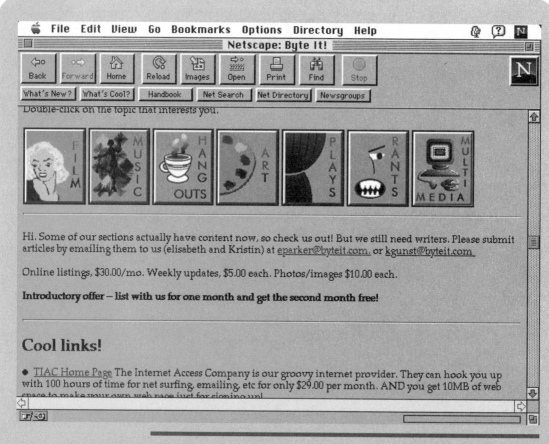

Figure 5.23 Graphical links for jumping to sections of an electronic magazine.

```
<P>Double-click on the topic that interests you. </P>
<A HREF="film.HTM"><IMG SRC="film.gif"></A>
<A HREF="music.HTM"> <IMG SRC="music.gif"></A>
<A HREF="hangout.HTM"><IMG SRC="hangout.gif"></A>
<A HREF="art.HTM"><IMG SRC="art.gif"></A>
<A HREF="plays.HTM"><IMG SRC="plays.gif"></A>
<A HREF="ranting.HTM"><IMG SRC="ranting.gif"></A>
<A HREF="multi.HTM"><IMG SRC="multi.gif"></A>
<HR>
<P>Hi. Some of our sections actually have content now, so
check us out! But we still need writers. Please submit arti-
cles by emailing them to us (elisabeth and Kristin) at <A
HREF="mailto: eparker@tiac.net">eparker@byteit.com.</
A> or <A HREF="mailto:
kgunst@tiac.net">kgunst@byteit.com </A></P>
```

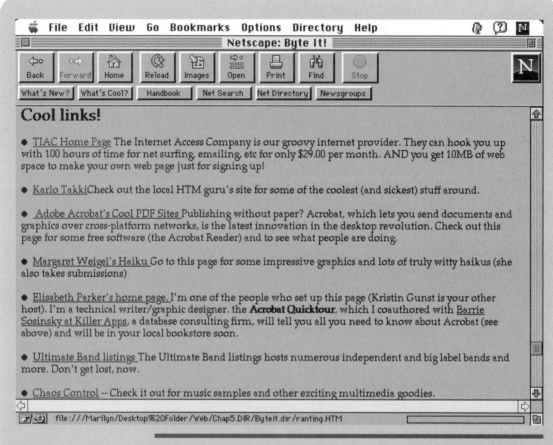

Figure 5.24 When in doubt, always link. *Byte It!* offers links to other cool web pages and resources on the Web.

```
<HR>
<H2>Cool links!</H2>
```

The appearance of the <LI> tag below implies the existence of a <UL> prior to it. It works to create the unordered list (or bulleted list), but it is a nonstandard tag structure.

```
<LI><A HREF=" http://www.tiac.net/">TIAC Home Page
</A> The Internet Access Company is our groovy internet
provider. They can hook you up with 100 hours of time for
net surfing, emailing, etc for only $29.00 per month. AND
you get 10MB of web space to make your own web page
just for signing up!
<BR>
<BR>
<LI><A HREF="http://www.xensei.com:80/users/
ktakki/">Karlo Takki</A>Check out the local HTM guru's
site for some of the coolest (and sickest) stuff around.
<BR>
<BR>
<LI><A HREF="http://www.adobe.com/Acrobat/PDF-
sites.HTM"> Adobe Acrobat's Cool PDF Sites </A> Publish-
ing without paper? Acrobat, which lets you send documents
and graphics over cross-platform networks, is the latest
innovation in the desktop revolution. Check out this page
for some free software (the Acrobat Reader) and to see what
people are doing.
<BR>
<BR>
<LI><A HREF="http://www.mit.edu:8001/people/mawei-
gel/MA.HTM">Margaret Weigel's Haiku </A> Go to this
page for some impressive graphics and lots of truly witty
haikus (she also takes submissions)
<BR>
```

<u>
</u>
<u><LI><A HREF="http://www.tiac.net/users/eparker/</u>
<u>index.HTM">Elisabeth Parker's home page. </A> I'm one of</u>
<u>the people who set up this page (Kristin Gunst is your other</u>
<u>host). I'm a technical writer/graphic designer. The</u>

We haven't used it before, but there are a set of logical styles you can use in HTML that let the browsers define the emphasis placed on text. The two most common of these styles are <EM> ... </EM> for emphasis, and <STRONG> ... </STRONG> for stronger emphasis. Some browsers italicize the former and bold the later. The next line shows its use.

<u><Strong>Acrobat Quicktour</Strong>, which I coauthored</u>
<u>with <A HREF=" http://www.tiac.net/users/basman/</u>
<u>index.HTM"> Barrie Sosinsky at Killer Apps</A>, a data-</u>
<u>base consulting firm, will tell you all you need to know</u>
<u>about Acrobat (see above) and will be in your local book-</u>
<u>store soon.</u>
<u>
</u>
<u>
</u>
<u><LI><A HREF="http://american.recordings.com/wwwofmu-</u>
<u>sic/alp_reg.HTM">Ultimate Band listings </A> The Ulti-</u>
<u>mate Band listings hosts numerous independent and big</u>
<u>label bands and more. Don't get lost, now.</u>
<u>
</u>

```
<BR>
<LI><A HREF="http://www.ids.net/~chaos/
chaos.html">Chaos Control</A> -- Check it out for music
samples and other exciting multimedia goodies.
<BR>
<BR>
<LI><A HREF=" http://cafeliberty.com/liberty.HTM
"> Cafe Liberty</A> A bunch of MIT graduates started a cof-
feehouse in Central Square, Cambridge, MA and voila--a
fun, cozy cybercafe with a fabulous selection of coffee
drinks. They also host bands and performances. And they
have computers so you can browse the world wide web for
only about $6.00 per hour.

</BODY>
</HTML>
```

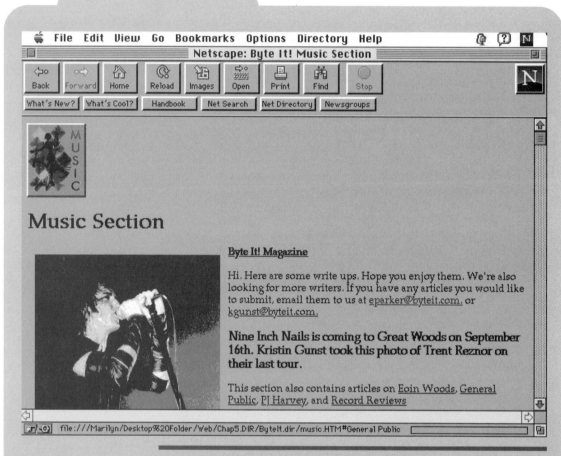

Figure 5.25 *Byte It!* link to the Music section.

MUSIC SECTION

If you click on the music section icon on the *Byte It!* page, you will see a screen similar to the one in Figure 5.25. To view the script, go into the **Chap5.DIR/Byteit.DIR/Music.HTM** document.

```
<HTML>

<HEAD>
<TITLE>Byte It! Music Section</TITLE>
</HEAD>

<BODY>
<IMG SRC="music.gif">
<H1>Music Section</H1>
<IMG SRC="NIN.GIF" ALIGN=LEFT HSPACE="10"
VSPACE="10">
<A HREF="index.HTM"><P><STRONG>Byte It! Maga-
zine</STRONG></P></A>
<P>Hi. Here are some write ups. Hope you enjoy them.
We're also looking for more writers. If you have any articles
you would like to submit, email them to us at
<A HREF="mailto: eparker@tiac.net">eparker@byteit.com.
</A> or <A HREF="mailto:
kgunst@tiac.net">kgunst@byteit.com.</A></P>
<H3>Nine Inch Nails is coming to Great Woods on Sep-
tember 16th. Kristin Gunst took this photo of Trent Reznor
on their last tour.</H3>
```

<P>This section also contains articles on
<A HREF="#Eoin">Eoin Woods</A>, <A HREF="#General
Public"">General Public</A>, <A HREF="#PJ"> PJ Har-
vey</A>, and <A HREF="#Rev">Record Reviews
</A><P>Byte It! features sections on
<A HREF="Art.HTM">art</A>, <A HREF=Plays.HTM">per-
formance</A>, <A HREF="Rants">rantings and ravings
</A>, <A HREF="Multi.HTM">multimedia</A>,
<A HREF="Hangouts.HTM">Hangouts</A> and more. Go
<A HREF="index.HTM">Home!</A>...

And the script continues.

○ SUMMARY

Now that we have explored an array of templates for creating impressive Web pages, you're ready to begin piecing them together on your own. Create a home page, and link it to your other Web pages. You now know how to link up an electronic magazine, create a basic business Web site, solicit input from your visitors with interactive forms, encourage visitors to send you e-mail, and you've even learned a bit about working with graphics. Those skills will take you far in Cyberspace.

But how do people find out about your Web site once you've built it? In Chapter 6, you will learn how to add your Web page to directories like Yahoo and search engines like WebCrawler and Lycos so that your topics and content are more easily located. You'll also learn how to announce your work over the Internet to various newsgroups so that it appears in everyone's "What's New" listings.

chapter

6

THIS CHAPTER WILL COVER THE FOLLOWING:

- An overview of the post-production process
- Putting your pages on a Web server
- Troubleshooting your home page
- Announce your home page to the millions of Cybernauts who long for them

SETTING THE TABLE: GETTING YOUR WEB PAGES POSTED

Now that you've created your Web page, it's time to check them out and get them posted to your Web server. Some final checks will make sure that your Web pages display the way you want them to and that all of your links work. Then you have to serve up your pages onto the Web and let people know your page exists. And finally, you have to maintain your page and update your information periodically.

○ AN OVERVIEW OF THE PROCESS

After generating a home page and related pages for your Web site, you must check them for potential problems. Then you physically copy your files to your Web server. Finally, it's time to spread the word that your home page exists. Let's take a brief look at these steps before we move on to more detailed explanations:

- ■ ***Check, check and double check:*** *One of the really nice things about working with HTML pages is that you can see your work displayed as you develop it. Visually, it's pretty*

269

easy to spot problems in your browser. The problem is, not everyone is using your particular browser. Therefore, test your Web page and see how it looks in at least a couple of different browsers.

The things you want to pay particular attention to are graphic alignment and text display, any Netscape extensions you used, graphical links, and the way your page looks in text-only browsers like Lynx. Remember, we discussed adding alternatives (ALT clauses) in Chapter 5, "Sample Meals," for text-based users. You also don't want to embarrass yourself with links that lead to nowhere—a cardinal HTML sin.

If possible, you should even have some other people test your pages for additional feedback on errors (bugs?) and suggestions for better methods of construction. Hopefully, they'll examine your site with different equipment (slower computers or modems), different browsers, and a different mindset. There's always more than one way to skin a cat.

- **Find a Web server:** *Perhaps your Web server is just across your office at work. Most Internet access providers, whether they are a commercial provider, your company, or your school, offer disk space to their clients for their Web pages. Often a certain amount of disk space (like 10 MB) is offered free as part of your monthly fee. More space is either negotiable or available for extra cost.*

CAUTION

Some Internet providers charge you based on how many "hits" you get—meaning how much bandwidth gets taken up on their server due to people visiting your page. Since you have little or no control over how many guests you may have, this could get you into some financial hot water if your page becomes popular. If this is the case, you might want to add a counter that measures the number of hits your home page gets. Also make sure that having the page up and running benefits you financially, and that the charges are worth it.

■ **Upload your content:** *Once your home page seems fine and dandy, it's time to serve it up.*

■ **Announce your new home page:** *What use is having a Web page if nobody knows it's there? If a Web page is posted in the forest and nobody sees it, was it ever posted at all? There are ways to announce your presence by posting your site with appropriate news groups, notifying search engines and directory listings, and posting a listing using on-line forms like the one shown in Figures 6.1 and 6.1a. It also helps to get people at other Web sites to add links to your site.*

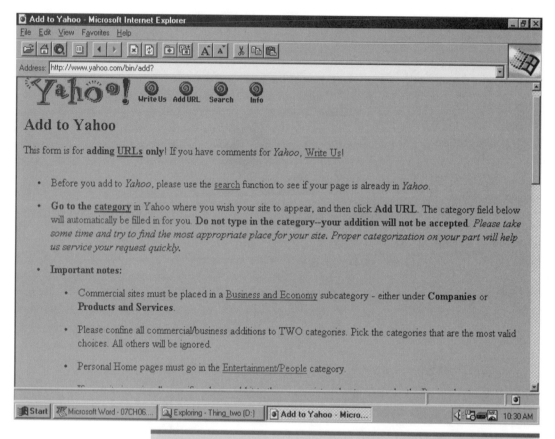

Figure 6.1 Yahoo invites you to tell them about your new home page with an on-line form accessed from the Add URL button. (Text and artwork copyright ©1996 YAHOO!, Inc. All rights reserved. YAHOO! and the YAHOO! logo are trademarks of YAHOO!, Inc.)

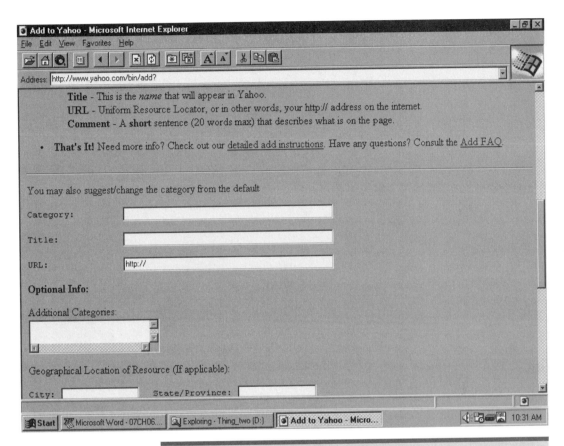

Figure 6.2   The forms section of Yahoo's Add URL section. (Text and artwork copyright ©1996 YAHOO!, Inc. All rights reserved. YAHOO! and the YAHOO! logo are trademarks of YAHOO!, Inc.)

To view home pages in Yahoo, check out the directory listing Society and Culture: People: Personal Home Pages. From the central White Pages directory listing for personal home pages in Yahoo, shown in Figure 6.3, you can access people's pages by alphabetical listing. Figure 6.4 shows you a typical page in the Personal Home Pages, which each contains many hundreds and hundreds of listings at the moment. If you click on the Click Here: Send a Message to the World, you go to the AT&T True Choice Message Center. The Yahoo White Pages maintains a commercial directory of listings if you are trying to post a commercial venture's home page.

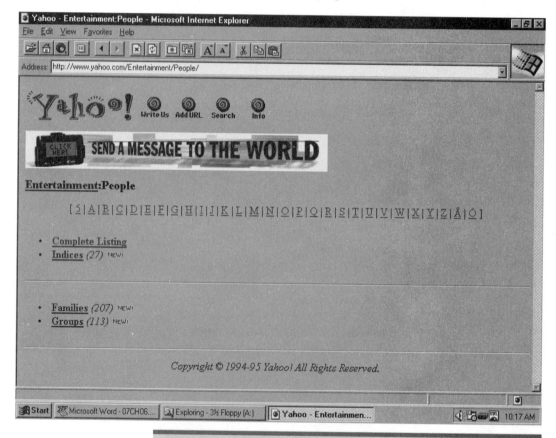

Figure 6.3   The Yahoo White Pages directory. (Text and artwork copyright ©1996 YAHOO!, Inc. All rights reserved. YAHOO! and the YAHOO! logo are trademarks of YAHOO!, Inc.)

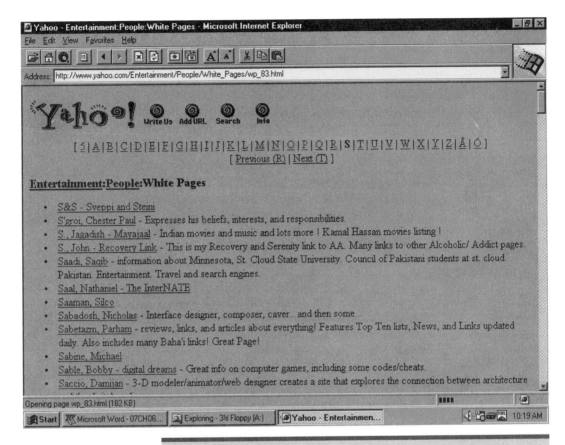

Figure 6.4 A typical page in Yahoo's White Pages with hundreds of home pages listed. (Text and artwork copyright ©1996 YAHOO!, Inc. All rights reserved. YAHOO! and the YAHOO! logo are trademarks of YAHOO!, Inc.)

■ *Maintain your home page:* Home pages require some maintenance from time to time. Add new content as often as possible so your visitors don't get bored. If you have links to other sites, check them occasionally and make sure they still work. For all you know, someone may have changed servers or stopped publishing their Web page entirely.

275

The incredibly dynamic nature of the World Wide Web makes it a certainty that Web pages come and go. You'll probably want to change the content of your Web pages every so often. You should take this fact into account when you plan the location of your documents.

TIP

If changing the location of your pages, and particularly your home page (i.e., their URLs), try to leave a page on the Web for a while announcing your Web page's new location. Then your viewers can note the new location and change any bookmarks or links that they have to your site. If not, your location will be considered a "dropout", and your viewers will think you have gone out of business.

What are you to do if you are posting a personal home page and want people to know about it and visit it?

○ PUTTING YOUR PAGES ON A WEB SERVER

Most Internet service providers either give you or let you purchase space on their Web server for a flat monthly fee. The big on-line services are experimenting with their Internet programs, and some (like Prodigy) already offer a place to post your pages. We expect that all the on-line services will offer this to their users beginning sometime in 1996.

As an example of this, America Online has a People section in its Internet Connection area where there will be a searchable database of their membership. They have posted some personal home pages of their employees as an experiment. Figure 6.5 shows you the table of contents for those Web pages, and Figure 6.6 shows you Amy Arnold's AOL home page.

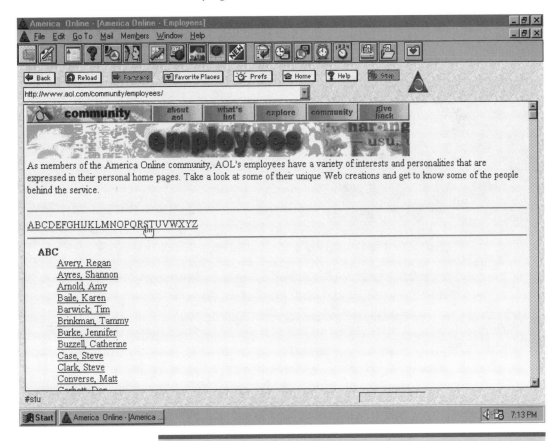

Figure 6.5   The table of contents to employees' home pages on America Online. (Copyright 1995–1996 America Online, Inc. All rights reserved.)

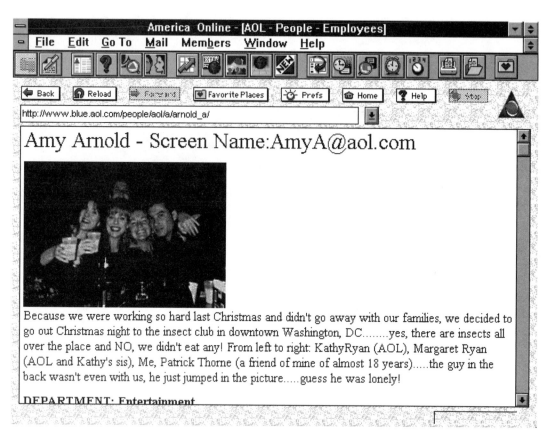

Many corporations are finding the Web to be a great
way to provide wide area networking (WAN) capabilities
to their staff. My editor describes the Web as a poor
corporation's Lotus Notes. If you have the company's Web
server nearby, great! Nothing could be easier to set up your
pages on.

Go have a chat with your Web administrator, if one exists, to find out what the file requirements are. Then string up your sneakers, copy your files to a floppy, and follow the Sneakernet over to the Web server. All you have to do is to copy your files to your directory on the server. (Yes, it can be that easy!) It your server isn't physically available to you, it's just a little more work.

As we discussed in Chapter 1, "What's Cooking on the Web?" many Internet service providers give you as much as 10 MB of disk space as part of your service package. That's the case with our Internet provider (The Internet Access Service, or TIAC). When you sign up, your service provider will provide you with a folder which typically has your login or company name.

We log onto the server using an FTP utility (like Fetch for the Mac or Trumpet TCP for Windows) and upload our files to our folder. When logging onto the server, it's typical to use your on-line name and your service provider password for the logon. Do not log onto the server in the standard FTP method as an anonymous user with no password (or your user name as password); you will be denied access. Figure 6.7 shows you the login screen for Fetch, the Macintosh FTP program.

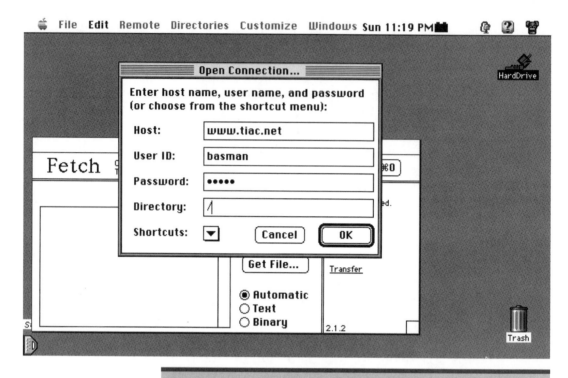

Figure 6.7 Logging into your Web server using Fetch.

Once you're logged in, the files appear in the file list,. Move to your folder in the file list, as shown in Figure 6.8 for Barrie's folder (BASMAN). Then open that folder by double clicking on it. Use the Put Folder or Files command to transfer the files or folders you desire to your Web site.

Figure 6.9 shows you this command. Of course, if you use another FTP program the exact command name will be different, but the procedure is substantially the same. Consult the documentation or on-line help for the program you are using.

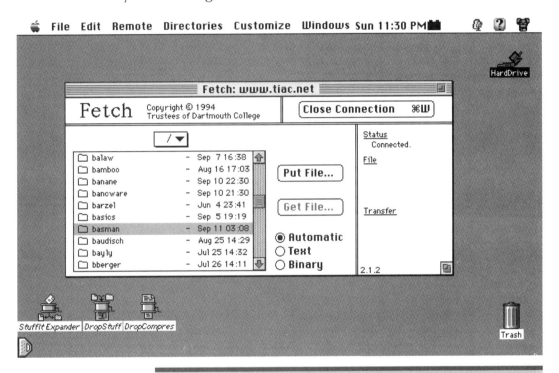

Figure 6.8   The file listing for a Web server in Fetch.

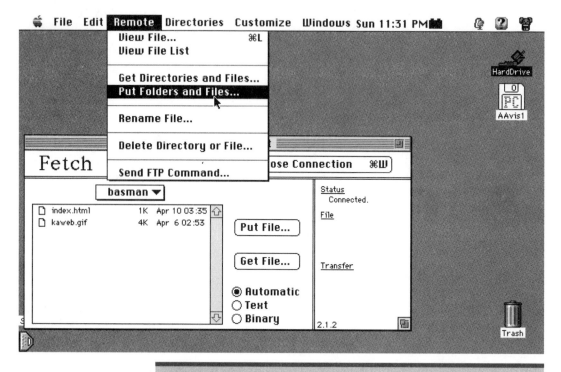

Figure 6.9   The Put Folders or File command in Fetch.

FTP programs were discussed in Chapter 1, "What's Cooking on the Web?" You can download an FTP program from your service provider, or from a number of archive sites on the Internet with your browser. Once you upload the content to your server, you should be able to view your home page on-line as it appears in your browser.

NOTE

If you're replacing new files with old ones, don't forget to select your browser's "Reload" option. Otherwise, you'll wonder why the browser keeps displaying your old files.

Unless you plan on having more than 1000 people visiting your home page every day, there's no reason to set up your own Web server. For most people, using a local Internet provider is the most affordable solution. Internet access providers tend to be more flexible, letting you upgrade your capabilities as needed. Most access companies offer very competitive prices, much better than you can get from the on-line service.

However, it's been our experience that you shouldn't expect a lot of technical support from your Internet service provider. They won't help you much with designing your Web pages or configuring your site. Most access providers are hardware guys. Some of the bigger Internet service providers offer classes to their users that you might want to investigate.

You can also overload a small Internet access provider if your site becomes very popular and pulls a lot of traffic. If you plan on expanding, you may want to sign up with one of the large national commercial providers instead of the smaller Mom and Pop outfits that abound in the landscape of Cyberspace.

If you want to check out what the on-line services are currently offering, they can be reached at:

- *America Online: (http://www.aol.com); (800) 827-6364.*

- *Compuserve: (http://www.compuserve.com); (800) 858-0411.*

- *Prodigy: (http://www.prodigy.com); (800) 776-3449.*

- *Delphi: (http://www.delphi.com); (800) 695-4005.*

TROUBLESHOOTING YOUR HOME PAGE

It is impossible to overemphasize the importance of troubleshooting your home page. Until you get the hang of working with Web documents and uploading files, home pages can be tricky critters. Here are some common things that go wrong, and how to correct these problems.

■ ***Your links don't work!*** *Since Web pages are connected by links, it is important that all your links work correctly. Test them all before serving your home page. In order for your links to work, the file names entered in the anchor tags must have quotation marks around them, and must match the actual file name exactly. Remember, all browsers require that upper and lower case letters must match in your URLs.*

TIP

Remember that if your links reference documents at your Web site, when you post them to your server they will continue to work correctly if the relative positions of documents haven't changed. However, links to absolute locations must be exactly correct to function.

■ ***Your graphics don't display!*** *Once again, all file names entered within the <IMG SRC="..."> must match the actual file name exactly and must have quotation marks around them.*

■ ***Your browser won't open up my HTML file at all!*** *Remember that browsers can only read plain-text documents. Make sure that you saved your HTML document in your word processing application as a text-only file.*

■ **All these strange characters keep showing up!** *If weird O's with ligatures and other strange characters keep showing up on your home page, smart quotes (curly quotation marks) are probably the culprits. Refer back to the discussion in Chapter 4, "Some Sample Dishes," to make sure that all special characters are stripped from your HTML document. Also turn off the Smart Quotes option in your word processor.*

CAUTION

Some Web servers require you to name your primary Web document in a specific way. For example, our Internet provider requires us to name our home page "Index.HTM." However, we can name secondary documents whatever we want. Make sure you know what the requirements of your server software are before you upload your files.

■ **All of your stuff looks fine in your tests, but they're not showing up on my Web site!** *When FTPing your files, make sure you upload your files with the correct format. Images should be sent as raw data—your FTP program may automatically assume that you want to compress them, in which case your browser won't be able to display them. Text files should be FTPed in text-only format using the .HTM file extension.*

■ **Your text is showing up in extra-large type!** *You probably forgot to close one of your header tags. Remember that all HTML formatting tags must be opened and closed.*

■ **Your Web page looked fabulous in Netscape, but terrible in my other browser!** *Although Netscape extensions let you create truly beautiful home pages, you must make sure that your home page still looks OK in other browsers.*

For example, not all browsers support the graphics alignment settings. This means that without Netscape, your images may butt up against each other and not align correctly with your text. Refer back to the discussion in Chapter 5 on Netscape extensions for more details.

Now that you've cleared up the little glitches, you're ready to tell the world about your Web page!

○ EXTRA EXTRA, READ ALL ABOUT IT! ANNOUNCING YOUR WEB PAGE

As an important step in the process, you need to let people know that your Web page and/or site is up and running. There are several ways that you can do this. In this section we cover the primary methods you should consider. There's a lot of interest in the World Wide Web, lots of lists of new sites people are compiling, and you can get this publicity with little work and at an almost insignificant cost. Compare that with advertising any business or product in your big city newspaper or glossy magazine. The Web is electronic publishing at its best.

Here are some of the common ways of announcing your Web site:

■ **Register with the search engines and directory services:** *Many of the search engines and directory services we discussed back in Chapter 1, "What's Cooking on the Web?" let you submit your site for indexing in their databases.*

All of the Web search sites offer on-line forms for telling them about your Web page. They will ask you to enter a category, the title and URL of your page, and some of them will even request your name and e-mail address and a brief description. After you submit your form, the system administrators will check out your home page and add you to the list. The process takes anywhere between a week and four weeks, depending.

How the search engines index your site is different for each engine. Some search engines just look at your URL and index your brief description. Other search engines use software robots (or agents) to visit your Web site and index the text it finds. The more thorough robots will check out all of your links and generate a lot of site activity. However, there is a protocol for robots that limits what a good robot will do. Most of the better content-based search engines (like WebCrawler) adhere to these standards.

■ ***Try the "What's New" pages:*** *In addition to the large, searchable databases and directory services, the Web abounds with listings of new pages. Registering with these "What's New" listings is identical to registering with a search engine. You go to the Web site and fill out a form.*

We would like to recommend to you four locations that keep active lists of new Web sites. Getting onto one or all of these sites is a great way to get noticed. Here are the four best lists of new Web sites:

The World Wide Web Virtual Library (http://wwww.w3.org/ hypertext/DataSources/bySubject/Overview.html) is kept at the University of Geneva/CERN site in Geneva, Switzerland.

The Global Online Directory (http://www.cityscape.co.uk/ gold/indexdir.html) keeps a list of new locations for 90 days.

NCSA Mosaic's What's New Page, as shown in Figure 6.10 (http://www.ncsa.uiuc.edu/SDG/Software/Mosaic/Docs/ whats-new.html), is probably the best known of all the new listing sites. It is located at the University of Illinois' super-computing center.

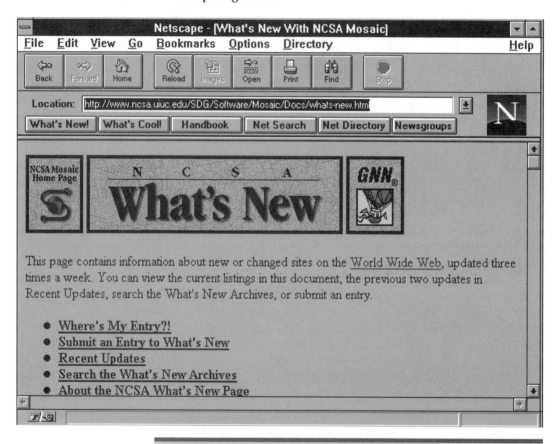

Figure 6.10 The NCSA What's New page.

The Global Network Navigator (GNN) home page (http://gnn.com/gnn/GNNhome.html) is also well known. It is maintained by O'Reilly and Associates, a technical book and software publisher. GNN appears in Figure 6.11.

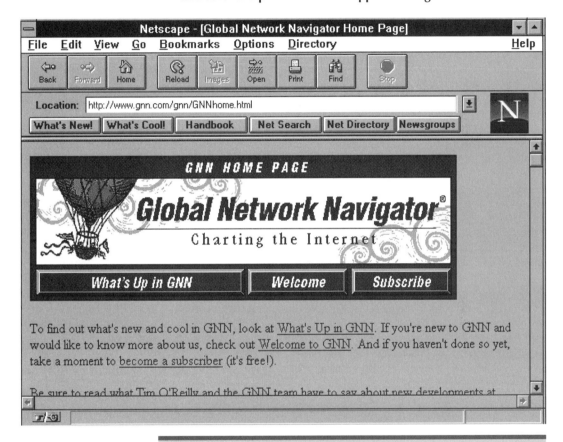

Figure 6.11 The GNN home page.

From these pages you will also find links to other "What's New" pages. It's our impression that these new listings draw a lot of immediate attention. We see the best of new sites listed in InfoWorld and other specialty magazines.

Check out the compiled lists at What's New (http://home.mcom.com/escapes/whats_new.html), kept at the Netscape server.

Also, for an archive of lists going way, way, way back (1994 and 1993), strap on your way-back machine and check out the archives at The What's New Archives (http://www.ncsa.uiuc.edu/SDG/Software/Mosaic/Docs/archives).

Announcing your site to appropriate USENET lists also can generate interest. If you have a Web site that specializes in a particular area, then:

- **Post announcements in USENET newsgroups:** *Posting to USENET groups is an effective way to promote your site, but it can be tricky for two reasons. Depending on your Internet provider, you may only have access to a limited number of newsgroups. You must also be extremely careful about where you post your announcements and how you phrase them, especially if you run a business page, because the Internet community resents any sort of blatant advertising and self promotion.*

TIP

Write your USENET announcements the same way you would write a press release. Keep your information concise and to the point, and make it relevant to the community to whom you're announcing it.

The information you offer must be relevant to the topics discussed in a particular newsgroup, and useful to its users. In other words, a newsgroup focused on sports would probably love to know about your Obscure Baseball Trivia home page, but they might not want to hear about your company's new inflatable sneaker product line. To get a feel for what is or isn't appropriate, look before you leap, and peruse the postings for a few days before making your announcement. You should also be aware of a newsgroup's rules. Some groups require that your announcement be OK'd by an administrator before you can post it.

CAUTION

Don't get flamed! Posting useless or inappropriate announcements is called "spamming"—and avoid anything that even remotely sounds like an advertisement, since that truly angers people in the Internet community. And when they get angry, they "flame" you with barrages of hostile e-mail— sometimes enough to crash your Web server.

Here are some additional tricks to try:

- **_Link up with other Web sites:_** _Get friends with home pages to add links to your Web site in exchange for your creating a link to theirs, and forge new relationships. Search the Web for addresses on similar topics, check out the sites, then e-mail the Webmasters, explain what your page does (don't forget to give them your URL), and work out an arrangement with them._

- **_Send announcements via e-mail:_** _Send announcements to everyone on your e-mail list, and ask that your friends forward your news to everyone on their mailing list. And don't forget to add your URL in your e-mail Signature line._

- **_Good old-fashioned schmoozing:_** _Just because someone's not wired yet doesn't mean they won't be. Send out press releases to local newspapers, put up posters, hand out fliers, and talk to people about it the same way as you would if you were promoting a non-Cyberspace endeavor._

The last one on our list is Elisabeth and Barrie's least favorite means of generating interest. Here real dollars change hands instead of Cyberbucks.

Now that we've done all of our post-production follow-up, we can move on to Chapter 7, "Coffee and Dessert: Learning More about the Web," which tells you how to become a true Webmaster.

○ SUMMARY

In this chapter, we learned about what to do with our Web pages once we're finished creating them. We addressed troubleshooting issues, discussed some common Web page troubles and what to do about them, talked about finding a Web server and what the Internet giants are doing, and concluded with how to let other people know you're out there.

chapter

7

THIS CHAPTER WILL COVER THE FOLLOWING:

- MORE ABOUT HOW TO BECOME A WEB PAGE EXPERT

- HTML CONVERSION PROGRAMS AND SOFTWARE CREATION TOOLS

- AN INTRODUCTION TO GATEWAY SCRIPTS

- SOME THOUGHTS ABOUT THE FUTURE OF THE WEB

COFFEE AND DESSERT: LEARNING MORE ABOUT THE WEB

By now, you can create some fairly sophisticated Web pages. But perhaps you would like to take it further and become a true Webmaster. To do this, you will want to start exploring the Web for information that will help you learn more about how the Web works. Fortunately, the Web offers a wealth of resources.

○ HOW TO BECOME A WEB PAGE EXPERT

Becoming a Web expert requires time, a desire to learn, and the willingness to become somewhat of a techno-weenie. Generating home pages is creative and fun; even the nontechnical among us can offer up an attractive, intriguing home page. However, fully utilizing the Web's powerful capabilities takes some technical know-how. Don't let that discourage you; you don't need a Master's Degree in computer science to weave the Web.

To be a true Webmaster, you may want to do some of the following:

- **Set up a Virtual Domain:** *Most Internet service providers now offer a virtual domain on their servers. That includes mail access, serious amounts of disk space, even CGI scripts for a fraction of the cost you would pay for your own installation. This is the most cost-effective solution.*

- **Set up a Web server:** *The next step up the cost ladder is setting up your own server. Having your own server increases your simultaneous connections to users, and becomes more cost-effective as activity on your domain increases. You can connect your Web server to an Internet service provider.*

- **Get high-speed leased lines:** *When you have your own server and a very active site, you will probably want to take the next step up and get a high-speed special connection from the telephone company. Then your Web server can handle large quantities of data. You will need a successful site before you want to assume this cost.*

To set up a server, you need to get a computer. That used to mean purchasing an extremely expensive UNIX workstation like a Sun workstation. Over time the price of workstations has diminished to the point that a Sun computer doesn't cost a whole lot more than a well-equipped top model Pentium computer. Still, a UNIX workstation requires that you work with the UNIX operating system, which might not be to your liking.

Using the right software, which is now readily available, you can turn an ordinary Windows or Macintosh machine into your own Web server. You don't need a really fast machine, a 80486 DX2/66, a Pentium 75 computer, or a fast 68030 Macintosh is adequate. A good system does require significant amounts of installed RAM, and the communication interface has to be first rate.

Although you can buy commercial software to set up a Web server, you can also download decent software in the public domain to do the task. Windows NT is the preferred solution on IBM PC-compatible computers, and now Apple even offers a prepackaged Macintosh with software as a Web server if you want a turnkey operation. There are several books on the subject, but two you might want to check out are *Build a Web Site* by Net.Genesis and Devra Hall, 1995, Prima Publishing, Rocklin, CA; and *Running A Perfect Web Site* by David Chandler, 1995, Que Books, Indianapolis, IN.

■ ***Common Gateway Interface (CGI) scripts:*** *Also known as Gateway scripts, CGI offers powerful tools for generating interaction between users, browsers, and Web servers. With CGI, you can index your Web pages for easy reference, create image maps where people can click on different parts of a graphic to go places, track how many people visit your page, and more.*

■ ***UNIX:*** *Most of the servers on the Internet use UNIX, and it will remain the standard for some time to come. UNIX is a powerful, but not particularly user-friendly,* *operating system. While you don't need to become a UNIX programmer—especially since there are good Windows and Macintosh solutions either available or just around the corner—some of the best and lowest-cost solutions for Web software are still to be found in the UNIX world.*

You may want to purchase some more advanced HTML books (see Chapter 1 for a list of alternative texts), take a few courses, and search for resources on the Web.

○ RESOURCES FOR LEARNING MORE

The people who launched the Web are far from snobbish—in fact, they seem to enjoy sharing their knowledge so everyone can join their global network. The Web offers many resources for learning more about HTML, setting up file servers, using CGI scripts, and obtaining the software you need to do so. Although the Web abounds with sites offering an eclectic array of information, we have selected a choice few.

To become a Webmaster, go to:

■ *Web 66 (http://web66.coled.umn.edu): If you're just getting your feet wet, this is a good place to start. The Web 66 site, as shown in Figure 7.1, was set up to help schools and educational programs create home pages. Here, you can find out about everything from writing HTML to setting up a server to finding clip art for using on your page.*

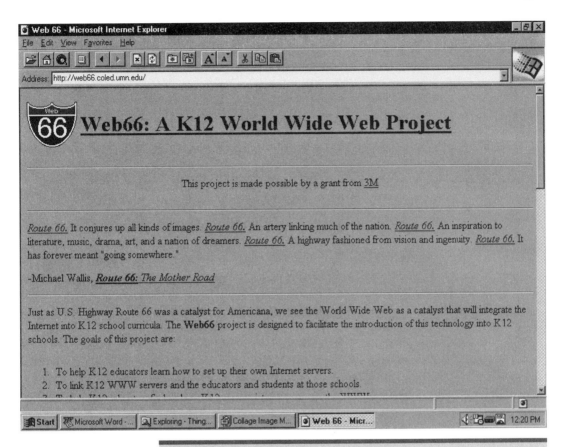

Figure 7.1 Web 66 is a good place to start on the road to becoming a Webmaster.

■ **W3C** *(http://www.w3.org): When you have enough technical knowledge to delve a little deeper, go to W3C. This is the World Wide Web Consortium site, so of course you'll find many Web resources. You can find HTML-related software, documentation on HTML and CGI scripts, a history of the Web, related sites, and more. The W3C site is shown in Figure 7.2.*

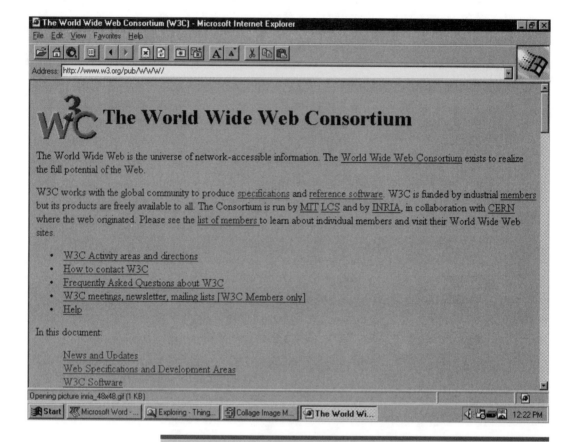

Figure 7.2   The World Wide Web Consortium is loaded with Web resources for the budding Webmeister.

■ *NCSA (http://www.ncsa.uiuc.edu): The creators of Mosaic at the University of Illinois Supercomputing Center also have impressive offerings for the would-be Webmaster as shown in Figure 7.3. They're a little hipper than the W3C and can also point you towards other places to go for information.*

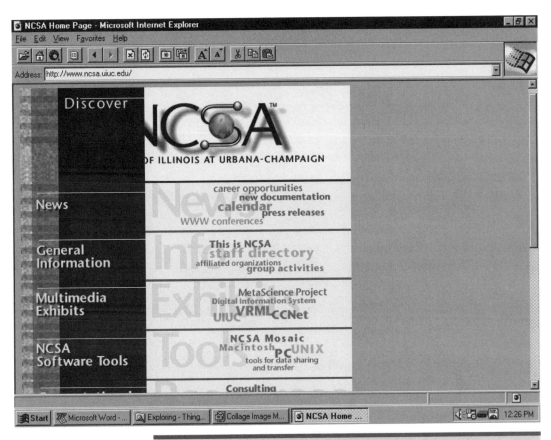

Figure 7.3 NCSA has many useful software tools and information for establishing a Web site.

■ *The Web Developer's Virtual Library* (http://www.stars. com), shown in Figure 7.4, is a treasure trove of information for anyone creating and supporting a Web site. It is extensively cross-linked to other resources throughout the Internet.

301

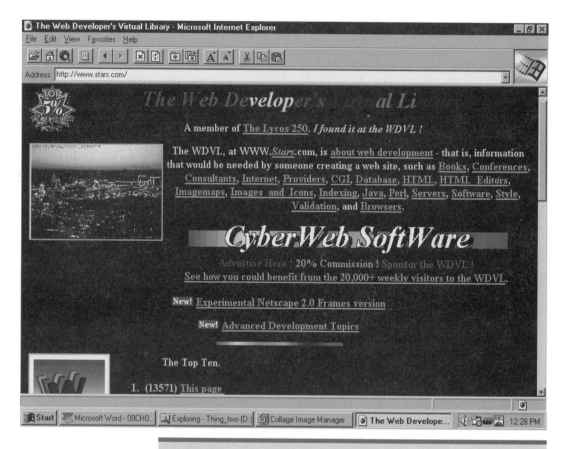

Figure 7.4   The Web Developer's Virtual Library.

We think that these are four of the very best sites on the Web, and that you should visit them all just to get a look at what's there. Make sure you bookmark them in your browser, or add them to your list of favorite places. Once you start mastering the Web, there'll be no limit to what you can do with it.

○ HTML CONVERSION AND EDITING PROGRAMS

If you become a Web expert, chances are it will be the result of creating lots of home pages; and if you do this a lot, entering each markup tag by hand will grow very tiresome. Face it, checking each tag to see that it is opened and closed in pairs is a drag. Fortunately, there are a wide array of HTML conversion and editing programs which can make tedious work go a little faster. Some are freeware, some are shareware, and there are some good commercial offerings. Also, the ability to read and write to the HTML format is being built into or added to popular word processors.

Some of these programs are stand-alone applications. They let you enter text, then add the markup tags by highlighting letters with your mouse and selecting a markup from a list of tags. This process is similar to how you would format text in a regular word processor. This means you don't have to spend time adding both the beginning and closing tags. You can also open plain-text documents that you have already created and mark them up. Other programs add markup tags to existing text within other applications.

Windows users can choose from the following:

- ***HTML Editor* and *HTML Writer*** *are shareware stand-alone editors that have toolbars, provide lists of markup tags, let you cut and paste text, help you create links, and save files as templates. HTMLed can even be configured to launch your browser so you can test the page. You can* find HTML Editor at ftp://pringle.mta.ca/pub/HTMLed and HTML Writer at http://lal.cs.byu.edu/people/nosack/.

■ **Web Wizard:** *This freeware offers a graphical interface and lets you enter text into dialog boxes following prompts, as shown in Figure 7.5. This is great for beginners, but allows no flexibility for the more advanced HTML generator. Download it at http://www.halcyon.com/artamedia/webwizard/.*

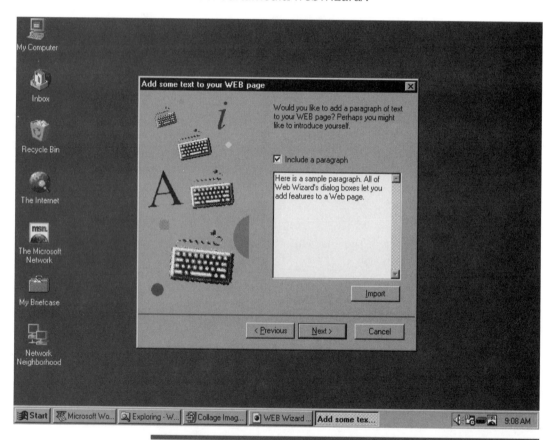

Figure 7.5 Entering text in Web Wizard.

- **HoTMetaL:** *This stand-alone program comes in freeware and commercial (HotMetaL Pro, $195) versions by Soft-Quad ((416)239-4801 or hotmetal@sq.com). Both versions guide you through the Web creation process, and the commercial version even includes a spell checker and a utility that lets you create HTML tables. However, you need to give HoTMetaL 6 MB RAM to run. A Macintosh version of this product exists, but the Windows version is more advanced at the moment. Obtain these products at http://www.sq.com.*

- **MS Word Internet Assistant:** *You can turn your ordinary Microsoft Word document into an HTML document by using this add-on application. Markup tags are added according to text styles in the style sheet. This is a freeware application for those with Microsoft Word version 6.0 or higher. Grab it at http://www.microsoft.com/msoffice/ freestuf/msword/download/ia/default.htm.*

- **AmiPro Tool Kit (Amiweb14.exe) and WordPerfect to HTML (WPTOHTML.EXE):** *These freeware packages enable you to author HTML documents with Ami Pro or WordPerfect, and they work along the same lines as the MS Word Internet Assistant. WordPerfect to HTML can be found at http://www.lib.ox.ac.uk/~hunter/. The AmiPro Tool Kit can be had for the price of a download at http:// www.cs.nott.ac.uk/~sbx/amiweb.html.*

Macintosh users should check out a linked site on HTML software at http://www.macuser.ziff.com/~ma-cuser/mu_1095/pub1.html. Also, noncommercial Macintosh software can be had at ftp://ftp.tidbits.com/pub/ tidbits/tisk/html/. Macintosh users can choose from the following software offerings:

- **Arachnid:** *Arachnid is a freeware stand-alone application similar to Web Wizard. It makes creating home pages easy and offers a pleasing interface. However, it offers* *only limited capabilities. You can get Arachnid on the Web at http://sec-loc.uiowa.edu/about/projects/arachnid-page.html.*

■ ***HoTMetaL:*** *You can also get the HoTMetaL freeware and commercial versions for your Macintosh. Most graphical HTML applications look more like HoTMetaL, as shown in Figure 7.6, than Web Wizard. You can get HoTMetaL at http://www.sq.com. There is a freeware version of the product, and a commercial version called HoTMetaL Pro 2.0.*

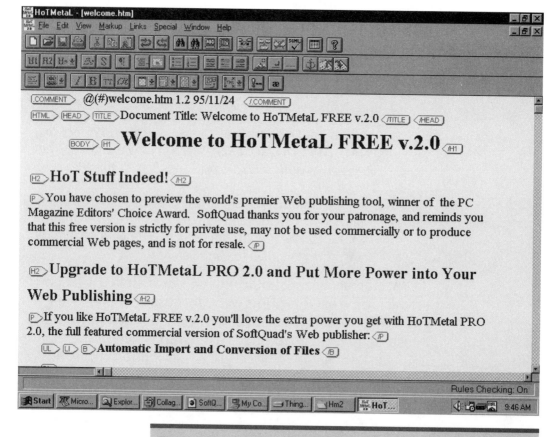

Figure 7.6 Creating HTML documents in HoTMetaL.

- **BBEdit:** *This has been a popular tool for a while and will continue to be popular because it is easy to use. It is available for $119 from Bare Bones Software ((508)651-3561 or bbsw@netcom.com). You can also get the this freeware Macintosh editor from ftp://world.std.com/pub/bbedit or at ftp://ftp.uwtc.washington.edu/pub/Mac/Text/.*

    For Web page creation, you'll certainly want to get the HTML Extensions for BBEdit. They were developed by The Web Project at the Universitat Jaume I in Spain. Download the Extensions from http://www.uji.es/bbedit-html-extensions.html. Another set of HTML tools for BBEdit are BBEdit Tools, which you can download at http://ctip-sych.york.ac.uk/WWW/BBEditTools.html.

- **RTF.TO.HTML:** *If you save your word processing document in a Text Interchange (.RTF) file format, the rtftohtml filter will take the tags set from when you added formatting attributes to the text, and change them to hypertext markup tags. You can get it at ftp://ftp.cray.com/src/WWWstuff/RTF/rtftohtml_overview.html.*

- **WebWeaver:** *HTML WebWeaver 2.5.3 is a shareware text editor that lets you write HTML and add markups, and includes a menu of tags. Although it can run slow, it is easy and flexible to use, and it lets you see how your text will look on the Web page, as shown in Figure 7.7. The World Wide Web Weaver for Macintosh is a design tool. Download both Web Weavers at http://www.north-net.org/best/.*

307

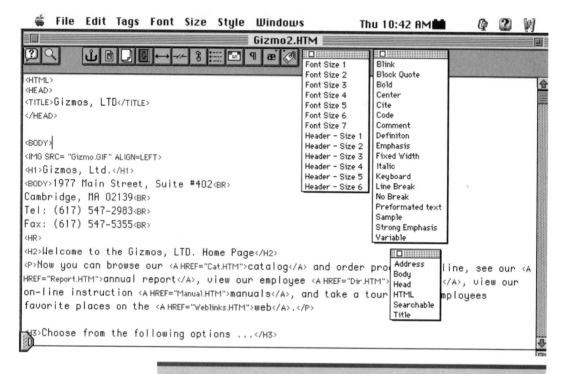

Figure 7.7 HTML written in Web Weaver.

○ PLUG-INS

In addition to these shareware and freeware applications, you'll find that many text-intensive commercial page layout programs like Aldus PageMaker and QuarkXPress have special "plug-ins" to format text into HTML in their text editor. Plug-ins work similarly to the HTML assistants which add tags within a separate application. More and more commercial software providers will make plug-ins available as more and more people put publications on the Web. Here are some filters on the Macintosh you might want to try out:

> **For PageMaker: Dave or WebSucker. You should note that PageMaker 6.0 saves directly to HTML format.**
>
> **For QuarkXPress: BeyondPress ($595) from Astrobyte ((303) 534-6344), Quark To HTML, or HTML Xport.**
>
> **For Claris software: HTML+ works with any program that has a Claris XTND translator, such as WordPerfect or Claris-Works.**

○ COMMON GATEWAY INTERFACE SCRIPTS

As we explained earlier in this chapter, Common Gateway Interface (CGI) scripts are simple but powerful programs that enable your browser to communicate with Web Servers. You can use CGI to generate extensive searchable indexes, create image maps on your page that give visitors visible links, and more.

Before you get intimidated by all of this and say, "But I'm not a programmer …"—surprise! You already know how CGI scripts work because we created a couple of forms back in Chapter 5, "Some Sample Meals." Forms are one of the most common uses for CGI scripts. The search engines we talked about back in Chapter 1, "What's Cooking on the Web?" also use CGI scripts to search indexes and respond to your search queries.

When someone fills out your form and you receive the information by e-mail, the following is happening:

- *The form-related tags tell your browser to search for the URL of the appropriate CGI script on your Web server (if your server does not provide the scripts, you can get them from the W3C home page mentioned earlier in this chapter).*

- *The CGI script responds to your browser's query by processing the appropriate information, as set in the markup tags you created—in this case, by sending the form along to your electronic mail box.*

309

The browser then displays the CGI script's response; in this case, it would notify your visitor that the form has been sent.

In case this process seems confusing, Figure 7.8 may help illustrate it more clearly for you.

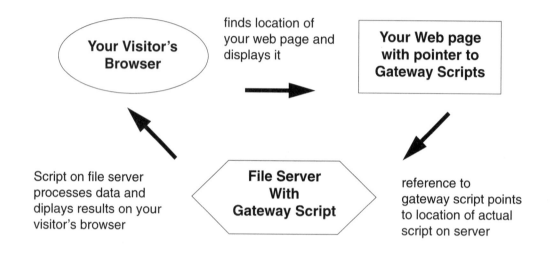

Figure 7.8   How Gateway scripts fit in the picture.

○ CREATING CLICKABLE IMAGE MAPS

Here's another thing we can try. Alas, we can't guarantee that it will work unless your server offers scripts for image mapping. Clickable image maps are similar to graphical links, only you have one graphic and different places to click on within this single graphic. As you move your cursor about the regions of an image map, the link changes. Therefore, you can pack a lot of links into a small and more easily recognizable graphic than you could do with text. Image maps are the cat's meow.

To create an image map, you need the following:

■ **An image:** *Like the one you'll find in the Chapter 7.DIR/ Gizmo.DIR/icons.GIF., shown in Figure 7.9. Yep, it's the same button bar we used for the Gizmos Ltd. home page back in Chapter 5, "Some Sample Meals," only it's all one graphic instead of separate buttons.*

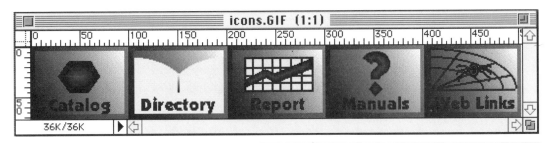

Figure 7.9   With the ruler in Photoshop you can measure the coordinates of a graphic like the button bar to create clickable areas.

■ **A "map" file:** *Now here's the hard part. You will have to open the graphic in an application so you can measure it by pixels, and set the coordinates so the CGI script knows what part of the image links to where.*

■ **An anchor tag that defines the links:** *You also have to tell your Web server that this image is a map.*

What makes things even more difficult is that there are two types of servers: CERN HTTPD and NCSA HTTPD. And image maps work slightly differently on each one.

To tell your browser that the image is a map, you would have do the following:

- *Define the map in the image source tag by entering <IMG SRC="Icons.GIF"> in place of all the current image tags for the individual buttons.*

- *Change all of the <A HREF="...">...</A> tags to link to a single map file, <A HREF="Gizmo.MAP">.*

- *Define the coordinates of each section of the image and link it to the appropriate URL.*

- *Define the shape and size of the hot spot: a circle, oval, rectangle, polygon, or point.*

To get a mapping program and to find out more, check out the NCSA and CERN (W3C) sites. Some programs that get mentions are Mapedit for Windows and WebMap for the Macintosh.

Also be sure to check out the MapMaker home page at http://www.tns.lcs.mit.edu/cgi-bin/mapmaker. This little beauty might just do the trick for you when you want to create an image map. The MapMaker site, shown in Figure 7.10, runs you through the process of creating an image map. Give that site a try if you are trying to create an image map; it accesses the URL you give it and lets you define the vertices of your hot spots. At the moment, MapMaker will not work with Netscape or Mosaic on the Macintosh.

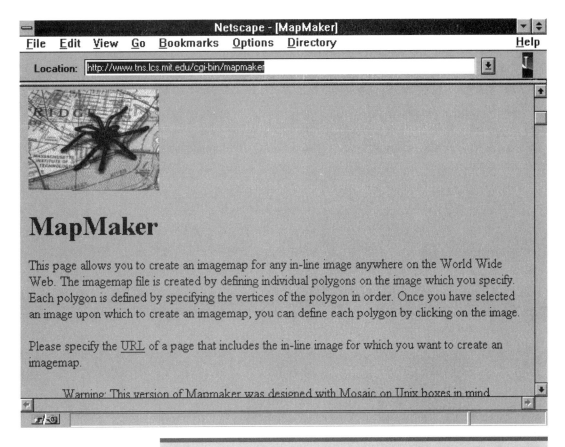

Figure 7.10 The MapMaker home page automates image map making—cool! (courtesy TNS Group and David Bacher)

However, be aware that the generation of image maps involves considerable activity. We expect to see some good software appear that will make the creation of image maps much easier and more elegant than it is at the moment, which is one reason that we are not covering the rather kludgy and fragmented way these special links are created.

It's worth your trouble to keep abreast of activities in this area, because image maps are really elegant. Just to show you what's possible, consider the image map for the Star Trek

Voyager's home page (http://voyager.paramount.com/cgi-bin/display?VoyagerMenu.html) shown in Figure 7.11. This is a single graphic (you can tell because it has the black border), and each button is part of an image map. As you move the cursor over each button, the location of the URL for the button appears in the lower bar of the Netscape browser.

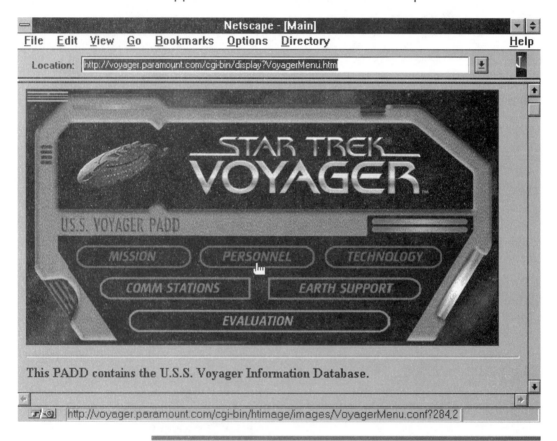

Figure 7.11 The Star Trek Voyager home page.

Here are some other sites you can visit to get graphic resources:

The Graphics Archive site (http://www.best.com/~bryanw).

For bullets, buttons, and bows: (http://coney.gsfc.nasa.gov/www/sswg/gizmos.html).

The Kansas State University interactive graphics generator at http://www.eece.ksu.edu/IGR/intro.html lets you roll your own bullets and icons.

The University of Minnesota Gallery of Interactive Online Geometry at http://www.geom.umn.edu/apps/gallery.html lets you create complex graphics in either GIF or PostScript format. Check this one out late at night with the house lights off. You may not use the images in your image maps, but you'll have a good time. Figure 7.12 shows you the Gallery's Web page.

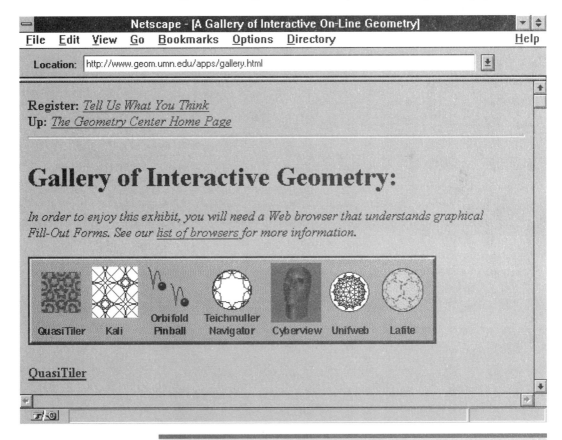

Figure 7.12 The University of Minnesota Gallery of Interactive Online Geometry. (Copyright by The Geometry Center, University of Minnesota.)

○ WHAT NEXT?

Hypertext Markup Language and the World Wide Web change so rapidly it's difficult to keep up—which is part of what makes the Web such an exciting place to visit. Faster computers, speedier telephone lines and modems, and prolific computer book writers, along with the constant global brainstorming session the Web encourages, point towards a future of more elaborate and interesting Web page content.

Here's some samples of what's cooking on the Web tomorrow:

- **HTML Plus:** *In the new version of Hypertext Markup Language, you will see more formatting capabilities and easier-to-enter markup tags—however, some of the markups you're using now may not be entered the same way, so keep a look out!*

- **Paperless publishing:** *The Web now lets us download .PDF files for later viewing, but something's in the works ....*
  A collaborative project between the Adobe Acrobat and Netscape people points towards publishing hyperlinked documents that look as good as printed ones on the Web. With PostScript as the underlying language, the quality of Web graphics would take a quantum leap; and the Adobe Portable Document Format (PDF) would provide a means to print out at high quality on any computer, whether you have the software that created the document or not.

And just think of the ramifications of being able to "print" a gorgeous, full-color magazine with photos and fancy display fonts—without having to spend money on paper! We have publishers who plan to send us Acrobat PDF files to use to edit the books we write.

- **VRML (Virtual Reality Markup Language):** *Many of us don't even know what "virtual reality" is, and people are already collaborating on a markup language for it! (Barrie* *knows, he thinks it's where he gets to put on a cool head-set and play great computer games; Elisabeth knows and thinks it's where she gets loving fan mail from the many Web robots that read her on-line magazine.)*

Keep on the lookout for three-dimensional images in motion while browsing the Web. To find out more about what's going on in this area, check out the VRML Repository home page at http://www.sdsc.edu/vrml, as shown in Figure 7.13.

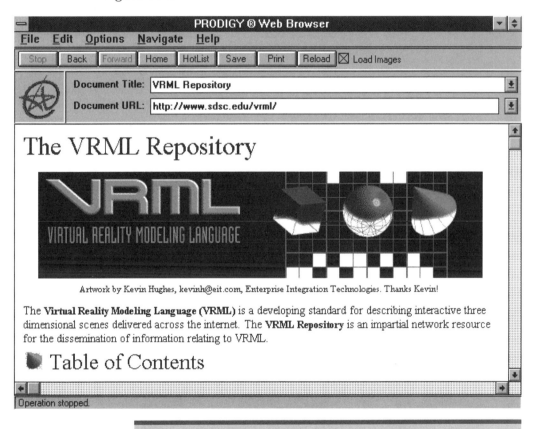

Figure 7.13 The VMRL Repository home page.

- **Java**: *Things happen so quickly on the Web that it can be hard to keep up. Over the past few months Sun's Java programming language has become a de facto standard for creating applets that enhance Internet browsers. This language is portable, platform-neutral, object-oriented, multithreaded, yatta, yatta, yatta ... all of the buzzwords that make professional programmers smile.*

Netscape is apparently standardizing on Java, which makes Java both happening and important. Netscape 2.0 will come with a Java plug-in. JavaScript will replace Netscape's LiveScript as a way of letting developers create Java applets by scripting instead of programming. Spyglass also plans to have Java support for its Enhanced Mosaic browser in early 1996.

Java not only adds functions to browsers, but supplies support for streaming automation and new client tools. Since Java is run in a Virtual Machine program, applets are small (5 to 10 KB) and highly portable (UNIX, Windows 95, and Macintosh). In a sense, the Virtual Machine program is almost like an operating system unto itself.

You can learn more about Java, including downloading the HotJava browser and Developer's kit from http://java.sun.com. Figure 7.14 shows you the Java home page. We believe that many important commercial systems on the Internet (like electronic banking) will be and are being programmed in Java.

- **And more:** *Maybe the Web will someday enable us to see television shows from around the world and people's home movies, and to have actual face-to-face chats with our long-distance friends; the possibilities are endless.*

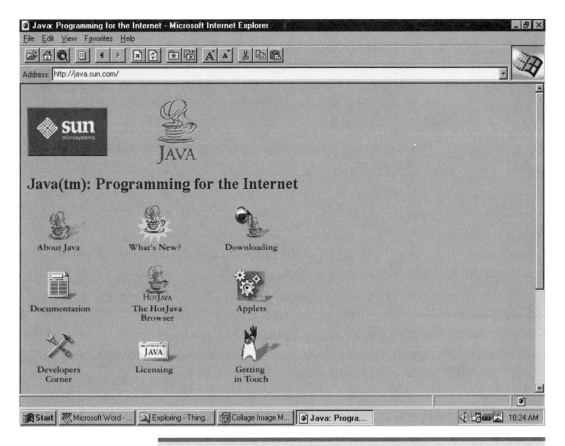

Figure 7.14 The Java home page. (Copyright ©1996, Sun Microsystems, Inc. used with permission.)

○ SUMMARY

Now that we've introduced you to the wondrous world of Web publishing, you're ready to strike out on your own. The appendix has a glossary in case you get stuck on a particular term, a table of HTML tags for convenient quick reference, and a complete list of what you'll find on the CD-ROM so you can start creating. Happy Web weaving!

Appendix A
Glossary of Terms

Attribute: A named characteristic within an HTML markup tag.

Bookmark: An option in your browser that lets you save the URLs of Web sites you would like to visit again to a list.

Browser: An application that lets you navigate the World Wide Web and view home pages.

Case-sensitive: When a program, interface, operating system or server can tell the difference between upper and lower case letters in file names.

Cello: A graphical Windows browser available from the Cornell Law School Web site.

Common Gateway Interface (CGI): The specification for how browsers interact with Web servers, and how information is input and transferred.

Cross-platform: Refers to files, protocols, and applications that can be viewed, used, or otherwise interacted with regardless of what type of computer someone is using.

Directory Service: A directory service is a database of listings on the Internet, organized by category. Yahoo is the prime example of a directory service. See also "Search engines" for a related topic.

Document: A single HTML file within a directory.

DOS naming convention: All files created on DOS or MS-DOS (Windows) platforms must have a file name of eight characters or less, followed by a three-character suffix, or file extension, such as FILENAME.HTM.

Downloading: The act of transferring files by modem from a server to your computer.

Electronic publication: Any literature that is produced and distributed on-line.

Element: A part of an HTML script or markup tag.

E-'zine: Slang for a magazine that is produced electronically and distributed on-line.

External links: Links that anchor either to other documents in your directory or to other Web sites.

File extension: Refers to the three-character suffix appended to files created on DOS or Windows platforms.

Flame: To send someone a hostile message.

Forms: Refers to forms that are generated on the World Wide Web to be filled in and sent to you when people visit your site.

FTP (File Transfer Protocol): A means of transferring files on-line. FTP is quick and efficient, but many FTP programs are hard to use because they don't have a graphical interface or support the ability to read documents or view files on-line.

.GIF (Graphic Interchange Format): The most commonly used format for producing and viewing graphics on the Web. .GIF is a proprietary compression format owned by CompuServe.

Graphical interface: An operating system, application, or protocol that supports display graphics. In the "graphical user interface" or GUI (pronounced "gooey") the system uses a noun-verb interaction. You pick an object and specify an action; then the system responds. Many people refer to this as a "point and click" environment, although keyboard entry is also supported. Both the Macintosh and Windows operating systems are examples of GUIs.

Helper applications: External programs necessary for viewing or launching some types of content on the Web, such as multimedia files.

Home page: Synonymous with Web page. Refers to an HTML document or set of HTML documents produced by a single organization or individual.

HTTP (Hypertext Transfer Protocol): A means of transferring hypertext files formatted as HTML documents.

Hypertext link: An item of text or a graphic on a Web page that can be clicked on to jump to another location. Locations can be another part of an HTML document, another HTML document, another directory, or even a location on a different Web server.

Hypertext Markup Language (HTML): A standard language for creating markup tags that tell browsers and web servers how to display and process information.

Image map: A single image with multiple graphical links that correspond with points on the image.

Internal links: Hypertext links within a single HTML document.

Internet: A global network of servers that are tied together by networking protocols. The Internet is a network of networks that you can access.

Internet Provider: A commercial, government, academic, or other organization that offers users access to the Internet.

.JPEG/.JPG (Joint Photography Experts Group): A graphic format commonly used on Web pages because it enables generation of compressed, high-resolution images and is viewable across platforms.

Jump maps: A nonlinear outline or storyboard sketched out by Webmasters to determine how they will organize complex documents.

kbps (kilobits per second): A measurement for the speed at which data is transferred. For example, a relatively fast modem transfers information at a speed of 14.4 kbps or 28.8 kbps.

To browse the Web, you should have either a 14.4 or 28.8 kbps-capable modem.

Links: Short for hypertext links.

Lynx: A text-only Web browser developed at the University of Kansas.

MacWeb: A graphical browser created by Microelectronics and Computing Corporation (MCC), a trade organization based in Texas.

Map file: A document which specifies the coordinates for an image map and where the coordinates link to.

Markups: HTML tags which tell browsers how to display and process information.

Mosaic: The first Web browser, from the National Center for Supercomputing Applications (NCSA) at the University of Illinois.

MPEG/MPG (Motion Pictures Expert Group): A commonly used, cross-platform compression format for digitized video.

Navigate: Finding your way around the Web using hypertext links and search engines.

NCSA (National Center for Supercomputing Applications): A development group, based at the University of Illinois, which developed Mosaic, the first graphical Web browser.

Nettiquette: Internet etiquette, an informal structure of rules regarding how people should interact and present information on the Internet to be considered responsible members of a global on-line community.

On-line: Refers to files, communications, and interactions that are transferred electronically via the Internet or networks.

Plain text: Nonformatted text that can be read across platforms.

PPP (Point to Point Protocol): A communications protocol that allows your computer to directly connect to the Internet using your modem. You generally need either a PPP or SLIP account to access the Web, and PPP is newer and more efficient than SLIP.

Protocol: A set of universal standards for communications and data transfer.

Resource: Information, downloadable software, images, and anything else available on the Web.

Search engines: Large, searchable databases like WebCrawler and Lycos, which help you find Web sites by entering topics, company/organizational names, or URLs. A related concept: directory services, which also let you search a database of listings on the Internet, organized by category. Yahoo is a directory service.

SLIP (Serial Line Interface Protocol): A communications protocol that allows your computer to directly connect to the Internet using your modem. You generally need either a PPP or SLIP account to access the Web. SLIP is older than PPP, and lacks some of the error checking that PPP does.

Server: A computer that is capable of processing enormous amounts of data quickly, and is dedicated to handling communications and data transfer over the Internet. Most servers are UNIX platform machines, but Macintosh and Windows also offer software that makes their machines competitive.

Tag: The HTML markups enclosed in the <> brackets.

TCP/IP (Transmission Control Protocol/Internet Protocol): A set of networking protocols that determine how information is transferred from server to client, and visa versa.

Transparent .GIF (.GIF 89): .GIF images that appear to float on a Web page because they have no background.

UNIX: A highly powerful operating system capable of handling the massive amounts of data that travels through a large server. Most of the Internet still runs on UNIX.

URL (Uniform Resource Locator): Specifies the location of Internet sites, including your Web page.

Web: Short for the World Wide Web.

Web page: Synonymous with home page, refers to a single HTML document or group of HTML documents generated by single individuals or organizations.

WinWeb: A graphical browser created by Microelectronics and Computing Corporation (MCC), a trade organization based in Texas.

Appendix B
HTML Tags

Tags	Descriptions

PUT ON EVERY HOMEPAGE...

<HTML>...</HTML>	Identifies your Web page as an HTML document and closes your HTML document
<TITLE>...</TITLE>	Displays document title in browser window
<HEADER>...</HEADER>	Blocks out the header section of your document
<BODY>...</BODY>	Blocks out the body section of your document

Tags	Descriptions

TEXT FORMATTING...

 	Creates a forced line break
<P>...</P>	Automatically inserts space between paragraphs
<B>...</B>	Bolds text
<I>...</I>	Italicizes text
<U>...</U>	Underlines text (use sparingly, doesn't always work and is nonstandard)
<BLOCKQUOTE>...<BLOCKQUOTE>	Indents text

HEADERS...

<H1>...</H1>	Level one header
<H2>...</H2>	Level two header
<H3>...</H3>	Level three header
<H4>...</H4>	Level four header
<H5>...</H5>	Level five header
<H6>...</H6>	Level six header

LISTS...

<UL>...</UL>	Unordered (bulleted) list
<OL>...</OL>	Ordered (numbered) list
<LI>...</LI>	Indicates list items within unordered or ordered list tags

Tags	Descriptions
<DL>...</DL>	Definition list
<DT>	Unindented definition term within definition list
<DD>	Indented definition description tion underneath definition term and within definition list.

ANCHOR TAGS

<A HREF="DOC.HTM">...</A>	Links text or graphic to a separate HTML document within the same directory
<A HREF="../DOC.HTM">...</A>	Links text or graphic to a separate HTML document in the directory directly above the one you're in
<A HREF="DIR.DIR/DOC.HTM">...</A>	Links text or graphic to a separate HTML document in a different directory
<A HREF="http://...">...</A>	Links text or graphic to a different Web page
<A HREF="#NAME">...</A>	Links text or graphic to a different location within the same HTML document
<A NAME="...">...</A>	Defines a location within an HTML document for creating links within a document

Tags	Descriptions

IMAGES

<IMG SRC="IMAGE.GIF">	Displays a .GIF-formatted graphic file
<IMG SRC="IMAGE.JPG">	Displays a .JPG-formatted graphic file
<IMG SRC="..." ALT="NAME">	Displays a text alternative for those without graphical browsers
<IMG SRC="..." ISMAP>	Defines a graphic as an image map
<IMG SRC="Name.GIF">	Aligns image on the left side of your screen and with the baseline of the next line of text
<IMG SRC="Name.GIF" ALIGN=Left>	Aligns image to the left side of your screen. The following text will align to the right side of the image
<IMG SRC="Name.GIF" ALIGN=Right>	Aligns your image to the right side of the screen. The following text will align to the right side of the image
<IMG SRC="Name.GIF" ALIGN=Top>	Aligns the image with the top of the tallest item in the following line
<IMG SRC="Name.GIF" ALIGN=Bottom>	Aligns the image with the baseline of the following text
<IMG SRC="Name.GIF" ALIGN=Baseline>	Same as ALIGN=Bottom

Tags	Descriptions
<IMG SRC="Name.GIF" ALIGN=Middle>	Aligns the middle of the image with the baseline of the following text
<IMG SRC="Name.GIF" ALIGN=TextTop>	Aligns the image with the tallest letters of the following text
<IMG SRC="Name.GIF" ALIGN=AbsMiddle>	Aligns the middle of the image with the middle of the text in the following line

FORMS

<FORM>...</FORM>	Defines a document or section of a document as a form
<FORM METHOD="Post" Action= "mailto: email address">	Tells form how to send you the information
<p>Input field: <input name= "Input field" size="...">	Displays text next to an input field where your visitors can fill in information like their name and address. You must specify the text next to the input field, the name of the input field, and the size of the input field (measured in pixels).
<Select Name="..."> <Option>Option One <Option>Option Two <Option>Option Three <Option>Option Four </Select>	Displays pulldown menu for which you enter options

Tags	Descriptions
<INPUT TYPE="radio" NAME="Radio Button 1" VALUE= "Radio Button One"> Radio Button One	Displays radio buttons for which you enter values
<textarea name="comments" rows=8 cols= 60></textarea>	Displays an area for entering text for comments, etc.
<p><INPUT TYPE="submit" VALUE="Send">	Displays a "Send" button for submitting the form
<input type=Reset> for clearing the form	Displays a "Reset" button

NETSCAPE EXTENSIONS

Tags	Descriptions
<BODY BACKGROUND="NAME.JPG">	Displays an image which repeats to create a background
<BLINK>...</BLINK>	Displays text in a blinking box
<IMG SRC="..." HSPACE="...">	Sets horizontal space between the image and surrounding text
<IMG SRC-"..." VSPACE="..."	Sets vertical space between the image and surrounding text
<BASEFONT ="...">...</BASEFONT>	Changes the default font size
<FONT SIZE="+...">...</FONT>	Increases default font size incrementally
<FONT SIZE="-...">...</FONT>	Decreases default font size incrementally
<CENTER>...</CENTER>	Aligns text to center of page

APPENDIX C
WHAT'S ON THE
CD-ROM?

The CD-ROM contains all of the samples we've worked with throughout the book, along with an array of templates, graphics, and photographs you can use for creating your own homepage. To view the contents of the CD-ROM, you need a graphical browser like Netscape or Mosaic. Browsers and other Internet-related software are generally available through your Internet provider's Software library. You will find a more detailed description of the CD-ROM's contents in the following pages.

NOTE

You can work with the CD-ROM material even if you're not hooked up! Get a copy of Mosaic, which is freely distributable, from a friend. Although you may get error messages because Mosaic can't find your modem connection, it will let you view local files. After launching Mosaic, press either the Control+. (Windows) or Command+. (Macintosh) key combinations, and Mosaic will allow you to proceed. You can then select the Open Local option through the File menu.

You'll find several directories with freeware and shareware programs on it. These versions contain the latest versions of browsers, HTML editors, filters and converters, and other text documents that you may find interesting to view. You can learn a lot by reading and browsing the contents of this CD-ROM. To view any file with an HTML file extension, open your browser and view the file. Some links to other places on the Web should be active, although many links that rely on relative links will not operate correctly. You can always copy the links, paste them into your browser's URL address box, and go directly to them with your connection active. Text files (.TXT extension) can be viewed with a text editor, word processor, or even more conveniently using your Web browser.

○ CHAP4.DIR

- **Charactr.DIR:** *Contains the numeric and character entities required for entering accented letters and other special characters on your home page. We also added some internal links to this home page to make navigating the document easier. If you like the graphics we made for the letters, we have an entire alphabet available in the Graphics.DIR/Letters.DIR directory.*

- **Family.DIR:** *This is the sample family home page we looked at in Chapter Four. Here, we create a basic home page with text links and a "fancy" page with graphical links. In addition, the directory contains Mom, Dad, Sister, brother, and baby icons to fit your family members' respective cultural backgrounds (African-American, Asian-American, Caucasian-American, and Latin-American).*

- **Gizmo.DIR:** *This example from Chapter Four is a good model for organizing your own company home page.*

- **Poetry.DIR:** *This example, courtesy of Margaret Weigel from the Massachusetts Institute of Technology Seagrant Program, explores formatting text and using Netscape extensions for a fancier home page. Poetry.HTM offers a basic poetry page in standard HTML, and Poetry2.HTM shows what you can do with Netscape Extensions. Feel free to explore the material, but please do not distribute for any profit-related purposes.*

○ CHAP5.DIR

- **ByteIt.DIR:** *Byte It! is an example of a real electronic magazine with complex links. All photos for this section, with the exception of the multimedia section, are by Kristin Gunst. Sarah.GIF courtesy of Sarah McLaughlin, whose CD-ROM was reviewed in Byte It! Feel free to explore the material, but please do not distribute for any profit-related purposes.*

- **Chaos.DIR:** *Chaos Control is another example of a real electronic magazine with a form and downloadable multimedia files. Chaos Control and its accompanying multimedia files are created and published by Bob Gourley. Feel free to explore, but please do not distribute any of this material for profit-related purposes.*

- **Chaos9.DIR:** *Interactive multimedia magazine created by Bob Gourley (Mac only).*

- **Chaosbore.DIR:** *Interactive game centered around the Boredoms, a popular alternative rock band, created by Bob Gourley (Mac only).*

- **Gizmo2.DIR:** *Here, we add an order form to the Gizmo, LTD. home page that we started working on in Chapter 4.*

- ***Kelley.DIR:*** *We took some photos and scanned them to show you how you can set up an electronic photo album. All photographs are by Kelley Hurst. Feel free to explore the material, but please do not distribute for any profit-related purposes.*

- ***Madge.DIR:*** *This gives us a real-life example of an on-line Résumé. All material supplied by Margaret Weigel.*

- ***Resume.DIR:*** *This example shows how you can publish your résumé on the World Wide Web and link it to your home page.*

○ CHAP7.DIR

- ***Gizmo3.DIR:*** *This directory will let you play with image maps. To make this work on your Web page, you'll need an image map program. Windows users can download the latest MapEdit at http://sunsite.unc.edu/boutell/mapedit/mapedit.html. Macintosh users can dowload the latest HyperMap Edit at ftp://sumex-aim.stanford.edu/info-mac/comm/tcp/. When generating image maps, you should also know that the way in which coordinates are entered differs with NCSA and CERN servers. We wrote ours for an NCSA server.*

○ DOCS.DIR

The Docs directory contains a number of useful text and HTML documents detailing various aspects of the Web. You'll find the following in the DOC directory:

- ***Books.HTML:*** *A listing of books on the Web.*

- ***HTML*.HTML:*** *HTML specifications for level two and three HTML and a style guide.*

- ***TCPHIST.HTML:*** *A history of the Web.*

- **LISTS?.HTML:** *Maintained database containing lists of subjects about the Web.*

- **NewsGrps:** *Names of USENET Newsgroups you can join to participate in discussions on the Web.*

- **WWW*.*:** *Discussions on background, frequently asked questions (.FAQ), etc. on the Web.*

○ MUSIC.DIR

Contained in this directory are the following Curvector programs: CURVE folder with the Windows program and the Curvector program for the Macintosh.

To view the catalog, do the following:

1. *Launch the application.*

2. *When the animated CD covers appear, click with your mouse on the one you're interested in to hear a sample of the music on the CD and see a picture of the band.*

3. *Click anywhere on the screen with your mouse to return to the main part of the catalog.*

4. *To exit the catalog, hit the Escape key in Windows, or the Command-Q keystroke on the Macintosh.*

The multimedia catalogs were created by Conrad Warre.

○ PARTS.DIR

The following parts are included for your use in templates:

- **01HTML.DOC:** *Basic shell for a home page*

- **02TEXT.DOC:** *Body text, paragraph, and block-quoted text*

- **03HEAD.DOC:** *Header tags*

- **04LISTS.DOC:** *Unordered, ordered, and definition lists*

- **05FORMAT.DOC:** *Text formatting options*

- **06NETSC.DOC:** *Netscape extensions*

- **07CHAR.DOC:** *List of numeric and text entities for special characters*

- **08LINKS.DOC:** *Internal and external links*

- **09IMAGE.DOC:** *Options for placing and aligning images*

- **10FORM.DOC:** *Basic form template*

- **11PRE1.DOC:** *Preformatted chart sample*

- **12Pre2.DOC:** *Second preformatted chart sample*

○ SHAREWAR.DIR

Some of the software in these two directories are freeware. That is, they are freely distributed for your use. Other software is shareware, and their developers request a fee after a certain trial period. Shareware often comes with a built-in registration form that you can use. Registering shareware gets you free upgrades, copies with fuller feature sets, and other benefits. It also enables developers to continue to improve their products.

○ IMAGES.DIR

This directory includes a number of freeware images that you can use for non-commercial use in your Web pages. To obtain a much larger collection, check out the resources accessed from http://www.yahoo.com and go to their WWW sections. There is a section on graphics there that leads you to collections of icons, backgrounds, bars, buttons, and so on that you can view and download individually. Note that many of these images are only available for non-commercial use.

○ MAC.DIR

- **2.unzip1.10:** *Extracts files compressed in WinZip (a Windows utility).*

- **Jpeg.view3.1:** *Enables you to view JPEG/JPG files. You should also know that this is "Postcard-ware," meaning that if you like the software, developer Aaron Giles wants you to send him a postcard.*

- **MapServe:** *A utility for creating image maps for an NCSA Web server.*

- **NIH Image:** *A freeware image editing program of high quality.*

- **NCSA Mosaic(Mac) 2.0.1:** *Developed by the National Center for Supercomputing Applications (NCSA), Mosaic was the first graphical browser.*

- **rtf.to.html.2.7.3:** *Converts Rich Text Formatted (RTF) wordprocessing documents to HTML.*

- **Sparkle2.1.4:** *Plays back .MPEG movies and saves them to QuickTime format. Created by Simen Lange.*

○ PC.DIR

- **AMI_WEB:** *The AmiPro Toolkit (AMIWEB.EXE) for authoring HTML documents. Includes style sheets, macros, icons and HTML converter.*

- **CELLO:** *A text-mainly Web browser for Windows.*

- **GOLDWAVE:** *Plays and converts Sun/NEXT, AU, WAV, Mac SND, AIFF, AmigaIFF, Matlab MAT and VOC files.*

- **GRAPHWRKS:** *The shareware program Graphics Workshop, a very capable image editor and file conversion program.*

- **HoTMetaL:** *HoTMetaL Pro, an HTML editor.*

- **INTPUBL:** *The Internet Publisher from Novell is an add-on for creating HTML pages in WordPerfect 6.1 for Windows.*

- **LView:** *A popular Windows graphics viewer and utility. NCSA's recommendation for GIF and JPEG images with Mosaic. This program also works with TIF, PCX, and others.*

- **LYNX:** *The DOS version of the WWW client made popular in the UNIX world.*

- **MOSAIC:** *Contains mosaic.2.1.1, developed by the National Center for Supercomputing Applications (NCSA), Mosaic was the first graphical browser.*

- **PAINTSHP:** *Paint Shop Pro is a paint program and image editing software.*

- **PM2HTML:** *This addition to Aldus PageMaker 5.0 lets you convert PageMaker pages to HTML pages.*

- **RTF2HML:** *This program converts files in the Microsoft Rich Text Format to HTML format. The two programs in this directory are RTF2HTM, the DOS version; and WRTF2HTM, the Windows version.*

- **VIDWIN:** *A MPEG video player for playing Microsoft Video for Windows Runtime 1.1. This player is required for viewing AVI Video files in Windows.*

- **WINWEB:** *An ideal HTML editor for beginners generating simple home pages.*

○ GRAPHICS.DIR

- **Animals.DIR:** *An assortment of animals which you can view by opening up 00Animal.HTM with your browser application.*

- **Backgr.DIR:** *Backgrounds you can view with Netscape version 1.1 or higher. To view the backgrounds, open up the HTML files in your browser application.*

- **Bullets.DIR:** *Bullets you can use for lists instead of list tags. To view them, open up 00Bullets.HTM in your browser application.*

- **Holiday.DIR:** *Festive images you can use on your home page. To view these images, open up the 00Holid.HTM file from your browser application.*

- **Icons.DIR:** *A variety of symbols you can use to add interest to your home pages. To view these images, open up the 00Icons.HTM file from your browser application.*

- **Kelley.DIR:** *Some more of Kelley's photos. Due to the large size of these images, we have not created an HTML file for displaying them.*

- **Letters.DIR:** *Some fancy uppercase letters you can use for graphics or section headings, along with matching horizontal rules. To view these images, open up 00Letters.HTM from your browser application.*

- **Lines.DIR:** *Lines you can use instead of <HR> Horizontal Rule tags. To view these images, open 00Lines.HTM from your browser application.*

○ TEMPLATE.DIR

Here are some of the templates we developed in this book:

- **Basic.DIR:** *Basic HTML template with external link to another HTML script.*

- **Biz.DIR:** *Templates for home businesses, including accounting/bookkeeping, graphic design, paralegal, computer consulting, marketing/promotions, cleaning services, babysitting, daycare, landscaping, catering, crafts, and interior decorating.*

- **Events.DIR:** *Templates for events listings, including theater; film; classical, jazz and rock music; church; synagogue; library; art and school.*

- **Fun.DIR:** *Templates for family recipes, gardening tips, advice column, and tips and hints.*

- **Nonprof.DIR:** *Templates for medical/health organization, animal shelter, environmental, consumer advocacy, political campaign (Democrat), political campaign (Republican), community action, and help line.*

- **Pubs.DIR:** *Templates for office newsletter, casual newsletter, wild -n- funky newsletter, and literary journal.*

- **Resume.DIR:** *Templates for résumés with different looks.*

INDEX

A

"&#...;" character strings, 145
"&...;" character strings, 145
<A>...</A> anchor tags, 123
Accented characters, 147
Acrobat, 18, 78, 316
Acrobat Reader, 18, 77–78
ACTION clause, 197
Adobe Photoshop, 64, 65
Adobe Systems site, 18
<A HREF="DIR.DIR/DOC.HTM">...</A>, 329
<A HREF="DOC.HTM">...</A>, 329
<A HREF="../DOC.HTM">...</A>, 329
<A HREF="http://...">...</A>, 329
<A HREF="MAIL TO:...></A>" clause, 190–91
<A HREF="#NAME:>...</A>, 329
<A HREF="address or location">...</A> tags, 68–70, 127, 151
<A HREF="http:"//...Ó>...</A>, 169 , 329
<A HREF="MAIL TO:youruser-

name@site.com">Send e-mail!</A>, 190
<A HREF="Name.HTM">Linked item</A> tags, 169
.aiff format, 202
Aldus PageMaker plug-ins, 308–9
ALIGN=BOTTOM option, 179, 183
ALIGN=LEFT option, 179, 180, 181
ALIGN=MIDDLE option, 179, 183
ALIGN=TOP option, 179, 183
Alignment clauses, 178–79
Alignment options, 184–85
Alphabet jump map, 70
ALT="..." clause, 208–9
America Online, 45, 68, 283
    browser, 29–30
    employee home pages, 277–78
    home page, 31
    People section, 276–77
AMI_WEB, 305, 339
AmiPro Tool Kit, 305
<A NAME="...">...</A> anchor tags, 69–70, 152, 329
Anchor tags, 150–57

343

W

LICENSE AGREEMENT AND LIMITED WARRANTY

READ THE FOLLOWING TERMS AND CONDITIONS CAREFULLY BEFORE OPENING THIS DISK PACKAGE. THIS LEGAL DOCUMENT IS AN AGREEMENT BETWEEN YOU AND PRENTICE-HALL, INC. (THE "COMPANY"). BY OPENING THIS SEALED DISK PACKAGE, YOU ARE AGREEING TO BE BOUND BY THESE TERMS AND CONDITIONS. IF YOU DO NOT AGREE WITH THESE TERMS AND CONDITIONS, DO NOT OPEN THE DISK PACKAGE. PROMPTLY RETURN THE UNOPENED DISK PACKAGE AND ALL ACCOMPANYING ITEMS TO THE PLACE YOU OBTAINED THEM FOR A FULL REFUND OF ANY SUMS YOU HAVE PAID.

1.   **GRANT OF LICENSE:** In consideration of your payment of the license fee, which is part of the price you paid for this product, and your agreement to abide by the terms and conditions of this Agreement, the Company grants to you a nonexclusive right to use and display the copy of the enclosed software program (hereinafter the "SOFT-WARE") on a single computer (i.e., with a single CPU) at a single location so long as you comply with the terms of this Agreement. The Company reserves all rights not expressly granted to you under this Agreement.

2.   **OWNERSHIP OF SOFTWARE:** You own only the magnetic or physical media (the enclosed disks) on which the SOFTWARE is recorded or fixed, but the Company retains all the rights, title, and ownership to the SOFT-WARE recorded on the original disk copy(ies) and all subsequent copies of the SOFTWARE, regardless of the form or media on which the original or other copies may exist. This license is not a sale of the original SOFTWARE or any copy to you.

3.   **COPY RESTRICTIONS:** This SOFTWARE and the accompanying printed materials and user manual (the "Documentation") are the subject of copyright. You may not copy the Documentation or the SOFTWARE, except that you may make a single copy of the SOFTWARE for backup or archival purposes only. You may be held legally responsible for any copying or copyright infringement which is caused or encouraged by your failure to abide by the terms of this restriction.

4.   **USE RESTRICTIONS:** You may not network the SOFTWARE or otherwise use it on more than one computer or computer terminal at the same time. You may physically transfer the SOFTWARE from one computer to another provided that the SOFTWARE is used on only one computer at a time. You may not distribute copies of the SOFTWARE or Documentation to others. You may not reverse engineer, disassemble, decompile, modify, adapt, translate, or create derivative works based on the SOFTWARE or the Documentation without the prior written consent of the Company.

5.   **TRANSFER RESTRICTIONS:** The enclosed SOFTWARE is licensed only to you and may not be transferred to any one else without the prior written consent of the Company. Any unauthorized transfer of the SOFT-WARE shall result in the immediate termination of this Agreement.

6.   **TERMINATION:** This license is effective until terminated. This license will terminate automatically without notice from the Company and become null and void if you fail to comply with any provisions or limitations of this license. Upon termination, you shall destroy the Documentation and all copies of the SOFTWARE. All provisions of this Agreement as to warranties, limitation of liability, remedies or damages, and our ownership rights shall survive termination.

7.   **MISCELLANEOUS:** This Agreement shall be construed in accordance with the laws of the United States of America and the State of New York and shall benefit the Company, its affiliates, and assignees.

8.   **LIMITED WARRANTY AND DISCLAIMER OF WARRANTY:** The Company warrants that the SOFTWARE, when properly used in accordance with the Documentation, will operate in substantial conformity with the description of the SOFTWARE set forth in the Documentation. The Company does not warrant that the SOFT-

WARE will meet your requirements or that the operation of the SOFTWARE will be uninterrupted or error-free. The Company warrants that the media on which the SOFTWARE is delivered shall be free from defects in materials and workmanship under normal use for a period of thirty (30) days from the date of your purchase. Your only remedy and the Company's only obligation under these limited warranties is, at the Company's option, return of the warranted item for a refund of any amounts paid by you or replacement of the item. Any replacement of SOFTWARE or media under the warranties shall not extend the original warranty period. The limited warranty set forth above shall not apply to any SOFTWARE which the Company determines in good faith has been subject to misuse, neglect, improper installation, repair, alteration, or damage by you. EXCEPT FOR THE EXPRESSED WARRANTIES SET FORTH ABOVE, THE COMPANY DISCLAIMS ALL WARRANTIES, EXPRESS OR IMPLIED, INCLUDING WITHOUT LIMITATION, THE IMPLIED WARRANTIES OF MERCHANTABILITY AND FITNESS FOR A PARTICULAR PURPOSE. EXCEPT FOR THE EXPRESS WARRANTY SET FORTH ABOVE, THE COMPANY DOES NOT WARRANT, GUARANTEE, OR MAKE ANY REPRESENTATION REGARDING THE USE OR THE RESULTS OF THE USE OF THE SOFTWARE IN TERMS OF ITS CORRECTNESS, ACCURACY, RELIABILITY, CURRENTNESS, OR OTHERWISE.

IN NO EVENT, SHALL THE COMPANY OR ITS EMPLOYEES, AGENTS, SUPPLIERS, OR CONTRACTORS BE LIABLE FOR ANY INCIDENTAL, INDIRECT, SPECIAL, OR CONSEQUENTIAL DAMAGES ARISING OUT OF OR IN CONNECTION WITH THE LICENSE GRANTED UNDER THIS AGREEMENT, OR FOR LOSS OF USE, LOSS OF DATA, LOSS OF INCOME OR PROFIT, OR OTHER LOSSES, SUSTAINED AS A RESULT OF INJURY TO ANY PERSON, OR LOSS OF OR DAMAGE TO PROPERTY, OR CLAIMS OF THIRD PARTIES, EVEN IF THE COMPANY OR AN AUTHORIZED REPRESENTATIVE OF THE COMPANY HAS BEEN ADVISED OF THE POSSIBILITY OF SUCH DAMAGES. IN NO EVENT SHALL LIABILITY OF THE COMPANY FOR DAMAGES WITH RESPECT TO THE SOFTWARE EXCEED THE AMOUNTS ACTUALLY PAID BY YOU, IF ANY, FOR THE SOFTWARE.

SOME JURISDICTIONS DO NOT ALLOW THE LIMITATION OF IMPLIED WARRANTIES OR LIABILITY FOR INCIDENTAL, INDIRECT, SPECIAL, OR CONSEQUENTIAL DAMAGES, SO THE ABOVE LIMITATIONS MAY NOT ALWAYS APPLY. THE WARRANTIES IN THIS AGREEMENT GIVE YOU SPECIFIC LEGAL RIGHTS AND YOU MAY ALSO HAVE OTHER RIGHTS WHICH VARY IN ACCORDANCE WITH LOCAL LAW.

ACKNOWLEDGMENT

YOU ACKNOWLEDGE THAT YOU HAVE READ THIS AGREEMENT, UNDERSTAND IT, AND AGREE TO BE BOUND BY ITS TERMS AND CONDITIONS. YOU ALSO AGREE THAT THIS AGREEMENT IS THE COMPLETE AND EXCLUSIVE STATEMENT OF THE AGREEMENT BETWEEN YOU AND THE COMPANY AND SUPERSEDES ALL PROPOSALS OR PRIOR AGREEMENTS, ORAL, OR WRITTEN, AND ANY OTHER COMMUNICATIONS BETWEEN YOU AND THE COMPANY OR ANY REPRESENTATIVE OF THE COMPANY RELATING TO THE SUBJECT MATTER OF THIS AGREEMENT.

Should you have any questions concerning this Agreement or if you wish to contact the Company for any reason, please contact in writing at the address below.

Robin Short
Prentice Hall PTR
One Lake Street
Upper Saddle River, New Jersey 07458